Slavery

History Workshop Series

General Editor
Raphael Samuel, Ruskin College, Oxford

SLAVERY AND OTHER FORMS OF UNFREE LABOUR

Edited By
LÉONIE J. ARCHER

Routledge
London and New York

First published in 1988 by
Routledge
11 New Fetter Lane, London EC4P 4EE

Published in the USA by
Routledge
a division of Routledge, Chapman and Hall, Inc.
29 West 35th Street, New York, NY 10001

Set in 11/12 pt Bembo
by Witwell Ltd, Southport
and printed in Great Britain
by Billing & Sons Ltd, Worcester

Library of Congress Cataloging in Publication Data
Slavery and other forms of unfree labour/edited by Léonie Archer.
      p. cm. — (History Workshop series)
   Papers from a workshop held in Oxford.
   Bibliography: p.
   Includes index.
      1. Slavery — Congresses.   I. Archer, Léonie.   II. Series.
HT855.S57 1988
306'.362 — dc 19   87–31664

British Library CIP Data also available

ISBN 0 415 00203 6 (c)
ISBN 0 415 00204 4 (p)

Contents

Contributors

Robin Blackburn is editor of New Left Review and part-time Lecturer in Sociology at the Polytechnic of Central London. He edited *Ideology in Social Science* (London, 1977), and is shortly to publish *The Overthrow of Colonial Slavery: 1776–1848* (London, 1988).

Joan Burdon is a research student in the Department of Ancient History and Archaeology at the University of Birmingham. She is currently bringing to completion her PhD thesis on Roman criminal law, and is generally interested in all aspects of Greek and Roman social history.

Paul A. Cartledge is University Lecturer in Ancient History at the University of Cambridge and Fellow of Clare College, Cambridge. He is author of many articles and reviews on all aspects of Greek history, and is currently preparing a social and economic history of classical Greece. His publications relevant to this collection include *Sparta and Laconia: A Regional History c. 1300–362* (London, 1979 – Ch. 10 on Helotage), *Agesilaos and the Crisis of Sparta* (London, 1987 – Ch. 10 on Helotage), 'Rebels and sambos in classical Greece: a comparative view' in *History of Political Thought* VI I/2 (1985) and in Cartledge and Harvey (eds), *CRUX: Essays in Greek History Presented to G.E.M. de Ste. Croix on his 75th Birthday* (London, 1985).

L. Mee-Yan Cheung-Judge is an Organisation Development Consultant, with special interest in racial equality practices within social organisations. Following completion of her PhD in 1979 she lectured in sociology in Oxford, Hong Kong and various institutions in the United States. Her particular areas of interest are race and ethnic relations; modernisation and development studies; social psychology; and sociology of self-concept and identity studies, and her publications include 'Modernisation and ethnicity' (with T. Parming) in J. Dofny (ed.), *National and Ethnic Movements* (London, 1980), and 'Assimilation rate, community involvement, community importance and sex-role changes: the case of single Chinese-American women', in *Minority Women: Problems and Strategies* (forthcoming). She is presently working on two studies of Chinese slavery, and a general work on manumission.

R. J. Ellis is Senior Lecturer in American and Cultural Studies at North Staffordshire Polytechnic. His research interests are discourse, language and ideology, and Little Magazines in the UK and US: the 'production of poetry'. He is an active poet and is editor of Sow's Ear Poetry Pamphlet series, *Text and Context: A Journal of Interdisciplinary Studies* and a volume on contemporary approaches to science fiction criticism. He has published the following works of immediate relevance to this volume: 'Mark Twain and the language of slavery', *Praxis* no. 5 (1985); (with A. Munslow) 'Narrative, myth and the frontier thesis', *Journal of American Culture*, vol. 9 no. 2 (1986).

Susan Grayzel is currently enrolled on the MA/PhD programme in History at the University of California at Berkeley. Prior to this she taught Peace Studies at various academic institutions in the United States and worked at the Schlesinger Library (Radcliffe College) on the History of Women in America (Black Women Oral History Project). Her principal areas of interest are feminist history and the history and theory of pacificism and non-violence.

F. D. Harvey is Lecturer in Classics at the University of Exeter, and author of numerous reviews on Greek social and political subjects, including slavery. He is joint editor (with P. Cartledge) and contributor to *CRUX: Essays Presented to G.E.M. de Ste. Croix on his 75th Birthday* (London, 1985), and is currently preparing a commentary on Herodotus' Lydian logos. In addition to his work on Herodotus, his other areas of interest include women in antiquity and literacy in ancient Greece. He has held office in a number of associations for the promotion of Hellenic studies.

Gad Heuman is Lecturer in the Department of History at the University of Warwick, and member of the Centre for Caribbean Studies at the same University. He is interested generally in the transition from slavery to freedom in the Caribbean and is presently working on a study of the Morant Bay Rebellion in Jamaica. He is co-editor of *Slavery and Abolition: A Journal of Comparative Studies*, and has published the following works of relevance to this collection: *Between Black and White: Race, Politics and the Free Coloreds in Jamaica, 1792–1865* (1981), and, as editor, *Out of the House of Bondage: Runaways, Resistance and Marronage in Africa and the New World* (1986).

Bernard S. Jackson is Professor of Law, University of Kent at Canterbury. Previous appointments include being Lady Davis Professor in the Department of Bible at the Hebrew University of Jerusalem, and Speaker's Lecturer in Biblical Studies at the University of Oxford. He has published widely in the field of legal history and Jewish studies, and is editor of *The Jewish Law Annual*. Particular works relevant to the present collection are *Theft in Early Jewish Law* (Oxford, 1972) and *Essays in Jewish and Comparative Legal History* (Leiden, 1975).

Wendy James is University Lecturer in Social Anthropology at the University of Oxford and Fellow of St Cross College, Oxford. She previously taught at the University of Khartoum. Of her many publications, the following are of particular relevance to this collection: '*Kwanim Pa: The Making of the Uduk People. An Ethnographic Study of Survival in the Sudan–Ethiopian Borderlands* (Oxford, 1979), 'The Funj mystique: approaches to a problem of Sudan history', in R.K. Jain (ed.), *Text and Context: The Social Anthropology of Tradition* (Philadelphia, 1972) and, with D. Donham (eds), *The Southern Marches of Imperial Ethiopia: Essays in History and Social Anthropology* (Cambridge, 1986). Her other areas of interest are history and comparative morality.

Douglas H. Johnson lives in Oxford where he pursues his research into the history of the southern Sudan and north east Africa. He was formerly Assistant Director for Archives, Southern Regional Government, Juba.

Alan Knight is currently Professor of History at the University of Texas, having previously worked at the University of Essex and later the Centre for US-Mexican Studies, La Jolla. His particular research areas are the modern history of Mexico and Latin America, and comparative analysis of agrarian societies, peasant movements and revolutions. He recently completed a large two volume work entitled *The Mexican Revolution* (Cambridge, 1986), and also published 'Mexican peonage: what was it and why was it?', *Journal of Latin American Studies*, vol. 18 (1986).

David Nicholls is Vicar of Littlemore, Oxford, and Senior Associate Member of St Antony's College at the University of

Oxford. Prior to coming to Oxford he was Lecturer in Government at the University of the West Indies, Trinidad. He is a specialist in Haitian history and has published the following books: *From Dessalines to Duvalier* (Cambridge, 1979), *Haiti in Caribbean Context* (London, 1985) and *The Pluralist State* (London, 1975).

Mechal Sobel is Associate Professor in the Department of History at the University of Haifa. Her particular area of interest is Afro-American history and the interpenetration of black and white culture in the southern United States. She recently completed a book which challenges most previously held notions in this area, *The Garden of the Lord: African Influence on Southern Culture* (Princeton, forthcoming), and earlier published *Trabelin' On: The Slave Journey to an Afro-Baptist Faith* (Greenwood, 1979).

G. E. M. de Ste. Croix is Honorary Fellow of New College, Oxford, where until his retirement in 1977 he was Fellow in Ancient History. His academic areas of interest are Greek and Roman history in general, and early Christianity. Of his many publications, the following are of particular relevance to this collection: *The Class Struggle in the Ancient Greek World, from the Archaic Age to the Arab Conquests* (London, 1981, 1983), and 'Early Christian attitudes to property and slavery', *Studies in Church History* 12 (1975). He is presently working on two books, *Heresy, Schism and Persecution in the Later Roman Empire*, and *Early Christian Attitudes to Women, Sex and Marriage*.

Michael Tadman is Lecturer in Economic and Social History at Liverpool University. His general area of interest is the history of ethnic minorities in Britain and America, and his publications include: 'Slave Trading in the ante-bellum South: an estimate of the extent of the inter-regional slave Trade', *Journal of American Studies*, vol. 13 (1979), and *Speculators and Slaves: Slave Trading, Accommodation and Resistance in the American South, 1790–1865* (University of Wisconsin, forthcoming). He teaches university courses on slavery in America; race, class and ethnicity in America; and British economic and social history.

Michael Twaddle is Lecturer in Commonwealth Studies at the University of London (Institute of Commonwealth Studies). He has written a number of articles on various aspects of Buganda, and in particular recently published an essay entitled, 'The politics of abolition in Buganda', in S. Miers and R. Roberts (eds), *The Ending of Slavery in Africa* (Madison, 1987). His other main area of interest is

Caribbean history. He is co-editor (with C. Abel) of *Caribbean Societies* vols. 1 and 2 (1980 and 1983), and co-author with Abel of a survey of nineteenth- and twentieth-century Caribbean history (to be published by James Currey, London 1988).

David Wiles is Lecturer in Drama and Theatre Studies at the University of London (Royal Holloway and Bedford New college), having previously been based at University College of Wales, Aberystwyth. His doctoral thesis was on master-servant relationships in classical and Renaissance popular comedy with special reference to role reversal, and he is presently working on a book on classical new comedy which focuses on the relations between text and performance, theatre and social structure. He is generally interested in theoretical approaches to popular culture, and has published monographs on the Tudor Robin Hood plays and on the Elizabethan clown.

Introduction

The papers in this book are the result of a two-day workshop held in Oxford in April 1985 under the auspices of the History Workshop Centre for Social History. The purpose of the workshop was to bring together a wide variety of papers under the umbrella title 'Slavery and Other Forms of Unfree Labour'. The formal notice to prospective speakers read:

> The intention is for it to be an interdisciplinary event, treating slavery in its broadest definition, within any culture and from any period (ancient and modern); to seek definitions of 'slavery'; and to encourage a cross-fertilisation of ideas, and bring together usually isolated disciplines and areas of research.

The desire to make the meeting interdisciplinary was central to the whole project: not only was it hoped to bring together normally self-contained areas of research and encourage that exchange of ideas out-lined in the brief, it was also hoped that the interdisciplinary character would be a means of opening up and moving forward the current debate in respect of slavery. Speakers at the workshop therefore included social anthropologists; economic, social and legal historians; psychologists; artists; literature and drama critics; and sociologists; together with a representative from a contemporary slavery abolition society and a researcher from Oxfam.

Some of the contributors were attached full time to academic institutions, others worked outside of the formal academy; some had already published extensively in their own fields, others were at the start of their writing career or not especially interested in publication; all brought a diversity of interests and skills to the meeting. Talks included specific case studies; general methodological discussions; work on women's history and oral history; cross-cultural material on the social and political construction of ideology; critiques of Marx, Engels, Genovese and Foucault; and suggestions in general as to new ways of looking at slavery. Speakers from the various disciplines addressed the wider (and shared) theoretical implications of slavery, and questioned the traditionally accepted and often over-worked notions and paradigms.

The coverage on time and place was also extensive. Geographic areas looked at included West, South and East Africa; the United States; the Caribbean; Mexico; the Near East; and Europe; and papers ranged from antiquity to the present day. The inclusion of material from the ancient world was one particularly exciting aspect of the workshop, as it is relatively rare for ancient historians to meet on the same platform as other historians. Also unusual was the fact that the workshop occurred in this country. For a variety of reasons, most of the current slavery debate takes place in America and through American publications. To have the meeting here was both welcome and exciting. All in all, therefore, the workshop was a stimulating and sharing event; much was learnt of recent work in other areas; and, it is hoped, the debate was moved forward somewhat.

This book represents the proceedings from the conference. Over the two days, twenty-five speakers addressed their own areas of research and shared their ideas about 'Slavery and Other Forms of Unfree Labour'. All agreed that it would be a good idea to publish the material and continue the sharing process, though seven speakers, due to pressure of work or the nature of their talks, felt unable to contribute. Whilst their material, therefore, cannot unfortunately be included in this volume, many thanks are due to them for their valuable contribution to the workshop: Belinda Coote for her insightful and disturbing examination of present-day exploitation by British companies of sugar plantation workers in Jamaica and the Philippines; Teri Bullen for her illustrated analysis – entitled 'Culture under Oppression' – of the quilts and quilt-making of women in America and Soweto; Duncan Macleod for leading a discussion on the methodological problems surrounding the interpretation of slavery in the United States; Stanley Trapido for his talk on nineteenth-century Boer society; Howard Temperley on the European forced labour experience; and Richard Rathbone and Richard Hart on slave resistance in West Africa and the Caribbean. The eighteen papers which are published here represent proceedings from the conference, i.e. simply written-up versions of the original oral deliveries, the only additions being editorial revision in consultation with the authors to make the texts as accessible as possible to specialist and non-specialist readers alike, some explanatory annotation, and a list of suggested further reading appended to each paper. To further encourage the interdisciplinary idea-swap, footnotes have been arranged according to a Harvard system of citation: for full publication details of works referenced, the reader must look beyond a specific paper or area of immediate interest and consult the extended bibliography compiled from all of the papers at the back of the book.

The book, like the workshop, takes its title from the plenary address by *Geoffrey de Ste. Croix* which opened the meeting. The focus of his paper was with definitions of slavery, one of the principal concerns of the original brief and something picked up on, directly or indirectly, by all of the contributors. He starts by giving a broad three-fold classification of unfree labour: chattel slavery, serfdom, and debt bondage, purposefully omitting such problematic areas as indentured and forced labour which are examined by other contributors (see, for example, Joan Burdon on criminal law in the later Roman Empire). These three headings, covering the bulk of unfree labour, form the basis of his analysis of slave societies in general and of classical antiquity in particular. Drawing upon the work of two international conventions on slavery (League of Nations, 1926; United Nations, 1956), Ste. Croix presents three working definitions of his principal slavery categories (pp. 21–3): of chattel slavery as being 'the status or condition of a person over whom any or all of the powers attaching to the right of ownership are exercised'; of debt bondage as 'the status or condition arising from a pledge by a debtor of his personal services or those of a third person under his control as a security for a debt, where the value reasonably assessed of those services rendered is not applied towards the liquidation of the debt or the length and nature of those services are not respectively limited and defined'; of serfdom as 'the tenure of land whereby the tenant is by law, custom or agreement bound to live and labour on land belonging to another person and render some determinate services to such other person, whether for reward or not, and is not free to change his status'. These definitions, as Ste. Croix points out, are clever and careful pieces of legal drafting, designed to embrace all forms of slavery and allow for no escape on technical grounds. Nevertheless, as the case studies in this volume show, they can be honed down even further, revised and supplemented when applied within the context of a particular society (see, for example, Alan Knight's analysis of debt bondage in Mexico, and in particular Robin Blackburn's direct challenge to the definition of chattel slavery).

As in *Class Struggle in the Ancient Greek World*, Ste. Croix sites his examination within a Marxist framework, his concern lying with modes of production, class and exploitation. Starting from the standpoint of 'the most distinguishing feature of a given mode of production is not so much *how the bulk of the labour production is done*, as *how the dominant propertied classes... ensure the extraction of the surplus* which makes their leisured existence possible' (p. 20, author's italics), he confounds the popular view that in the world of Greek and Roman antiquity slaves did most of the actual work of production and demonstrates instead that that world was a slave economy by virtue of the fact that its dominant classes derived the surplus for their leisured existence from unfree labour. Having established his terms of reference, Ste. Croix goes on to compare the relative states and statuses of slaves, serfs and debt bondsmen in antiquity, mentioning *en passant* certain characteristics which it would seem are shared across the ages and not confined to the ancient slave system (for example, the fact that from the slave's point of view the greatest possible misfortune was separation from family, a fact picked up upon repeatedly by all of the contributors). He notes the hierarchy which existed within full slavery depending on whose slave you were, and the way in which imperial slaves in the Roman Empire amassed great personal wealth and were themselves served by retinues of slaves – all of which had a considerable bearing upon the levels, processes and consequences of manumission (when it occurred), a fact noted by Ste. Croix and further analysed in terms of status inconsistency by Mee-Yan Cheung-Judge. He points out that the category of serfdom *per se* did not exist in the ancient world before the fourth century AD except in a few local societies, the most notable of which being Sparta where a system of state serfdom was imposed upon the surrounding populace. This system is analysed in further detail by Paul Cartledge.

Ste. Croix concludes with some remarks about the ideology of slavery, an area elaborated upon within the context of ancient drama by David Wiles. He argues that the much vaunted theory of 'natural slavery', although found in the writings of Plato and Aristotle, was not in fact in general circulation in the ancient world and indeed did not really gain wide acceptance until the sixteenth century when, for example, it was used with such devastating effect by Spain in respect to the American Indians. Instead there was an almost universal belief in the perhaps even more insidious theory that slavery, in the sense of our analysis, did not exist: the good and wise person is never 'really' a slave despite external appearances; one can only be enslaved by one's faults and lusts. This rather convenient belief was adopted by the Early Church with the result that no general condemnation of slavery as an institution is to be found within Christianity until the late seventeenth century. As Ste. Croix concludes, this then theologised notion of slavery provided ideal propaganda for the pro-slavery lobby of North America in the eighteenth and nineteenth centuries.

Paul Cartledge's analysis continues with the world of classical antiquity and with questions of definition. He too highlights the continuing academic controversy as to whether classical Greece was a slave society or characterised by the slave mode of production, and for the non-classicist he gives a useful and welcome outline of what constituted 'Greece', the terminological difficulties surrounding the word for that 'far-flung and politically heterogeneous aggregation of well over a thousand individuated ...communities extending from the east coast of Spain to the eastern end of the Black Sea, from south Russia to Libya' (p. 33). He notes that the difficulties of reaching an overarching definition of classical slavery by the modern historian are further confounded by the ancients' own terminological imprecision and lack of overt systematisation with respect to their various categories of unfree (see also Ste. Croix; Harvey). As Cartledge writes, 'although classical Greek was exceptionally rich in words for the unfree, the dozen or so separate terms in current use... were used with a bewildering, almost nonchalant inconsistency' (p.34), no apparent distinction being made between what we would define as separate servile classes or groupings. He briefly looks at the historical rise of chattel slavery – the main form of servile labour in classical antiquity – and, within the context of Athens, shows the necessary connection which existed between this rise and the abolition of citizen debt bondage in the sixth century, an abolition which obliged rich Athenians to look elsewhere for the labour exploitation necessary to yield the surplus required to maintain them as a leisured ruling class (see Ste. Croix).

The main concern of Cartledge's paper, however, is not with general questions of definition and evolution, but with an analysis of the system of state exploitation which pertained at Sparta and the siting on the spectrum of free–unfree of the exploited people, the Helots. Working his way through the confused and ambiguous writings of the ancients, and then arguing against the conclusions of such modern scholars as Olivia, Lotze and Garlan, Cartledge concludes – with Ste. Croix – that the Helots (called in Greek simply 'slaves') were in fact serfs, or more particularly 'state serfs', sharing the characteristics of serfdom as defined by the United Nations and owned by the Spartan state. He ends by saying that within the analysis of ancient slavery these 'slaves' at least must be viewed in terms of a class engaged in class struggle to gain political power and freedom from personal bondage and economic exploitation. The successful revolt of the Helots in 369 BC, which, as Cartledge notes, was unique in the annals of Greek servitude, may be compared to that of the slaves on Saint Dominique in the eighteenth century (see Nicholls): both revolted into personal liberty and sovereign, autonomous polity.

Basing himself upon the writings of the ancient historian Herodotus (fifth century BC), *David Harvey* widens the geographic coverage of slavery in antiquity from that examined by Ste. Croix and Cartledge. His concern is not so much with definition and *post hoc* analysis, but with the ancients' own perceptions of slavery and the lifestyles of (chattel) slaves. His paper looks, in anecdotal fashion, at such aspects as modes of acquisition; where slaves originated; their tasks and treatment; given names; and signs of unrest, and he covers the ancient world from the Greek mainland and islands through to Asia Minor, Mesopotamia, Phoenicia, Egypt, south Russia and Italy. From the evidence of Herodotus, he suggests that modern classical scholarship may have seriously underestimated the amount of slave labour employed in agriculture in the Greek world (cf., the warnings of Ste. Croix that some Marxists have skewed the picture in the other direction), and he tentatively suggests that there may have been chattel slaves at Sparta as well as the state serfs discussed by Cartledge. Harvey concludes by examining Herodotus' own attitude to slavery. In common with so many other writers and societies, Herodotus only found loss of liberty abhorrent when it occurred at a state level such as, in his time, the subjection of Greeks to Persians. He did not question loss of individual freedom; saw enslavement as the will of the gods; and placed slaves at the bottom of the hierarchy of personal belongings after wives, children and non-human chattels. Like other cultures, his only caveat was that nationals should not enslave fellow nationals: they should only look to 'barbarians' for their slave labour.

Following on from this contempt for barbarians and working within a slightly later period, *David Wiles* has as his forum of analysis the Greek theatre, the place where 'citizens celebrated and debated their systems of values', values which made them 'decent, civilised human beings: the opposite, that is, of barbarians' (p. 53). The concern of this paper is with the ideology and legitimation of slavery as revealed in popular comedy of the Hellenistic period, in particular the works of the playwright Menander (fl. c. 300 BC). Quite rightly, Wiles uses the plays not for any extrapolation of concrete information about slaves, but as a vehicle for insight into a given social system at a given moment in time: reality and ideology may differ widely in detail, but the latter is nevertheless a support for the former and both are part of a self-reproducing system. This is a theme elaborated upon in the context of southern state American slavery by Dick Ellis.

Pointing to the new cosmopolitanism and individualism of the Hellenistic world, Wiles shows that the moral discourse of Menander's time was no longer about the state and the good citizen (cf., Herodotus), but about the good human being, with slavery being perceived as some kind of problematic to be explained (though not of course abolished). Working within the framework of Aristotle's theory of natural slavery – labelled by Ste. Croix as 'intellectually disreputable' and by Wiles as a mere 'rationalisation of gut feelings about the superiority of the Greek race and Greek culture' – Wiles points to the connections which existed between the Aristotelian science of physiognomy and philosophy and Menander's dramaturgy with its system of masks and role typology. He describes how the masks were categorised and divided according to an assumed system of relationships or hierarchical 'natural' order of age before youth, free before slave, male before female, and how the masks in turn provided the structural framework of the comedies. Stereotyped visuals characterised the masks rendering each actor and role readily identifiable to the audience. Slaves were characterised by racial indicators (for example, red hair) and by a stylised asymmetry (for example, one raised eyebrow) indicative of mental disharmony and moral deviance. Stock classificatory names (the ancient equivalent of 'Paddy') were then added to the character. As Wiles demonstrates, these theatrical constructions had little to do with observable reality, where slaves could in fact bear neutral Greek names and did not derive from one racial pool, but were based upon the logic of a conceptual system: the visual image was to serve as a constant reminder to the spectator of the 'natural' baseness of the slave, no matter what fine sentiments the character might in fact display in the course of the play. He makes similar and interesting connections regarding the position and role of women, contrasting them with the representation of men and noting that within the category of female masks, unlike for men, slavery and freedom were not presented as polarities but as the basis of a continuum.

From all of this, Wiles concludes, in opposition to Ste. Croix, that Aristotle's theory of natural slavery did continue to be influential in the Hellenistic and Roman period. The standard philosophical position may well have been that of Fortune not Nature dictating an individual's circumstances and of external conditions being irrelevant to inner character, but on a popular level the Aristotelian view remained prominent, as evidenced by the comedies of Menander which remained for several centuries part of the dominant culture, reflecting and shaping popular perceptions.

Joan Burdon's paper moves us from ideology to law and focuses upon Roman antiquity. Spanning approximately eight centuries of history and working from the standpoint of a legal historian, she presents a detailed analysis of the institution of penal slavery in the Roman Republic and Empire. She notes that with the growth of the Empire a system of state punishment arose to replace earlier civil settlements, and that within the state system differentiation was made with regard both to choice of punishment and conditions of servitude according to whether the criminal was of high or low status (see also Jackson). She examines the way in which some of the penalties involved a reduction to slave status whilst others did not, and tries to assess what in real terms was the quality of freedom retained in the latter case. Having explored the hierarchy in status and punishment which existed in Roman law (particularly the separation between penal slavery and other punishments of forced labour), Burdon describes the conditions of life of the penal slave, and concludes that the extreme conditions of the penal slave (who had no owner and whose punishment was limitless) served in some sense to define the position and 'rights' of the ordinary slave.

The final paper in the book's survey of antiquity – again a treatment of legal material – focuses upon the ancient Near East and has several points of contact with the papers presented thus far. *Bernard Jackson* considers the two paradigms of slavery to be found in the earliest of the biblical law codes, those of captives and of debt-slaves, and through a combination of detailed textual work and utilisation of comparative material from other ancient societies, traces the oppositional typologies of the two groups and the historical crisis in labelling which that opposition generated (i.e., the increasing unwillingness to apply the concept 'slave' to debt-slaves; see also Burdon on the process of re-classification).

Basing himself on an overview of slavery and debt bondage in the early historical periods of Greece and Rome (in which he provides a mini-critique of the work of Moses Finley and Lévy-Bruhl), Jackson presents a typology based upon the structural opposition between the insider and the outsider: when the result of war or capture, slavery was permanent and applied to the outsider; when the product of debt, it was temporary and applied to the citizen or insider. Within the context of this typlogy and of broader Near Eastern material, Jackson analyses the provisions of *Exodus* 21 and demonstrates that the laws there were concerned with debt bondage. The labelling of the debt bondsman as a 'slave' proved problematic to later Hebrew legislators who reordered and reclassified this earlier material and made explicit the insider-outside opposition (cf., Blackburn). As in Greece and Rome, the term 'slave' was now reserved for the foreign captive, whilst 'hired servant' or its equivalent was used for the citizen debt defaulter. Jackson explores the various possible reasons for this reclassification in the final part of his paper.

Alan Knight's paper, which opens the survey of unfree labour in the modern period, continues with the subject of debt bondage and elaborates, within a different geographical and historical context, upon points made in some of the earlier essays (see in particular Ste. Croix). Focusing upon debt peonage in Latin America (particularly Mexico) and carefully combining historical and theoretical perspectives, diachronic and regional, he presents a detailed analysis of the nature of that institution and also argues for appropriate modes of analysis regarding the spectrum of unfree labour in general. Posing the question, was the debt peon a surrogate slave or a surrogate proletarian, Knight draws upon the work of various Marxist theorists in an attempt to break down the 'broad spectrum of unfreedom' into its constituent parts and to demonstrate that debt peonage ought not be viewed as an homogeneous, unified category. He demonstrates that Genovese's three criteria for differentiating the character of New World slavery may be of use in separating out Mexican peonage, and he examines the confusion which, in terms of grand theory, surrounds discussion of pre-capitalist social formation. In particular he criticises the way in which many theorists and historians have conflated the two distinct dimensions of 'form of surplus labour' and 'mode of exploitation'.

Drawing upon the analysis in this respect of Gerry Cohen, and historical processes within and outside of Mexico, Knight argues for three distinct types of debt peon: (1) voluntaristic – those who were really (temporary) wage labourers whose debts were advances to attract them to the plantations and who evolved into a rural proletariat; (2) 'traditional' peons whose debts could be seen as more of an inducement than a bond and whose position of being 'tied' to the land could be viewed as both enviable and secure; (3) coercive debt peons forcibly brought into underpopulated territory in response to fresh and powerful (usually short-term) market demands. Knight concludes by showing that only the last category, on the basis of Genovese's criteria, could be called slavery (in fact, the coerced peon's condition could be worse than that of the formal chattel slave), and demonstrates that only it was vulnerable to political action/reform/revolution, the others not.

The next three papers all address the continent of Africa. *Michael Twaddle* starts off by looking at Buganda, a country which has largely been neglected in studies of African slavery. He underlines the way in which study of the momentous changes in that kingdom in the nineteenth century have been distorted by (exclusive) concentration upon the political changes following the overthrow of Kabaka Mwanga II and the impact of Islam and Christianity to the neglect of research into the socio-economic changes associated with the East Africa slave trade. Contrary to other studies, Twaddle points to the importance of slavery as a distinct institution in pre-colonial Buganda; demonstrates that its character was not of the integrative kind described by anthropologists for the period of the British protectorate; and examines the internal tensions and societal shifts and revolts which external control, British labour demands and imposed changes in the trade generated within Buganda society.

Wendy James elaborates upon a theme touched on by all of the contributors, that of the slave as foreigner or outsider. She argues that examination of the customs and views of slave-raided areas, rather than the traditional focus on the slave-holding society, can reveal much regarding the politico-historical relationship and the character of slavery in a given area. As she says, in line with Goody and Foucault, 'it is at the far extremities that the nature of the power relations involved can be seen most directly. Those who have evaded or escaped the tentacles of the system, or who have otherwise managed to survive on its margins, can see its distinctive features more accurately than those who control, or theorise about, its workings from the centre. At the furthest territorial limits of the old slaving systems, we can still seek that "subjugated knowledge"... the communities of the marginal regions may not only remember these acts of disruption and bodily alienation... but also may have built a moral world around these memories' (p. 139). Working within the context of the Sudan–Ethiopian border, an area exploited for slaves for many centuries both from the Nile Valley and the Ethiopian Plateau, James examines some of the internal features of Gummuz society. On the basis of her own fieldwork, she discusses their distinctive concepts of freedom, myth-making and language. She notes the way in which chiefs are not allowed to build up much authority; marriage arrangements are on the basis of a protective and mutual exchange of sisters with no bride-price payment; and special kinship systems/concepts exist to allow for the reabsorption of individuals previously lost to the community. All of these, James concludes, reflect certain chosen systems of alliance and particular features of that area's slave-raided past.

Douglas Johnson's paper stays with East Africa and again picks up on some of the major themes of the volume, i.e., definitions of slavery; the fostered 'otherness' of the slave; notions of enslaveable peoples; and the structuring of political relationships and shifting interstate power dynamic. The particular focus of his study is Sudanese military slavery during the eighteenth, nineteenth and twentieth centuries, and he draws from this some wider implications for the study of military slavery in general. He points to the fact that military slavery as an institution has been either neglected or misrepresented, with analyses concentrating on remote origins or treating slave armies as early stages in political and social evolution. Johnson argues instead that it is 'an institution of long endurance and continuity which is crucial to the understanding of political relations of dependency and marginality within the regions where it was practised' (p. 142). He highlights the apparent contradiction of the armed slave and the ambiguity of that slave's position (drawing interesting parallels with the so-called 'free' enlisted soldier), and points to the need to distinguish between the institution and the individual in any discussion of the subject. With regard to his specific study, Johnson charts in detail the history, spread and endurance of Sudanese military slavery and demonstrates the institution's importance in the formation of colonial states. He also explores the nature of the 'martial race' syndrome (the combination of marginality and dependency which made areas ideal suppliers of so-called martial races); the fostered distinctiveness of the slave soldier; and the ethnic ambiguity surrounding military slave communities (the 'Nubi' factor).

Like David Wiles, *Dick Ellis*'s concern is with the ideological supports to the institution of slavery, and his particular context is the post-bellum ideology of the southern United States in the 1880s which allowed for the emergence of a reconstituted form of slavery (debt-peonage) after formal abolition. Moving far beyond Genovese's concentration upon hegemonic structure and institutional manifestations (see also Mechal Sobel), Ellis takes as his focus language, and in particular the writings of Mark Twain. Drawing upon the work of John B. Thompson, M. Foucault, the Russian formalists, F. K. Stanzel and P. Ricoeur, he analyses *Huckleberry Finn* and *Life on the Mississippi*, approaching both texts by means of the 'discursive analysis of linguistic constructions and the social analysis of the conditions of discursive production'. He contrasts the simple narrative structure of *Life on the Mississippi* (a structure which both constrained Twain and rendered the text open to censorship) with the deeply ironic, multilayered (and self-protective) complexity of *Huckleberry Finn*. Ellis demonstrates the way in which, in the latter work, the ideological complicity of language is revealed and how the whole stands as a profound critique of ante-bellum slavery, with clear implications that the ideology continued in the post-emancipation period.

Mechal Sobel's paper, 'All Americans Are Part African', challenges the view held by most analysts that the black and white cultures of the slave period were different and separate, with any influence only being of white on black (see, for example, Tadman, this volume). As Sobel points out, little research has been done on African and Afro-American influence on whites, and it is still widely assumed that blacks did not influence white culture to any significant extent. Even the seminal studies of Genovese in this respect are limited by his obsession with ruling class hegemony and the consequent belief that blacks could not have influenced whites beyond a certain point. Basing herself on data from the eighteenth century South – the period when large numbers of English and Africans were coming in contact with each other for the first time, and before the segregation policies of the nineteenth century – Sobel challenges these assumptions and presents, to use her own words, a 'radically different view'. She traces the extent of interaction and interrelationship between whites and blacks at work, home, in family life and recreation, and shows that whilst slaves were not equals, neither were they just 'acted upon'. Regarding value interpenetration, she argues for a pervasiveness of black influence and discusses two areas in particular: the English–African world views of time and causality, and the domain of religion (the Great Awakening). For the first she demonstrates the way blacks both reinforced and subtly Africanised the old English view, whilst for the latter she charts the considerable extent to which blacks introduced their cultural perspectives and were held up as role models in the mixed revival churches. Sobel concludes, in opposition to other analysts, that 'blacks and whites [together] forged a new Anglo–American culture pool, from which both took the value of the other' (p. 185).

Mike Tadman, an economic historian, also addresses the question of master–slave mentalities and interrelationships in the old American South but from a very different perspective and for a later period. His concern is to show the inappropriateness of the accommodation theories of Genovese, Fogel and Engerman as models of analysis for ante-bellum slavery, and he argues that the relationship between masters and slaves was far more jarring and segregated than these theories allow. He demonstrates that the theories rest heavily on inexact calculations and poor methodology regarding the extent and type of domestic slave movement in the eighteenth and nineteenth centuries. He calculates that the bulk of the movement comprised slave trading rather than planter migration and that it was an age-selective process rather than the sex-selective one which Fogel and Engerman had assumed from their work in the New Orleans area. According to Tadman, the pattern which emerges from this revised calculation is one of economic exploitation and deliberate separation of families – facts which run contrary both to the statements from the period itself and to the views of the above theorists, and which would suggest a slave attitude of intense hostility/resentment and a slave-holder attitude of uncaring business-first racism. From this analysis, and unlike Sobel, Tadman concludes that 'the worlds of masters and slaves would, it seems, while overlapping at points, have been largely separate and segregated. Segregation seems likely to have dated not from emancipation or "Jim Crow" laws but from slavery itself. A model of segregation combined with limited accommodation to power seems more useful for the ante-bellum South than the all-embracing accommodation models . . . During the seventeenth and eighteenth centuries, with a higher-born presence, slave-master adjustments would have been somewhat different from those of the ante-bellum period – but the African presence does not suggest a less segregated pattern' (p. 204).

Gad Heuman also points to the strength of the family in his examination of runaway slaves in nineteenth-century Barbados. Using the statistical evidence of advertisements in the Barbadian press (a source which, whilst problematic, is unbiased), he provides a comparative breakdown of the runaway populace in terms of sex; age; skills; colour; duration of absence; preferred month of flight; and place of hiding, and from this draws conclusions not only about individual runaways but also about the nature of Barbadian slavery in general. He brings out two aspects in particular. Firstly the way in which many slaves ran to their family (especially to parents rather than spouses or siblings), the members of which were not all necessarily slaves – a fact which suggests 'a complex pattern of relationships [providing] evidence of the existence of the slave family [which should] redirect efforts to examine the intricate and connected world of slave and free people' (p. 220). And secondly, the way in which slaves and runaways, either as troublemakers, valued labourers or no longer wanted workers whose recapture was not sought, brought pressure to bear in a variety of ways on their owners. As Heuman concludes, in line with Sidney Mintz and Richard Price, 'While runaway slaves were clearly resisting aspects of the slave society, they were also testimony to the "role of the powerless in affecting and even controlling important parts of the lives of the masters"' (p. 223).

Davis Nicholls' paper, which maps the history of Haiti between 1804 and 1825, returns to the theme of race and enslaveable peoples and in particular explores the links between slavery, race and colonial status. He traces the way in which slavery on the island was only finally abolished with the victory of Dessalines and the end of the colonial regime, despite its formal abolition some years previously, and demonstrates how 'independence thus came to be seen by Haitians as a necessary condition of freedom and was, moreover, for them as for many foreign observers...a symbol of racial equality and a challenge to slavery in the new world' (p. 225). He highlights the way in which national independence was quite explicitly seen by the Haitian leaders to be based on a conception of race, and he examines that concept both in terms of the situation which pertained in the colonial period and in the struggles to retain their freedom up until its formal declaration by France in 1825. Nicholls concludes by examining the Haitians 'highly ambivalent' attitude to Africa: regarding themselves as Africans and in no way racially inferior, they nevertheless still accepted the idea that real civilisation in the nineteenth century, through a series of historical and cultural factors, was to be found in Europe; their independence was a signal of hope to Africa, but conquest and colonisation of that continent for the purpose of civilisation was, in their eyes, to be welcomed.

Drawing to the end of the workshop and the book, Mee-Yan Cheung-Judge discusses manumission. She does this not from any anthropological, demographical or specifically historical standpoint (areas which have been well mapped already) but from a perspective which has to date received little documentation, that of the socio-psychological. Having resonances with many other papers in the book (see, for example, Ste. Croix, Burdon, Knight and Ellis), she explores in greater detail the way in which in all societies the ex-slave, although technically free, remains in various ways and to varying degrees inferior to other free members of the community. On the basis of this universal status inconsistency she presents a three-tiered subjective and objective model of the 'identity structure of the manumitted' (personal: self-esteem; social: ascribed status; collective: group identification), tracing the impact which the disjunction between expectation and reality can have on the manumitted's self-perception and interpersonal relations. She concludes by demonstrating that the response and level of self-esteem depend upon the significance to the individual of the label 'slave'; the value he/she places upon free status; and the level of collective involvement/re-inforcement.

Susan Grayzel continues with many of the same themes, although again from a different analytical perspective. Concerned with the lives of Afro-American women removed by one or two generations from the actual experience of slavery, she too looks at the dynamics of pride *vs* alienation, individual *vs* collective, powerlessness *vs* self-determination within the 'free' black community – not, however, from the standpoint of any 'grand history' but in terms of a particular and significant oral history project which set out to record the stories of (selected) women born between 1870 and 1920. From this archival material, Grayzel takes as her focus the influence which older women had on the interviewees' lives and the recognition that they as black women had (have) a double burden to bear with respect to discrimination. As far as possible letting the women speak for themselves through quotations from the interviews (unfortunately not all of the excerpts presented in the original oral delivery could be included here as permission to reproduce was refused by some of the interviewees), Grayzel examines the notions and types of group loyalties, and the ways in which the individual was seen to be working for the benefit of all. She highlights the fact that the experiences are described in terms of the family and the way in which the interviewees looked to their foremothers, recognising their strength and hardwork. Throughout the paper, Grayzel emphasises the importance of using oral history now before the record is lost to capture the voices of the disenfranchised and those left out of traditional history (a double likelihood in the case of black women), and, drawing upon specific examples from the interviews regarding particular struggles and the women's own explanations of their acts, she demonstrates how our understanding of the motive for 'significant acts' is often skewed by traditional modes of historiography and our own assumptions as to why individuals act in certain ways. As she stresses, what is needed is to listen to the voice of the participant, and, in this particular context, to recognise that oral history reaches back to African traditions and highlights the racism of historical societies and institutions.

The plenary address which closed the Oxford workshop was provided by *Robin Blackburn*. Like Ste. Croix's opening talk, and in line with the conference's brief, Blackburn focuses primarily on definitions of slavery. Ranging widely through the ages and touching upon virtually every area examined in microcosm by other contributors to the volume, he poses two fundamental questions: is there a core of features common to the slave status beyond the great diversity of uses to which slaves have been put, and, what distinguishes slavery from other forms of social oppression? He starts by giving various dictionary definitions of slavery, and then moves on through the work of Marx, Engels, Orlando Patterson, Lévy-Bruhl and Moses Finley to the League of Nations conclusions which opened this volume (Ste. Croix). One of Blackburn's particular concerns is to compare and contrast the relations of slavery with those based on marriage and kinship. Marx and Engels argued that primitive slavery was itself a product of family relations in the early phase of tribal ownership, that the domination of women by men had a slave-like character and represented the germ of slavery proper. As Blackburn notes, their theories pinpoint certain features common to all oppression/domination but the wholesale equation of family with slavery misses important dimensions of the slave relation. Women and childen have a fixed status, they help constitute the family and lineage and bring together different human groups: many of the important dimensions of the slave relation stem precisely from slavery's negation of family and kinship – their absolute dominion, no sense of belonging in terms of group membership, no group or individual identity, effaced origins and no continuing link. As Blackburn says, 'Unlike distinctions of gender or generation the slave status [is] a purely social construct' (p. 267). He demonstrates the fact that all slaves – whether enslaved by capture, barter, debt, natural disaster or crime – are perceived as owing their lives to the master, a state from which all else in their condition flows; he analyses the social significance and mechanics of natal alienation, a condition which paradoxically can be inherited; and he examines the means by which cross-culturally slave systems are maintained (punishment; ideology). Surveying from the ancient Greeks, Romans and Hebrews through to New World slavery, he concludes that what sets the slave apart from any other social relation is the comprehensiveness of the slave's domination and the property rights claimed by the slave holder. On this basis, and unlike Ste. Croix, he therefore rejects the definition of the 1926 Convention (above, p. 3): it is not a question of any or all of the rights of ownership being exercised (this could apply in some sense to employers and spouses in relation to their workers and marriage partners), but of all *and more* of those powers having application.

Blackburn ends his paper and this book with the following words, 'the slave status and condition has been a purely social construction – that of a social isolate, an outsider, a person without kin, a person subject to the complete and arbitrary authority of the master, a person who could be whipped or tortured or sexually abused, a piece of property, and, by virtue of the foregoing, an instrument. The very enumeration of such qualities must remind us that slavery was not a suprahistorical essence but had to be produced and perpetuated, enlisting the support of the free population and adapting the slave to the particular use required' – a salutary reminder to us of the nature and essential condition of slavery in all societies and ages, and one which brings together many of the themes touched upon in this book.

One

Slavery and Other Forms of Unfree Labour[1]

G. E. M. de Ste. Croix

I sent in the title of this talk, 'Slavery and Other Forms of Unfree Labour', in the hope that it might be adopted as the general title of this particular workshop, as it has been. While preparing the talk, I knew virtually nothing about the contents of the other contributions to the programme, and I cannot pretend to be giving a general introduction to the proceedings, which cover many aspects of slavery proper and a wide variety of forms of unfree labour from Greek and Roman times to the present day. I must explain that my own thought on these subjects has been formed largely on the basis of what I know about the Greek and Roman world as an ancient historian, roughly from the eighth century BC to the mid-seventh century of the Christian era; and I hope that those who are experts in the history of other societies will bear with me if I betray the limits of my own detailed knowledge rather too often. Fortunately, as it happens, the ancient world does provide a remarkable amount of solid evidence (not only literary); and in it we find not only the most severe form of slavery (chattel slavery, as it is usually called) but also all sorts of other kinds of unfree labour – to a far greater extent, I think, than most classical scholars and even ancient historians have realised. I therefore feel justified in confining myself mainly to the societies I know best: those of the Greeks and Romans.

I admit that I have a passion for defining the concepts I use as precisely as possible. So, after a few more introductory remarks, I shall state what I think is the most useful way of classifying the main categories of unfree labour under three general heads: chattel slavery, serfdom, and debt bondage, and then explain exactly what I mean when I speak of each of those three categories. I realise that this classification may omit certain forms of unfree labour which some people may immediately think of: indentured labour, for example, which existed even in the Greek and Roman world, at least as a particular form of what was called in Greek *paramonē*. So I freely admit that my definitions do not explicitly take into account all possible forms of unfree labour. But I do believe that they cover the great bulk of such forms, with one conspicuous exception: forced labour, imposed not by private individuals or organisations but by states, for example upon prisoners of war, or as a form of punishment or disciplinary treatment, for crime or for behaviour considered reprehensible by the state concerned – often, of course, behaviour which is considered legitimate in other states.[2] This is a well-known minefield; and it is not surprising that the whole question of forced labour exacted by states was carefully ignored by the two important International Conventions of 1926 and 1956, whose definitions I shall be adopting presently – the subject raised delicate questions on which different states can have fundamentally different opinions.

In presenting my definitions in a moment, I want to emphasise that they go right to the heart of the matter in their emphasis on labour. As a Marxist, the very first thing I want to know about any society above the most primitive level is the way in which the dominant classes extract unpaid surplus labour (in Marx's sense) from the primary producers.[3] So, for me, what has to be kept in the forefront all the time, in dealing with our subject today, is that slavery and the other systems I shall be discussing are forms of extraction of labour, and most are profitably considered from that point of view. Slavery and the other systems tend to have exceedingly unpleasant features; but the essence of them all, the basis on which they all rest, is extraction of labour for the master, the feudal lord, the creditor, etc.

At this point I want to say a brief word about what constitutes a slave society. If we proceed as I do, on Marxist principles, there can be no doubt about the conclusion; and the result agrees admirably with the way in which the expression has been applied to the Greek and Roman world, the American Old South, and other such indubitable slave societies. As I have indicated already, the most significant distinguishing feature of a given mode of production is not so much *how the bulk of the labour of production is done*, as *how the dominant propertied classes*, controlling the conditions of production, *ensure the extraction of the surplus* which makes their leisured existence possible. Some Marxists in the past have tried to pretend that in the Greek and Roman world slaves did most of the actual work of production; but this got the argument off in a seriously wrong direction, because in fact it is perfectly clear that most production in antiquity was done by free peasants and artisans, except perhaps for brief periods in parts of Italy and Sicily in about the last century BC. But, as I hope I have already demonstrated sufficiently in print,[4] the dominant classes in the Greek and Roman world derived the surplus on which their leisured existence was based from unfree labour, especially that of chattel slaves. It was that which made the Greek and Roman world a slave economy. A fundamental difference between antiquity and the modern world is that the propertied classes, which in capitalist society derive their surplus primarily from wage labour, derived it in antiquity from slave and (to a less extent) other unfree labour.

When in 1959 Sir Moses Finley published a much-quoted article with the title, 'Was Greek civilisation based on slave labour?',[5] he found himself unable to answer his own question, and eventually substituted a very different one: 'Not whether slavery was the basic element, or whether it caused this or that, but how it functioned' – an enormously wide and open-ended question, to which of course we can do no more than provide fragments of an answer. At that time Sir Moses was refusing to employ even the most basic Marxist categories of class and exploitation.[6] Yet he has always in fact spoken of the Greek and Roman world as a 'slave society'. And in recent years he has come round a little. In the early 1980s he proffered a definition of what he meant by a slave society: it was where 'slaves provided the bulk of the immediate income, from property, ... of the élites, economic, social and political'.[7] But 'élites', especially in that very broad sense, is an unfortunately imprecise term; and as it happens it is particularly inappropriate for Greek and Roman society, where many well-to-do and even middling peasants, whom no one could conceivably wish to number among an élite of any sort, might own slaves to do their farmwork, as might some quite humble people engaged in manufacture or trade.

It is time now to set out my three categories of unfree labour, and produce definitions. Fortunately, we have an excellent set of ready-made definitions from two international conventions: for slavery, the Slavery Convention of 1926, organised by the League of Nations, and, for the other two forms of unfree labour, the Supplementary Convention resulting from a conference at Geneva, organised by the United Nations in 1956, and attended by representatives of forty-eight nations. In a useful book called *Slavery*, published in 1958, a leading specialist on the subject, C.W.W. Greenidge, gives all the relevant texts, which I have also summarised and briefly discussed.[8]

Slavery in the full sense (often referred to as 'chattel slavery') is defined in the 1926 Convention as 'the status or condition of a person over whom any or all of the powers attaching to the right of ownership are exercised'.[9] This is a brilliant piece of drafting, because the essential purpose of the Slavery Convention was to prohibit, and help to stamp out, all forms of slavery, and not to allow any to escape on technical grounds. Now there have been forms of slavery in which individual slaves have not actually been the property of those whom they serve; but of course even they would be caught by the definition, which refers to persons 'over whom any or all of *the powers attaching to the right of ownership* are exercised' – so that it does not matter whether or not a master actually owns a particular slave, if he exercises powers over him that are normally associated with ownership.

In the 1956 Convention we have a definition of *debt bondage*, as 'the status or condition arising from a pledge by a debtor of his personal services or those of a third person under his control as a security for a debt, where the value reasonably assessed of those services rendered is not applied towards the liquidation of the debt or the length and nature of those services are not respectively limited and defined'. Notice that the debt bondsman is not a slave, even though his services, his labour, are to a considerable extent in practice (if not always in theory) at the disposal of his creditor. This, the fact that the debt bondsman is not a slave, can be very important, as it was in classical antiquity, where outright enslavement for debt did occur, but seems to have been increasingly replaced by debt bondage, where the debtor, if a free citizen, would remain a free citizen in theory and would regain his original status when he had worked off his debt, if indeed he ever did so.[10] It is impossible to say what proportion of Greek and Roman debt bondsmen were able to do this; but I suspect that many remained in bondage to the end of their lives, and probably their children after them, as still happens today, of course, in countries where debt bondage, even if in theory illegal, still persists. There are some fascinating Greek and especially Latin sources showing how thin the line could be between debt bondsman and slave; but at least in principle the bondsman was free rather than slave, and there was always the possibility that he might be able to become genuinely free by paying off his debt or getting a relative or friend to do so.

I referred earlier to the Greek institution of *paramonē*,[11] which can be conveniently grouped with debt bondage in general, because it was often a result of defaulting on a debt (and sometimes even of

incurring one), although its terminology could also be used for con-
tracts of service or apprenticeship; and in some of its forms it seems
to come near to what is usually called in English 'indentured labour',
something which in its modern forms I am afraid I know too little
about.

In the 1956 Convention *serfdom* is defined as 'the tenure of land
whereby the tenant is by law, custom or agreement bound to live and
labour on land belonging to another person and render some
determinate services to such other person, whether for reward or
not, and is not free to change his status'.[12] Here again it is the services
rendered by the serf to his lord, with the inability to move away or
liberate himself, on which the definition concentrates.

When I was teaching ancient history I often used to ask my pupils
how they would compare the lot of the slave and the serf; but I
hardly ever got a good answer. There are two elements to be
considered. First, the services that have to be provided by the serf,
above all of course the quantity of labour he must perform on his
lord's land, are nearly always limited – although of course the serf
may sometimes be unable to refuse a demand for additional labour.
But the second element is even more important: the serf,
paradoxically, just because of the most burdensome feature of his
condition, his being in effect 'bound to the soil', cannot be sold away
from the land he works, and *therefore* can marry (often officially) and
enjoy a family life, whereas the slave, who has rarely if ever been
granted any semblance of a legal right to marry, has no redress if his
master decides to sell him separately from the woman he regards as
his wife and her offspring. In this respect, then, the serf is far better
off than the slave.[13] There is much evidence from the American Old
South in particular that the breaking up of a slave family was felt as
the worst of all possible misfortunes.

At the peak periods of Greek and Roman history, slavery in the
strict sense was by far the most important form of unfree labour; and
it was only from the fourth century of the Christian era that serfdom,
in the form of the Later Roman colonate, became the most important
form of surplus extraction in large parts of the Roman Empire.[14]
Serfdom, as it happened, had been until then in the general sense an
institution entirely unknown to Greek and Roman law, and there
were no technical terms to express it; but there had been a few local
societies where it did exist, by local law and custom, down to the last
century or two BC, though hardly longer.[15]

The best known of these local societies is Sparta, where the Helots (of Messenia and Laconia),[16] who provided the bulk of the labour for their Spartiate masters, were state serfs, in that they belonged to the Spartan state, and were merely allocated to individual Spartiates, who had no right to free them, in the way that ordinary Greek slaves could always be freed by their masters – Helots could be freed only by the state, which did occasionally free them (even in quite considerable numbers) when they gave military assistance to Sparta. Being a Helot, however, was hardly better than being a slave; and slave terminology was sometimes applied to the Helots, as in a treaty between Sparta and Athens in 421 BC, where the Helots are referred to as *hē douleia*, the slave population (Thucydides V. 23.3). The Helots, according to Aristotle (*Politics* II.9, 1269^{a}38–9), lay in wait, as it were, to take advantage of the Spartans' misfortunes; and Spartan policy, in the opinion of Thucydides (IV.80.3), was always mainly governed by the necessity of taking precautions against the Helots. But perhaps the most remarkable piece of evidence of the implacable hostility between Spartans and Helots is the Spartan law, which we happen to know only from a fragment of Aristotle, preserved by Plutarch,[17] obliging the principal magistrates of Sparta, the ephors, on taking office each year, to make a formal declaration of war upon the Helots, so that they all became official enemies of the state, *polemioi*, and could then be killed as necessary, without bringing upon Sparta the religious pollution involved in putting to death anyone who was not a *polemios*, otherwise than by due process of law. Declaring war on one's own workforce is an extraordinary action, to which I know of no parallel.

I want to say something now about the subject of the manumission of slaves: the freeing of slaves individually. As someone else is dealing with the social-psychological analysis of manumission, I shall stick to the factual side, and to matters which I know well from the original source material.[18] The extent of manumission, and the forms which it has taken, have differed very widely in different slave societies; and there were important differences even between Greek and Roman practices. The Greeks, at least until they came under Roman rule and acquired many Roman habits and in due course the whole system of Roman law, seem to have made only very restricted use of manumission. Aristotle, in a statement in the *Politics* which is often overlooked,[19] actually advised that all slaves should be offered the ultimate reward of manumission; but unfortunately he never returned to the subject to give his reasons, as he said he was going to do. And I think I am right in saying that we do not know of any Greek city in which a formally manumitted slave automatically became a citizen of that city. In Rome, from a very early period, manumission in strict form did make the freed slave, the new freedman, into a citizen of Rome. His civic rights were severely limited in several ways, and he always remained a dependant, a *cliens*, of his former owner, now his *patronus*; but his children, if born after his manumission and therefore born free (*ingenui*), were not in any way legally different from other Romans, although of course certain snobbish persons might hold the servile origins of their fathers against them. This may seem very remarkable; but I believe myself that the explanation of this extraordinary apparent generosity to freed slaves is the one revealed by Dionysius of Halicarnassus: that it was the Roman system of patronage and clientship which made the turning of one's freed slaves into dependent *citizen* freedmen a most useful means of displaying the number of one's dependents and promoting one's own political career.[20]

I have often wondered what hard-hearted Romans did with their slaves when they became too old or too decrepit to perform useful tasks. That old ruffian, Cato the Elder, who died in 149 BC and was perhaps the archetypal Roman Republican aristocrat of the Old School, expressed an opinion on this subject which has been quoted again and again: in his book on agriculture he advises the landowner to reduce the rations of such slaves, and to sell off those who became old or diseased, just like decrepit oxen or worn-out tools or 'anything else that is superfluous' (*De Agric.* II.4, 7). Well, that might work as long as the slave was not too old or sick; but what would you do with a man who became entirely unserviceable? Unfortunately, I know of hardly any evidence on this point; and I hope that perhaps someone else will be able to provide some information from other slave societies. I strongly suspect that what you would do was to go up to the man, pat him on the shoulder, and tell him that you were now going to give him, as a reward for faithful service, the very best kind of golden handshake: his freedom. 'Of course', you would say to him, 'you can't expect me to go through a formal manumission ceremony, which is a fearful bother and involves paying a tax; but as far as I'm concerned you're a free man, and you can just get lost'. If you did this in front of others it might count as informal manumission *inter amicos*; but if there was no one to testify, and you later changed your mind, the wretched man might even find himself hauled back into slavery. And anyway, with informal manumission, the freed slave did not become a Roman citizen.

Very occasionally we hear in the Greek world of freedmen who acquired great wealth; but it is only in Rome, at the very end of the Republic and the beginning of the Principate (the last century BC and the first of our era) that we come across a number of freedmen who were conspicuously rich – mainly but not entirely imperial freedmen: men who had been slaves of the emperor or his family.[21] Narcissus and Pallas, freedmen who played a major part in administering the empire under the Emperors Claudius and Nero, in the first century, are credited in the literary sources with enormous fortunes, hardly ever equalled, at that period, by free men who were not members of the imperial family; but the figures we have may be greatly exaggerated. However, it was not only freedmen of the imperial household who might acquire great wealth: even before being freed, imperial slaves occupying lucrative administrative posts might become extraordinarily prosperous. I will limit myself to one example, which for once is certain, as it comes not from a literary source but from a contemporary inscription, of the reign of Tiberius (the early first century), commemorating an otherwise entirely unknown man, Musicus Scurranus, a mere cashier (*dispensator*) in a provincial treasury, who happened to die at Rome.[22] The inscription was set up by fifteen men and one woman 'from among the number of his *vicarii*, who were with him at Rome when he died'. In Roman law, *vicarii* were slaves belonging to a slave: strictly they were in the legal ownership of the slave's master (the emperor, in this case); but the remarkable Roman institution of the *peculium* enabled a slave to accumulate such possessions of his own as his master was prepared to allow him to retain: these were often used eventually to purchase his freedom. All the men in the inscription state their roles in the household of Musicus: there are three personal servants (*a manu*), two 'gentlemen of the bedchamber' (*a cubiculo*), two men who looked after Musicus's silver plate (*ab argento*), two footmen (*pedisequi*), two cooks, a doctor, a business manager (*negotiator*), a man who controlled the household expenditure (*sumptuarius*), and a valet (*a veste*). The one woman, Secunda, alone does not specify her function, and may well have been a concubine. I may say that Musicus is not the only imperial slave who is known to have possessed large quantities of silver plate.[23]

There has been much debate among scholars about the frequency of manumission in the Roman world. Of course, by far the most important consideration was the nature of the work done by the slave. I think everyone would agree that agricultural slaves, especially those on large estates, were always far less likely to be manumitted than those who functioned in urban households or work-shops, and that those who were most likely of all to obtain their freedom were those who performed personal services for their masters, above all as secretaries or accountants. In my opinion, it is impossible to make even an informed guess about the proportion of slaves who were manumitted at any time in the Greek and Roman world, although some scholars have tried to do this.

Although slaves were always, in principle, at the very bottom of the social pyramid, and were entirely without rights and completely at the disposition of their masters, not all slaves, by any means, were actually worse off economically than all free men and women. Much depended on whose slave you were: as we have seen, many Roman imperial slaves acquired great riches and importance; and the con-fidential servants of many leading Greeks and Romans made some progress in the same direction. Even the slaves of relatively poor men represented an investment which their masters would be likely to want to preserve. I know no better way of illustrating this than quoting a nice little story from the famous account by F. L. Olmsted of his journey on the steamboat *Fashion* up the Alabama River in 1855.[24] He saw some bales of cotton being thrown from a height down into the ship's hold: the men throwing the bales down were negroes, the men in the hold were Irishmen. Olmsted remarked on this to the mate of the ship. 'Oh', said the mate, 'the niggers are worth too much to be risked here; if the Paddies are knocked over-board or get their backs broke, nobody loses anything'.

Now I think we have to be careful here, because it is easy to make an unnecessary concession to one of the pro-slavery arguments that has been heard so often in slave societies: that of course most slaves will be well treated by their masters because they are a valuable property which their masters will naturally wish to preserve as such. Most slave societies have been characterised by frightful abuses and cruelties; and surely nothing can compensate for the total derogation of human dignity which must be suffered by every slave, even one with a benevolent and humane master. But it remains true that some of the very poor in antiquity, especially among wage labourers, may actually have been worse off than most slaves.[25] And in the brilliant and sophisticated analysis of the component parts (the *merē*) of the population of a Greek *polis*, which we find in Books IV and VI of Aristotle's *Politics*, the wage labourer comes off very badly indeed: he is almost at the very bottom of the heap, below everyone but the slave; and his condition is often referred to as having 'slavish' elements, because the hired man is helplessly dependent on his various employers for his livelihood.[26]

It is also interesting that we never find *free, hired* employees in high positions in the work process, either in agriculture or in manufacture. Almost without exception, the bailiffs or overseers or estate managers we hear about in classical Greece or republican Rome are slaves or freedmen; and this situation never changes throughout Greek and Roman history.[27] I began some time ago to make a collection of the references to the status of such men in later Roman sources, especially the Roman law books; and although by then slavery had declined somewhat in volume and importance, I found an overwhelming preponderance of men of servile origin, even if some of the more important of them had become freedmen.

I want to end with some remarks about the ideology of slavery, in Christian as well as pre-Christian times. It is often said that 'the Greeks' accepted the theory of 'natural slavery' (as it is called): the view that some men are slaves *by nature* (*kata physin*, in Greek). This inevitably involves the consequence that slavery is a good thing for them, just as much as for the 'natural' masters.[28] (It is all too easy for those who hold this view to see most of those who are *actually* slaves as '*natural*' slaves'.) This view was implicit in Plato, one of the greatest enemies of human freedom; but its earliest explicit formulation is by Aristotle, whose treatment of natural slavery is the most inadequate section of his great work, the *Politics*, and perhaps the feeblest part of his whole magnificent philosophical output. A more vivid and memorable expression of the essence of the views held by Plato and Aristotle on natural slavery than any they themselves formulated can be found in a remarkable book published in 1854 by a Virginia slave owner, George Fitzhugh: 'Men are not "born entitled to equal rights". It would be far nearer the truth to say that "some men were born with saddles on their backs, and others booted and spurred to ride them" – and the riding does them good. They need the reins, the bit and the spur'. The book in question has the interesting title, *Sociology for the South, or the Failure of Free Society*.[29] This was one of the earliest occasions, I believe, on which the word sociology, a compound of Latin and Greek roots, appeared in print on the other side of the Atlantic. (Incidentally, Fitzhugh must have been quoting, and contradicting, some famous words spoken on the scaffold by the English radical, Richard Rumbold, in 1685.[30] I have never been able to discover how Fitzhugh came to know Rumbold's words – was it through reading Jefferson, perhaps? If anyone has a solution to this puzzle, I shall be glad to hear it.)

But in reality the theory of natural slavery seems never to have caught on, and after Aristotle it almost disappears in antiquity, except in isolated passages such as that in which Cicero scornfully refers to Jews and Syrians as 'peoples born for slavery'.[31] Indeed, we have to wait until the sixteenth century before we find the theory of natural slavery widely accepted once more, explicitly on the authority of Aristotle, and in Spain, to such an extent that the great question whether the Spaniards might lawfully wage war upon American Indians and enslave them, before even preaching the Gospel to them, was decided by the experts in full acceptance of Aristotle's theory: the one problem was to decide whether the American Indians were in reality natural slaves – it was hardly doubted that negroes were.[32]

But we have jumped ahead many hundred years. Let us return to the last few centuries BC, when a new theory of slavery (already adumbrated by Aristotle) rapidly emerged and soon became almost universal: it was adopted by the Stoics in particular.[33] This is the theory that the good and wise man is never 'really' a slave, even if that happens to be his actual condition, but is 'really' free; the real slave is the bad man, who is in bondage to his own faults and lusts – gluttony, lechery, drink or foolish and costly ambitions, to quote Xenophon (*Oecon.* I.21–2). The state of slavery is the result of accident, of Fortune (*Fortuna, Tychē*) rather than Nature: in this way slavery resembles poverty and war on the one hand, and on the other, liberty, riches and peace. As I have remarked in dealing with this subject, I fancy that such austere philosophical notions are of greater assistance in the endurance of liberty, riches and peace, than of slavery, poverty and war. But it is obvious that the whole doctrine is perfectly adapted to the mentality of slaveowners.

Early Christianity, in its standard Pauline form, accepted *in toto* the view I have just described.[34] Too many people have misinterpreted a couple of New Testament texts which appear to deny any difference between slave and free: the more explicit one, *Galatians* III.28,[35] reads, 'There is neither Jew nor Greek, there is neither slave nor free, there is neither male nor female, for ye are all one in Christ Jesus'. But the statment is intended in a strictly spiritual sense: the equality exists in the sight of God and has no relation whatever to temporal affairs; the distinction between slave and master in this world is not seen as needing to be changed, any more than that between male and female. and on the lines of a text in *Ephesians* which tells slaves to obey their masters 'with fear and trembling, *as unto Christ*', two early Post-Apostolic works go beyond anything I know in pagan literature in formulating the subjection of the slave to his master in explicitly religious terms. The slave, in reverence and fear, must obey his master 'as a counterpart of God' (*hós typói Theou*).[36] All the evidence from the early Christian centuries is on the same lines. St Paul assures the slave who becomes a Christian that he is now 'Christ's freedman', just as the Christian who is a free man is 'Christ's slave'[37] – the way St Paul describes himself at the beginning of his *Epistle to the Romans*. I admit that I find it hard to estimate whether the Christian slave will have found this assurance more comforting than the pagan slave who was told by the philosophers that because he was a good man he was not really a slave at all; but it seems to me that the two conceptions, however different theologically, are philosophically indistinguishable. There is no evidence that slaves were better treated overall in the Christian Roman Empire than previously. Church councils continue to decree flogging as a standard penalty for slaves, male or female. Early in the fourth century the Council of Elvira in Spain punished with no more than seven years' excommunication even the intentional flogging to death by a mistress of her slave girl – presumably for accepting the sexual attentions of the woman's husband.[38] I have not been able to discover any general condemnation of slavery as an institution by Christians before the late seventeenth century.[39] Even those who admitted that slavery was an evil in principle, St Augustine in particular, accepted it as God's punishment upon mankind for the sin of Adam[40] – a highly indiscriminate method of collective punishment, which many people nowadays might shrink from attributing to the Almighty. And in the great debate in North America in the eighteenth and nineteenth centuries it seems to me that the pro-slavery propagandists easily had the better of the abolitionists, in so far as both appealed to the supreme authority of the Old and New Testaments.

There is one thing that particularly puzzles me in this sad story. Churchmen like Augustine and Ambrose felt that slavery might actually be good for the slave, an instructive form of correction, perhaps even a blessing, with the good slave being specially rewarded for triumphing over his disadvantages: St Ambrose explicitly says, 'The lower the station in life, the more exalted the virtue'.[41] So I am inclined to agree that perhaps on strictly Christian principles slavery cannot be wholly condemned, if one considers it only from 'the position of the slave. But what about the master, who is surely led into temptation' to an unparalleled degree, to commit acts of lust and cruelty, by having more or less unlimited power over fellow human beings? The use of slaves for sexual purposes, although condemned again and again by the Early Fathers, was an everyday phenomenon; and cruel punishments (flogging especially) were evidently all too common. Yet I have not been able to find this argument against slavery as an institution in any early Christian writer. My favourite example of it comes in *War and Peace*, Book Five, where Prince Andrey presses upon Pierre, as the major evil of serfdom, its brutalising effect upon those who owned the serfs.[42]

Notes

1 To avoid unnecessary detail I shall sometimes give references to ancient sources and modern works by citing my book *The Class Struggle in the Ancient Greek World, from the Archaic Age to the Arab Conquests*, London, Duckworth, 1981, corr. repr. (paperback) 1983, hereafter referred to as *CSAGW*, which has very full references throughout.

2 On 'forced labour', see *CSAGW* p. 134 (cf., p. 170), and, since that book was published, Millar (1984).

3 In *CSAGW* pp. 50–2 I have set out a series of passages from all three volumes of *Das Kapital* in which Marx makes clear the importance he attached to this consideration.

4 *CSAGW* pp. 52–5, 172–3.

5 Finley (1959). Cf., *CSAGW* p. 94.

6 See *CSAGW* pp. 58–9, 80, 91–4.

7 See Ste. Croix (1984), p. 109–10, citing two of Finley's works in note 54.

8 See *CSAGW* pp. 135–7.

9 See *CSAGW* pp. 135, 140–7; cf., IV.iii.

10 *CSAGW* pp. 136–7, pp. 162–70.

11 *CSAGW* p. 169.

12 See *CSAGW* pp. 135–6, 147–62; cf., VI.iii.
13 *CSAGW* pp. 147–8.
14 *CSAGW* pp. 226–59 (IV.iii).
15 *CSAGW* pp. 137–40, 147–50, etc.
16 See, briefly, *CSAGW* pp. 149–50, with p. 93; and, in more detail, Ste. Croix (1972), pp. 89–94.
17 Arist., fr. 538, in Plutarch, *Lycurgus* 28.7. See *CSAGW* pp. 61, 92.
18 On Greek and Roman freedmen, see *CSAGW* pp. 174–9 (III.iv).
19 Arist., *Pol.* VII.10, 1330^{a}32–3.
20 Dion. Hal., *Antiq. Rom.* IV.22.4 to 23.7.
21 *CSAGW* pp. 176–8, with p. 143.
22 Dessau, *Inscriptiones Latinae Selectae* 1514: see *CSAGW* p. 143.
23 See *CSAGW* p. 143, for Rotundus Drusillianus, in Pliny, *Nat. Hist.* XXXIII.145.
24 See *CSAGW* p. 142, with p. 563 n.12.
25 *CSAGW* pp. 185–8.
26 *CSAGW* p. 77.
27 *CSAGW* pp. 140, 144–5, 172, 173, 181–2, 256–8, 505–7.
28 'Natural slavery': *CSAGW* pp. 416–18.
29 See *CSAGW* p. 417.
30 *CSAGW* p. 638 n.13.
31 *CSAGW* pp. 417–18.
32 *CSAGW* p. 418.
33 *CSAGW* pp. 418–19.
34 See *CSAGW* pp. 419–25.
35 Cf., *Colossians* III.11.
36 *Ephesians* VI.5; *Epistle of Barnabas* XIX.7 and *Didache* IV.11.
37 *I Corinthians* VII.22. St Paul in *Romans* I.1 describes himself as a slave (*doulos*) of Jesus Christ.
38 *CSAGW* p.420, with p. 638 n.2.
39 *CSAGW* pp. 423–4.
40 Augustine, *De Civitate Dei* XIX.15–16, cf., 21. And see *CSAGW* p. 639 n.4.
41 *CSAGW* p. 421.
42 On Christian attitudes to slavery, see Ste. Croix (1975); *CSAGW*, pp. 419–25.

Two

Serfdom in Classical Greece
Paul A. Cartledge

Was classical Greek civilisation based on slavery? Was classical Greece a slave society, or characterised by the slave mode of production? These questions are hardly original neither have they lacked for answers in the scholarly literature.[1] But they remain more or less hotly controversial for empirical, theoretical and indeed ideological reasons. Empirical, for sheer lack of good contemporary evidence, above all from the side of the enslaved.[2] Theoretical, because of unresolved doubts about, for example, the applicability of the 'mode of production' concept to any society and the classification of any or all slaves in classical Greece as a 'class'.[3] Ideological, since although the lingering poison of slavery does not subtly contaminate the modern historiography of ancient Greece as it inevitably does that of New World slavery, there have always been ancient historians who find it hard to stomach the notion of slavery as an integral part, let alone the basis, of a civilisation they like to see as the fountainhead of everything most admirable in the entire western cultural tradition.[4]

Those sources of controversy are surely already daunting enough. Yet there are more, arising from ambiguities of terminology surrounding both 'Greece' and 'slavery'. In the fifth and fourth centuries BC the world of dominant Greek speech and culture was by no means confined within the frontiers of the present nation–state of Greece. Indeed, there was no state (or nation) of 'Hellas' in that epoch but rather a far-flung and politically heterogeneous aggregation of well over a thousand individuated Greek communities extending from the east coast of Spain to the eastern end of the Black Sea, from south Russia to Libya. Greekness, the antithesis of being a 'barbarian', was a matter of shared language, religion and social customs, not of membership in a unitary political organisation.[5] The absence of such an all-embracing union was deplored in the third quarter of the fourth century by Aristotle. But had one existed, his own great work of political theory and sociology would have been rendered superfluous. For Aristotle took the ideal (rarely an actuality) of the sovereign and autonomous Greek *polis* to be the end or goal, the final term, of all human social life and went so far as to define man as a *zoön politikon*, a living creature designed by its nature to attain its full development within the framework of the *polis* – hence his *Politics*, literally 'matters relating to the *polis*'. ('City-state', the conventional translation of *polis*, is a travesty, exaggerating the urban element at the expense of ignoring the rural-urban continuum and symbiosis that the *polis* typically embodied.) Moreover, as Aristotle was perfectly well aware, not all Greeks enjoyed the *polis* form of self-government, many preferring the more informal, less centralised, more broadly territorial framework of the *ethnos* or tribal state (where 'state' is appropriate) that prevailed especially in areas of mainland Greece to the north of the Corinthian Gulf.[6]

With this heterogeneity of polity went heterogeneity of society and economy. It is inconceivable, therefore, that one single type of slavery could have been practised by each and every classical Greek *polis* or *ethnos*. But although classical Greek was exceptionally rich in words for the unfree, the dozen or so separate terms in current use were unfortunately not employed with the kind of precision dear to the heart of a Roman lawyer – or the modern historian of ancient Greece. Instead they were used with a bewildering, almost nonchalant inconsistency. For example, the term meaning etymologically household slaves (*oiketai*) could be attached equally to slaves whose sole occupation was in the fields (as well as to free domestics); slaves labelled *andrapoda* (David Harvey's 'man-footed creatures': see next chapter, were not all war-captives by a long chalk, although the verb *andrapodizein* meant specifically to sell a conquered population into servitude; and, most seriously, the commonest term of all, *douloi*, was so far from having any precise juridical content that it was formally and publicly applied to the radically different servile populations of the no less sharply politically differentiated states of Athens and Sparta. (Athens represented an extreme version of radical democracy, whereas the political system of Sparta is best defined as a quite narrow form of oligarchy.)

Here we approach more closely to the nub of our subject. For in classical Athens of the fifth and fourth centuries BC, despite great internal gradations of economic and social status, all the perhaps 80–100,000 *douloi* of both sexes may be categorised precisely as chattel slaves, whereas the perhaps twice as numerous *douloi* of the Spartans were indubitably not chattels, whatever exactly their proper positive classification may be (below). In this respect the Helots, as the Spartan *douloi* were known, were very far from being unique, and if I shall be spending most of my time here on them, this is chiefly because theirs is easily the best documented of all the many sorts and conditions of non-chattel servitude in classical Greece (not that there is a great deal of evidence even for them.)

However, in order to comprehend the Helots' complex and confusingly hybrid status, it will be best to begin the discussion with the *douloi* of the kind enslaved within the Athenian *polis* and – if it is legitimate to make this inference from Aristotle's unfortunate attempt to defend the institution as a necessary component of the good life in the *polis* – many other classical Greek *polis* too.[7] For chattel slavery would seem to be the simplest category of unfreedom to grasp conceptually, simplest because most sharply defined. In a Weberian sense the chattel is the ideal type of the slave – the most unfree of the unfree, the most servile of the enslaved. In his or her typical classical Greek guise the chattel slave was most literally an outsider, being a barbarian (non-Greek, especially Phrygian, Carian or Thracian), torn from kith, kin and community, thrust through the medium of physical, commercial and psychological violence into an alien environment, there to be deprived of all or virtually all legally enforceable rights and even of many of the ordinary solaces of a human existence. The chattel, in short, was ideally a thing rather than a person, an implement (as Aristotle brutally put it) that happened incidentally to possess some sort of human personality, or – to change the image – 'a human being who is legally owned, used, sold, or otherwise disposed of as if he or she were a domestic animal'.[8]

Since classical Athens was by far the most populous Greek state, there were more chattel slaves here than anywhere else in the Greek world. They may have accounted for about a third of the total population at its peak in the third quarter of the fifth century. (Only wine-exporting Chios may have had a higher chattel slave density.) This proportion would be comparable to that statistically documented for the American Old South, Brazil and the Caribbean at their respective peaks. But whereas those three may certainly be classified as slave societies – that is, societies where an institutionalised system of large scale employment of slave labour in the basic productive sectors was integral to their functioning, reproduction and lifestyle – the evidence is such that it is strictly only an inference that the same was true of classical Athens (and some other Greek states). Nor do we have the evidence to explain conclusively why and how Athens became a slave society, if (as I believe) it did. But we can at least identify one of the necessary conditions, which takes us into a second major area of unfreedom in ancient Greece besides chattel slavery, an area that historically has been and is far more prevalent in the world as a whole.

In about 600 BC the reforming Athenian legislator Solon responded to a severe debt crisis by not only cancelling all existing debts but also outlawing for the future the practice of securing loans on the person of the debtor. This law was never revoked, with the result that 'legally' rich Athenian creditors (typically large landowners) were thereafter obliged to look elsewhere than to poor Athenian citizens for the compulsory, forced, involuntary, dependent or tied labour they had to exploit in order to yield the surplus required to maintain themselves as a leisured ruling class. By Solon's law poor Athenians were not of course guaranteed against falling into debt, but legally they could not again be reduced to the condition of debt bondsmen or debt slaves in their native land.[9]

Obviously legal prescription and actual social practice need not precisely coincide, as a recent survey of debt bondage in the modern world has made all too uncomfortably clear.[10] (One might add that there are reliably reckoned to be more slaves today than before abolitionism began to be translated into legal enactment.) Yet there is reason for thinking that the development of a trade in 'barbarian' slaves in the sixth century and the institution of a primitive democracy at Athens shortly before 500 would together have ensured that Solon's debt bondage law was not merely honoured in the breach. Elsewhere in the classical Greek world, though, we do not hear of precisely parallel legislation and on the contrary do learn of insistent calls for the cancellation of debts and (often simultaneously) the redistribution of land – the classic slogans of oppressed peasantries who we may suspect (for lack of direct evidence) found that indebtness arising out of inadequate harvests from insufficient land all too frequently entailed a greater or smaller, a milder or harsher, degree of personal bondage. That at any rate would be a wholly legitimate inference on comparative grounds.[11]

The few surviving (but probably representative) ancient Greek writers who bothered themselves with the origins of chattel slavery –

or indeed any historical aspects of any form of servitude – in Greece did not make this modern connection between the abolition of debt bondage and the rise of chattel slavery in Athens. They were, however, capable of drawing some distinctions, if only with the crudest of strokes, among the many hundreds of thousands of *douloi* in classical Greece. Reflection along these lines was given a strong stimulus by the unparalleled personal and political emancipation in 369 BC of perhaps as many as 100,000 Helots. Not only did this feat exacerbate existing philosophical disagreements about the justice of slavery (disagreements which, it must be added, gave rise to no categorical demands for abolition, let alone an abolitionist movement), but it also prompted attempts to clarify the differences between Helots and other *douloi* and even some rudimentary shots at classifying the type of servitude experienced by Helots and other *ex hypothesi* similar servile groups.[12]

Thus the historian Theopompos, himself a native of the island state of Chios and writing in the same period as Aristotle, averred with a certain 'national' pride that 'The Chians were the first Greeks after the Thessalians and Spartans to make use of *douloi*, but they did not acquire them in the same way as these. For the Spartans and Thessalians ... recruited their slave populations from the Greeks who previously inhabited the country they now control' – whereas the Chians allegedly inaugurated the characteristic classical practice of buying barbarians as *douloi* rather than enslaving local Greek populations by conquest.[13] This was an important, negative differentiation. What we would call chattel slaves were typically non-Greeks purchased in the market. Positively, Aristotle went a big step further on the basis of his and his pupils' extensive researches into the political and social arrangements of no less than 158 polities. The Kallikyrioi at Syracuse, he declared, 'are like the Spartans' Helots, the Thessalians' Penestai and the Cretans' Klarotai'. Unfortunately, though, the source who quoted this snippet from the Aristotelian 'Polity of the Syracusans' was not interested in saying precisely what the likeness consisted in indeed, the author of the 'Polity' may not have been either. It was left to a post-classical writer, who may have been the famous literary critic Aristophanes of Byzantion (where another, though not Greek, Helot-like population had been enslaved), to come up with the following: 'Between free people and *douloi* are the Helots of Lakonia, the Penestai of Thessaly, the Dorophoroi [of Herakleia on the Black Sea], the Gymnetes of Argos and the Korynephoroi of Sikyon'.

That classification is not, frankly, overwhelmingly persuasive as it stands, being both ambiguous and probably in part factually false.[14] By *douloi* must presumably be meant chattel *douloi*, interpreted in the manner adumbrated above. Yet not only were the Helots themselves regularly and officially referred to as *douloi*, but they too could be described by the extreme Athenian oligarch Kritias in the fifth century as '*douloi* to the greatest degree'. Another ancient definition of the Helots may therefore legitimately be called in evidence, late though it is. Some time after Helotage ceased following the Roman conquest of Greece the geographer Strabo, writing towards the end of the first century BC, remarked that the Spartans had held the Helots 'as *douloi* in a way of the community'. The 'in a way' was intended to convey the notion that, although Helots were not owned individually by Spartan masters or mistresses but by the Spartan state 'and so could only be manumitted by act of the Spartan assembly', it was to an individual Spartan that they were bound to hand over annually a certain amount of the produce from the private estate to which they were forcibly attached. This formula, however, helpful though it is, fails by itself to account for the 'between free people and *douloi*' tag. What grounds were there for supposing that the Helots, like the Penestai and so forth, should be located at some intermediate point along the spectrum between outright freedom and total bondage?

The fact that they were Greeks was clearly not decisive; others of the genuinely servile groups with whom they were compared or lumped were not Greek. What appears to lie behind the pseudo-definition therefore is the fact that the Helots and so on, unlike *douloi* pure and simple, enjoyed some sort of customary rights over their persons and over property, some kind of family life, some form of religious community, all these being based ultimately on varying degrees of ethnic solidarity (hence their collective names). It was arguably these elements of freedom, combined crucially with geographical distance, overwhelming numerical superiority, and a deep socio-political crisis among their Spartan masters (reflected in a decisive military defeat and a massive and unprecedented invasion of the Spartans' home territory by their Greek enemies), that enabled the majority of the Helots – those of Messenia – to revolt successfully and permanently in 369. This was something that no group of chattel slaves in classical Greece achieved or even, possibly, attempted.[15]

The Penestai, on the other hand, and some other comparable

ethnic servile groups did at least manage to revolt, though without achieving lasting success. But what made the Messenian Helots' revolt unique in the annals of Greek servitude is that, like the chattel slaves of Saint Dominque (Haiti) in the late eighteenth century, they revolted not only into personal liberty but into full political freedom as citizens of the (re)founded sovereign and autonomous *polis* of Messene. It was perhaps this precisely political dimension to the Messenians' desire to be free (which they shared with all servile groups) that accounts for the Spartans' equally unparalleled annual declaration of war (for ritual as well as police purposes) on their workforce.

Finally, how should *we* classify the Helots? Disagreement rages here no less fiercely than among the ancients. For the Czech scholar Olivia what they experienced was an 'undeveloped' form of slavery, but this is surely to confuse a difference in kind of servitude with a difference of 'progress' along a supposedly single evolutionary path.[16] The suggestion of the East German Lotze that they were 'collective' slaves is by contrast rather too bland and perhaps not as accurate or informative as Strabo's 'in a way public *douloi*'.[17] Far more promising at first sight is the French Marxist Garlan's classification of Helotage as a tributary species of intercommunal servitude, but this classification is achieved only at the cost of grouping Helots with very dissimilar kinds of unfree persons such as temple slaves.[18] On balance, therefore, it seems to me most fruitful to follow the lead of the English Marxist Ste. Croix, who finds a place for them among the third major category of the unfree besides chattel slaves and debt bondsmen. That scholar unhesitatingly defines the Helots as 'state serfs' – serfs, because they conform closely enough to the internationally agreed definition of serfdom as formulated by the United Nations Supplementary Convention on the Abolition of Slavery, the Slave Trade and Practices similar to Slavery (1956); and state serfs, because the Helots were owned and controlled collectively by the Spartan state which exerted an unparalleled degree of state coercion upon them.[19]

It is possible, indeed, to go further than merely defining the Helots's juridical status. It may be a matter for legitimate dispute whether Greek civilisation was based on slavery or the slave mode of production or whether any particular Greek *polis* or *ethnos* was a slave society. But there need be no prevarication in declaring that Spartan civilisation was based on the forced labour of the Helots, that the

Messenian Helots in particular constituted a class in an objective, economic sense, and that the struggle between them and their collective Spartan master was precisely a class struggle conducted with a view to their (re)gaining political power as well as escaping from personal bondage and economic exploitation.

Notes

1 Outstanding is Finley (1959)
2 This lack is demonstrated by the only available sourcebook, Wiedemann (1981), but it should be added that this is biased towards Roman slavery.
3 On the 'slave mode of production' contrast Anderson (1974), pp. 18–28 (pro) with Finley (1985), pp. 179–80 (con). On slaves as a 'class', Ste. Croix (1981) (pro) with Vidal-Naquet (1981) (con). My sympathies here lie with Anderson and Ste. Croix.
4 Finley (1979).
5 Walbank (1951); Finley (1975), Ch. 7.
6 The situation is graphically depicted for the immediately pre-classical 'archaic' period in Snodgrass (1980), fig. 9. See also Snodgrass (1984).
7 For a collection of evidence for slavery (especially agricultural) in the classical and Hellenistic periods see Ste. Croix (1981), pp. 505–9. For the contradictions in Aristotle's defence see Smith (1983).
8 Davis (1985).
9 Finley (1981), Ch. 9 ('Debt-bondage and the problem of slavery'), especially pp. 156–60; idem (1980), Ch. 3 ('The emergence of a slave society').
10 Ennew (1981).
11 On debt and debt bondage in the ancient (not just classical) Greek world see Ste. Croix (1981), Index s.v.
12 Vidal-Naquet (1981), pp. 223–48; Finley (1981), Ch 7 ('Between slavery and freedom') and Ch. 8 ('The servile statuses of ancient Greece').
13 This and the following translated passages are included in a much larger selection of ancient sources on the Helots in Cartledge (1979), Appendix 4.
14 That the Gymnetes and Korynephoroi were free is argued by Lotze (1959). The servile status of the Sikyonian Katonakophoroi seems better attested: Whitehead (1981); but see now Lotze (1985).
15 Cartledge (1985): for the purposes of comparison I focused especially on Genovese (1979).
16 Oliva (1971); *idem* (1981).
17 Lotze (1959)

18 Garlan (1982)
19 Ste. Croix (1981), p. 135, quotes the relevant Convention and attempts to apply it at pp. 147–62 (Helots at pp. 149–50).

Further reading

See Cartledge (1986), Ch. 10; Ducat (1974); *idem* (1978); Welwei (1974–77).

Three

Herodotus and the Man-Footed Creature[1]
F. D. Harvey

Herodotus of Halikarnassos was the world's first practitioner of the historian's craft. The Chinese generally manage to do things first, but Herodotus' history of the Persian invasions of Greece was written in the fifth century BC, some three centuries before Ssu-ma Ch'ien, the Chinese 'father of history', was born. Unlike the other Greek writers from whom we derive our information about ancient slavery, Herodotus travelled widely: to Asia Minor, Mesopotamia, Phoenicia, Egypt, south Russia, south Italy and Sicily, as well as all over the Greek world. His observations on slavery therefore constitute an important and unusual contribution to the historiography of the subject.

The Greek vocabulary for servile labour was large, and Herodotus uses most of it. The most general word is *doulos*, slave: Herodotus had unfortunately not read the United Nations Conventions, and uses the word of all forms of unfree labour, not only slavery (e.g., 7.155).[1] *Andrapodon*, the 'man-footed creature' of my title, is an unpleasant word formed on the analogy of 'four-footed creatures', i.e., cattle; it can mean either prisoner-of-war or slave. The other terms which Herodotus uses include *oiketēs*, a member of the household, frequently but not always a slave (see 7.170; 8.4, 41, 62, 106, 109); *therapōn*, a personal slave (synonymous with *oiketēs* at 2.113); *amphipolos*, a hand-maiden, who attends a woman; *hypēretēs*, a slave assistant, and *diēkonos*, a slave attendant.

What does Herodotus tell us about these people? Let us look in turn at the following topics: the early history of slavery; the methods of acquiring slaves; their place of origin; their names; their tasks; eunuch slaves; the treatment of slaves, and signs of unrest; and finally, Herodotus' own views on slavery. There are also interesting comments at 1.111, 1.173, 2.113, 6.83 and 8.68, which cannot be discussed here.

Early history

Not much is known about chattel slaves in Greece before the Persian invasion of 480 BC. Herodotus recounts an Athenian tradition that in the remote past their daughters were assaulted when they went to fetch water from a spring. The girls fetched water, he says, because at that time neither the Athenians nor any other Greeks had household slaves (6.137). The date implied is a century after the Trojan War, the early Dark Age in our terms; and given the catastrophic slump in the living conditions of most Greeks at that time, the tradition may well be correct. Again, there were once six cities on the island of Lesbos; but one of them turned the inhabitants of Arisba into man-footed creatures, and then there were five (1.151). This must have taken place at some time before the mid-sixth century, when all the cities of Lesbos began to issue coins – but not Arisba. The glamorous Rhodopis (2.134–5), of whom more later, constitutes good evidence that the slave trade between Thrace and Samos was already in progress in the early sixth century. In 499 BC a Persian satrap was told that there were many man-footed creatures on Naxos (5.31). If this is not merely sales-talk to entice him to attack the island, the remark attests a lively growth of slavery in the Aegean islands before that date. Chios was notorious for the size of its slave population (Thucydides 8.40); perhaps Naxos was not so far behind. Over in Sicily, the citizens of Zankle had plenty of slaves by 493 BC (6.23). At the battle of Plataia in 479, the booty included Persian concubines, who were distributed among the Greek states that had taken part; presumably they became slaves. The commander-in-chief received ten select women (besides ten camels and other goodies). We do not know whether he kept them as personal slaves (9.81).

Methods of acquisition

After a city had been captured in war, it was common practice (already established in the Homeric epics) to sell off the inhabitants. Although the horrors of warfare have of course increased immeasurably since Herodotus' day, this is one piece of inhumanity that has not survived. The Persians did it frequently (1.76, 156, 161; 4.203–4; 6.18–19, 96; 7.181). Captives taken from Eretria in 490 BC were marched off to the Persian capital, and settled at Arderikka, near an oil well of which Herodotus gives a careful description (6.94, 101, 106–7, 115, 119). This is represented as an act of mercy: no doubt the Persian king originally intended to have them executed, but Herodotus' language also suggests that they retained their personal freedom, though transported to what they must have regarded as the middle of nowhere. If so, they were exceptionally fortunate: elsewhere when prisoners-of-war are described as man-footed creatures, there is good reason to suppose that they became slaves. Generally they were sold on the spot (e.g., 1.156, 3.14): an army operating in hostile territory does not want to be encumbered with masses of prisoners. Herodotus does tell us of a Pharaoh who brought captives from his far-flung conquests back to Egypt, some even from Russia (2.107–8); but that is fiction, and strictly speaking they became not slaves, but forced labourers.

Greeks also enslaved other Greeks whom they captured in war. That is what happened at Arisba (1.151), to the Spartans taken at Tegea (1.66; early sixth century), and to Samian dissidents settled at Khania in Crete (3.59; late 520s BC). An aristocratic lady from Kos, concubine of a Persian commander who had brought her with him to help him conquer Greece, only escaped servitude by a personal appeal to the Greek commander-in-chief (9.76; 479 BC). In one instance, in Sicily, a tyrant was given half the man-footed creatures from a conquered city, and all those taken in the surrounding countryside, as a reward for his cooperation (6.23; 493 BC).

Many of these incidents involved whole cities, and warfare must have created thousands of unfree labourers in the Persian Empire. The communities that Herodotus says were captured by Greeks were comparatively small, but here again it was war which produced slaves.

In many societies kidnapping is a common method of acquiring slaves, but we meet only one instance of this in Herodotus, and that is mythical: Phoenicians are said to have carried off two Egyptian priestesses and to have sold them in Libya and north-west Greece (2.54–6). The Phoenicians, it seems, specialised in kidnaps (cf., 1.1). Rather different is the story of fifteen Persian grandees who were wrecked off the heel of Italy in the late sixth century; they were later discovered working as slaves for the natives, who were barbarians but not totally barbaric (3.138). The incident is bizarre, though not unparalleled.

One lot of slaves was obtained by trickery. Polykrates, tyrant of Samos, was lured to his death by a Persian satrap (c. 522 BC). The tyrant was accompanied by slaves and foreigners, and the satrap kept them as man-footed creatures. After he in turn was put to death, the slaves were transferred to the royal court at Susa (3.125, 129).

In Skythia (south Russia), the kings did not buy slaves for cash (by implication, then, that is what Greeks normally did); they chose them from their own subjects, you you and you. This was no joke: when the king died, his slaves were strangled (4.71–2).

Increasing the stock of slaves by breeding is never mentioned by Herodotus in a Greek context, though a folktale seems to imply it for the Medes (1.114; cf., 1.173 [Lycia]).

Place of origin

The passages already mentioned contain most of what Herodotus has to tell us about the places from which Greeks obtained slaves. In the Peloponnese and on Lesbos, they enslaved their neighbours and Aiginetans acquired Samian slaves from Crete (1.66, 151; 3.59). Uncharacteristically, no linguistic barrier will have separated these slaves from their masters, or prevented them from communicating with each other. Rhodopis came from Thrace to Samos (2.134); the story that the god Salmoxis was really a Thracian slave belonging to Pythagoras (4.95) is totally bogus, but taken from the right angle, so to speak, it shows that it was natural to think of Samians still getting slaves from Thrace a couple of generations later. Thrace, roughly equivalent to modern Bulgaria, was a rich source of slave labour: the inhabitants exported their own children (5.6).

Names

Herodotus mentions two dozen individual slaves, and tells us the names of six. The infant Cyrus (King of Persia 559–529 BC) is said to have been brought up by slaves called Mitradates and Spako (1.110); another folktale, but both are good Iranian names. Spako means 'bitch', and some said that Cyrus was literally brought up as the son of a bitch (1.122). The story implies that Median slaves were allowed to marry. Aisop (2.134; early sixth century) was well known for his fables; Rhodopis was a classy courtesan. Some said she built one of the pyramids, a notion which Herodotus solemnly refutes on economic and chronological grounds (2.134–5). Perhaps the story started as a joke: her immoral earnings were so vast that she could afford to build a Wonder of the World. Rhodopis, however, was not a slave when she amassed her spectacular fortune in Egypt: she had been freed by the brother of Sappho, who was infatuated with her. She and Aisop had been the property of the same Samian master: small world.

We are also told about Themistokles' household slave Sikinnos, who carried the message to Xerxes that enticed the Persians to disaster at Salamis in 480 BC. He was a *paidagōgos*, a trusted senior slave; and afterwards his master made him a citizen of Thespiai (8.75, cf. 110). The adult males of this little community had been wiped out at Thermopylai, and the town must have been desperate for citizens. A manumitted Greek slave did not normally acquire citizen rights, and it is worth noting that Sikinnos did not become a citizen of Athens, the *polis* in which he had been a slave.

Finally there is Skiton, the household slave of a doctor. Demokedes, the doctor, had cured Dareios (King of Persia 521–486 BC), and Dareios' many wives were so pleased that they each gave him a cupful of gold pieces. Demokedes' household slave, following behind, picked up the coins that fell from the cups and collected a fortune for himself (3.130).

These named slaves have little in common. Most of them make a great deal of money (so too Salmoxis, 4.95), and Herodotus likes stories about people who do that (e.g. 1.24, 29 ff.; 2.121; 4.152; 6.125; 9.80).

The names themselves tell us little. Aisop is opaque; Rhodopis, 'Rosycheeks', sounds like a professional name. Sappho calls her Doricha, 'little gift', a present to her Samian owner, perhaps. Sikinnos is the name of a satyr, a lustful irresponsible creature; it is cognate with *sikinnis*, a Thracian dance, but this does not prove that he came from Thrace. Skiton is supposed to mean 'worthless'; if so, not a very amusing name to be lumbered with. All these names, however, even Skiton (Demosthenes 21.182), were also borne by citizens, a striking example of the fact that slave names, courtesans' names and citizens' names were all drawn from the same stock.

Tasks

The tasks that unfree persons were required to perform range from domestic chores to murder. Slaves form a Greek tyrant's retinue (3.125); man-footed creatures work in the fields at Tegea (1.66). An Athenian household slave carries vital messages (8.75, 110); so too at

Sparta (6.63, 65), where one is a donkeyman (6.68). All Greeks use such slaves to fetch water (6.137). Samian personal slaves cut up fish and polish silver (3.42, 148). When king Demaratos flees from Sparta, his personal slaves accompany him (6.70). The lady of Kos is escorted by handmaidens (9.76). Slave attendants are required to prepare a dinner after the battle of Plataia (9.82).

The Helots, the serfs of the Spartans, took part in the mourning when a king died (6.58); one acts as a guard over a mad king who had been put in the stocks (6.75); they heap wood around a grove to set it alight, together with the refugees inside it (6.80); they are ordered to drag a priest from the altar and whip him (6.81); they attend their masters on campaign (7.229; 9.10, 28); they fight in battle (8.25, 9.85), and collect valuables left behind by the enemy (9.80). We think of Helots as essentially agricultural workers, but Herodotus should make us realise that their tasks – or at least the tasks assigned to the trusted elite – were in fact more varied. Indeed, he never mentions Helots working on the land; nor does he say anything about slaves employed in crafts, or trade, or in the mines: that is simply because his narrative happens not to touch on these matters.

In Persia we find man-footed creatures washing their masters' feet (6.19), household slaves cutting off the legs of a horse (7.88), and personal slaves being told to kill Croesus, the ex-king of Lydia (3.36). A personal slave of king Dareios had to remind him of the Athenians three times at every meal (5.105, 6.94) – an extremely boring job, but one that required tactful timing. Many personal slaves accompanied the Persian forces that invaded Greece in 480 (7.83, 184, 186). Among the Medes, we find a slave herdsman (1.110), slave escorts (1.111,116) and a slave who carries a message in the belly of a hare (1.123).

In Egypt, slaves carry water (3.14), and captives are forced to build a temple with massive stones, and to dig canals (2.108). In Asia Minor, a slave had a message tattooed on his head (5.35). Household slaves are present at a tricky interview between a queen of Lydia and a gentleman who had seen her undressing (1.11; folktale, allegedly c. 685 BC). Personal slaves conduct a visitor around the treasure-houses of Croesus (1.30; mid sixth century), and accompany Babylonian ladies required to prostitute themselves religiously (1.99). In Skythia, in a problematic passage, we are told that slaves milk the mares, and increase their output by blowing into their genitals through tubes (4.2).

Two points of particular interest emerge. First, it is usually believed that there were no chattel slaves at Sparta, only serfs. That may well be true, but some passages make one wonder whether the Spartan royal family may not have had personal slaves who were not Helots. The regent Pausanias, as we have seen, was awarded ten women (9.81): did he not keep them? Kings Ariston and Leotykhidas had household slaves (6.63, 65, 67); Demaratos had personal slaves (6.70); and Pausanias told 'his own' personal attendants to prepare a dinner (9.82). Or perhaps these were all Helots: Herodotus, who like all Greek writers is frequently loose and inconsistent in his use of slave terminology, certainly calls serfs slaves elsewhere (7.155).

Secondly, agricultural slavery. The vastly wealthy Pythios, who was probably a descendant of Croesus, offered his entire monetary fortune to the Persian King Xerxes, saying that he could live quite comfortably off his man-footed creatures and estates – an excellent example of exploitation (7.28; 480 BC). The tight verbal connection between 'slaves' and 'estates' here must imply that the slaves were working the estates, providing their master with food and an income from the sale of surplus. In the Peloponnese we find Spartan prisoners-of-war working the fields of the Tegeans (1.66; early sixth century). In Zankle, on the Sicilian side of the Straits of Messina, there are quantities of slaves in the countryside (6.23; c. 493). Then there is a striking anecdote about Cyrus, who made the Persians clear a large tract of land of thorn-bushes. The next day he gave them a lavish feast, and promised them that if they rebelled from the Medes, their whole life would be like the second day, and they would not be burdened with 'labour befitting a slave' (1.125–6; c. 549 BC). This story is written for a Greek audience, and the labour that Cyrus chooses as characteristically slave-like is work on the land. Not only that, but a one-off job, clearing thorns, which one would have thought was precisely the kind of job for which a farmer would have used hired labour. All these passages strongly support the view that we have hitherto seriously underestimated the amount of slave labour employed in agriculture in the Greek world.

Eunuch slaves

Eunuch slaves were not a feature of Greek life, but of Oriental courts. Herodotus tells us that Babylon provided five hundred eunuch boys to the Persian king each year (3.92). Periander, the tyrant of Corinth c. 625–585, sent three hundred upper-class boys from his colony on Corfu to Croesus' father to be castrated at Sardis (not in Greece). They took refuge on Samos, where the inhabitants prevented the Corinthians from starving them out by inventing a religious rite that involved feeding the boys with sesame and honey-cakes; and they all lived happily ever after (3.48). A character named Panionios from Chios made his living by castrating handsome boys and selling them at Sardis and Ephesus (the end of the Royal Road to the heart of the Persian Empire). The operation, performed without anaesthetics, can hardly have been very pleasant. Panionios, the only dealer in human wares mentioned by any of the Greek historians, was eventually forced by one of his victims to castrate his own four sons, who in turn were forced to castrate their father (8.104–6; 480 BC). Elsewhere in Herodotus, a Mede sends his eunuchs to ensure that a baby is dead (1.117); the Pharaoh sends a eunuch by ship to catch a man, who subsequently made his captors drunk and got away (3.4; c. 525); eunuchs carry messages at the Persian court (3.77, 130); and in 480 eunuchs accompanied Xerxes' invading army in vast numbers (7.187). Most but not all of these will have been slaves. One certainly had a master, called Sataspes, whom Xerxes sent to circumnavigate Africa. Sataspes found that the journey was longer than he had expected, and was executed for not completing it (4.43). But the eunuch who took the sensational revenge on the eunuch-dealer held a high position at the Persian court, and should certainly not be lumped together with menials (cf., 8.105).

How badly were slaves treated?

The Tegeates made their Spartan captives work their fields in chains; that was unusual in Greece, but as the Spartans had marched into battle carrying the chains all ready to put on the Tegeates, they were perhaps asking for it (1.66; early sixth century). Demokedes, the Greek doctor who cured Dareios (p. 46 above) was found among the slaves of an executed satrap in chains and rags (3.129); but maybe this detail is merely invented to provide dramatic contrast with his later brilliant career. In Egypt, the conquered Pharaoh's daughter was made to wear a slave's clothing (3.14; 525 BC). Herodotus obviously thought that a slave's clothes were distinctive, unlike the reactionary writer who grumbled that at Athens slaves dressed in such a way that they were indistinguishable from free men (pseudo-Xenophon, *Con-*

stitution of Athens 1.10). The Skythians are said to have blinded their slaves (4.2), which will hardly have increased their efficiency. As for punishments, when Kambyses, King of Persia (530–522 BC), ordered his personal slaves to kill Croesus, they hid him instead. Kambyses, as the slaves had expected, wanted to see Croesus again before long, and was delighted that he was still alive; but he executed his slaves for disobedience (3.36). If this story were true, which it almost certainly is not, Kambyses would have been violating a Persian custom: no one, not even the king, was permitted to put a man to death for a single offence. Furthermore, no Persian was permitted to do an irreparable injury to any of his household slaves for a single offence; he could give way to his temper only if he found that a slave's offences were more numerous than his services (1.137).

Signs of unrest

We are told a little about how slaves might react. The eunuch slave of the failed Persian circumnavigator ran away with a great deal of money when he heard that his master was dead; but a man on Samos, whose name Herodotus knows but refuses to divulge, grabbed the stolen cash (4.43). After the battle of Plataia (479 BC), the Helots were ordered to collect the valuables left behind by the Persians; they stole a lot of it and sold it to the Aiginetans. The Helots thought the gold was bronze, and that is how Aigina became so rich (9.80). The last bit is just a malicious fiction, but maybe the Helots did steal some of the booty. Both stories remind one of the frequent thefts by slaves in the southern United States, and of their belief that stealing from one's masters was not reprehensible.

Two unfree persons ran away: the circumnavigator's eunuch, who got from the Persian court to Samos, and a Helot who was instructed to lead a Spartan hoplite, who was suffering from eye disease, back to the battle of Thermopylai. He pushed off instead (7.229; 480 BC).

Herodotus' views on slavery

Herodotus was a slave owner himself, and took the institution for granted. 'The gods have made me your slave,' says Croesus to Cyrus (1.89), and the pious Herodotus no doubt believed that some men were slaves, and others not, because that was the will of the gods (cf. *Odyssey* 17. 322–3). The men of Methymna enslaved their neighbours 'although they were related by blood,' he says (1.151), thus almost foreshadowing Plato's belief that it was all right to enslave barbarians, but that Greek should not enslave Greek (*Republic* 469 BC). Herodotus does protest against the eunuch-maker's line of business, which he calls 'most unholy' (8.105). He does not say why, but in view of the importance which the Greeks attached to the perpetuation of the family, I imagine that the extinction of the family line was uppermost in his mind.

Word-order betrays Herodotus's scale of values: the men of Xanthos gathered their wives, children, belongings and household slaves into the acropolis (1.176); Asia contains gold, silver, bronze, luxury clothing, beasts of burden and man-footed creatures (5.49); Boges killed his children, wife, concubines and household slaves (7.107). Slaves regularly come last, after animals (7.55), money (5.31) and furniture (6.23): we are not so far from Aristotle's notion that a slave is a thing (*Politics*, 1253b32 etc.).

Herodotus recounts a story about the Skythians who were away from home campaigning for twenty-eight years. Their wives, no doubt because of the chilly Russian climate, had intercourse with their slaves. Their offspring fought the returning husbands successfully again and again, until one of the Skythians said: 'Look, we are killing our own slave force. Let us give up conventional weapons, and go at them with horse-whips: then they will know that we are their masters'. His advice was followed, and the slaves fled (4.1–4). This has been taken as a parable for Greek slave owners: don't treat slaves as your equals; horse-whip them, it's the only language they understand. But there is no reason to assume that this story must reflect Herodotus' own attitudes.

He does however give us his own view when he mentions the Persian custom forbidding a master to do an irreparable injury to his slave for a single offence. 'I approve of that,' he says (1.137). An irreparable injury is, presumably, one that maims him, lames him, blinds him or kills him. Not for a single offence: we must regretfully conclude that Herodotus had not objections to treating perpetual offenders in this brutal way.

Liberty, Herodotus believed, was a splendid thing; subjection was intolerable. That is, liberty and subjection at state level – the subjection, for example, of Greeks to Persians. It is sad that, like all his contemporaries, he never thought of transferring these notions to individuals, to the relationship between master and slave.

Notes

1 This is the text of the paper delivered on 28 April 1985, except that some cuts have been restored; I hope to publish a fuller discussion eventually. No one, I trust, will be offended by the occasionally light-hearted tone, which seemed appropriate to oral delivery. I am of course well aware of the horrors of slavery and the serious nature and implications of the subject. I am most grateful to Dr Paul Cartledge, Mrs Margaret McKie and Dr Léonie Archer for their helpful comments. Where no author's name is given, figures refer to book and chapter of Herodotus. Greekless readers can consult Herodotus most easily in the World's Classic translation by Harry Carter (Oxford, 1962); A de Sélincourt's Penguin version (second edition, 1972) is livelier, but the chapters are not numbered. Translations of the passages cited from Demosthenes and ps. – Xenophon can be found in the Loeb Classical Library (vols. 3 and 7 respectively), and of the other Greek sources in the Penguin Classics series.

Further reading

There are no discussions specifically devoted to slavery in Herodotus. The best recent general treatments of the historian are Hart (1982) and Waters (1985). On Greek slavery, see Ste. Croix (1981) *passim* (See Index, p. 727; slaves in agriculture at pp. 505–9); Finley (1981), Chs. 6–10 (Ch. 10 for slave trade); Garlan (1982). For prisoners of war, see Ducrey (1968); Pritchett (1971), Chs. 3–5. For terminology, Gschnitzer (1964); names, Masson (1973). Helots are discussed by P.A. Cartledge in this volume. For eunuchs, see A. Hug in Pauly-Wissowa, *Real-Encylopädie* Suppl. III (1918), 449–55 s.v. Eunuchen.

Four

Greek Theatre and the Legitimation of Slavery

David Wiles

As a teacher of drama, my interest lies in the ideological aspect of slavery: how drama works to legitimise (or undermine) a slave system. I shall be discussing mainly Menander, an Athenian comic dramatist who flourished around 300 BC, though I shall say a few words at the end about Plautus, the Roman actor-dramatist who wrote pastiches of Greek comedy about a century later.[1]

Menander is important sociologically because his work travelled so well and lasted so well. He wrote most of his plays for Athens in the first instance, but the age of touring theatre companies was beginning at this time, and the drama of Menander was quickly carried to all the cities of the Greek-speaking world. Theatre in this world was a focal cultural activity: it was an opportunity for citizens to celebrate and debate their systems of values.

Democracy was the normal Greek system of government in the Hellenistic period. The problem of democracy, always, was who should constitute the democratic body. The citizens were a male elite who for most purposes excluded foreign residents (unless by provision of some bilateral treaty), children of only one citizen parent (in Athens' case anyway), the poor (under certain regimes) and of course slaves. Many Greek cities were rich and sophisticated coastal enclaves with a hinterland of 'barbarians', which is to say non-Greek speakers. The overtly humanitarian values of Menander's plays had great appeal for Greek speakers who considered themselves to be decent, civilised human beings: the opposite, that is, of barbarians.

Menander wrote at a time when people's horizons were becoming cosmopolitan. In classical Greek drama a century earlier, the good of the individual city-state was a moral imperative, and drama regularly portrayed the conflict of interests between the state and the individual citizen. Slavery was not seen as an ethical problem in this context. However, when city-states became satellites of a Macedonian empire around the end of the fourth century, it became hard for individual citizens to feel the same sense of corporate obligation. A moral discourse about the good citizen gave way to a new discourse about the good human being, and slavery immediately became problematic.

It is a notorious paradox that the advance of democracy in classical Greece went hand in hand with the advance of chattel slavery. The subjection of citizen women in classical Athens is a closely related phenomenon. One man's freedom was another person's unfreedom. Drama helps us, I shall argue, to see how Greeks came to terms with this contradiction. Since they could not conceive of civilised life without slavery to support it, they found ways of convincing themselves that slavery was not a man-made but a natural institution.

Aristotle saw that slavery was the economic mainstay of a political system that he admired. To his credit, he had enough intellectual integrity to see the need to justify slavery. But his theory that the slave is a living tool, the human equivalent of an ox, is a shambles, 'intellectually disreputable' as Geoffrey de Ste. Croix terms it.[2] Aristotle's theory of 'natural slavery' is a rationalisation of gut feelings about the superiority of the Greek race and Greek culture. When we read his *Politics* today, it is hard to see how his disciples swallowed such stuff. A knowledge of drama helps, I think, to show why Aristotle's view of slavery was readily acceptable.

There are close links between philosophy and Hellenistic drama. Menander was educated in the Aristotelian school, and absorbed its values. His plays posit the Aristotelian mean as the solution to any given ethical problem. The science of physiognomy which developed in the Aristotelian school is closely related to Menander's dramaturgy. According to this science, specific features of the face and body signalled specific psychological traits. That is to say, specific physiological deviations from the ideal mean were deemed to correspond with specific types of mental disharmony. Menander's actors wore masks which allowed a character's psychological endowment to be analysed in these terms. A famous relief shows the dramatist gazing at a set of masks in order to decide what words to give them.

Menander wrote plays with domestic settings. He invited spectators to see a slightly idealised reflection of themselves in the theatre. He portrayed a citizen milieu that was slightly more prosperous than average but still acceptable as typical. He worked with a conventionalised repertory of characters (or mask types) and a conventionalised plot structure. His plots turn upon questions of birth and status. Greek democratic communities were obsessed by status – that is, by the degree of wealth and genetic purity that entitled someone to become a member of the democratic community – and Menander dramatised the profound tensions which democracy engendered. The plays culminate in marriage: that is to say, legal marriage, capable of producing citizen children. In Athenian life, a man married at about thirty, the age when he became capable of holding office. The plays dramatise the central rite of passage in a citizen's life, the point when he became a full member of the community, and set about its reproduction.

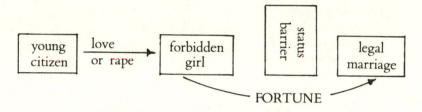

Table 1:   Menander's plot paradigm

The protagonist or subject of the narrative (see Table 1), is always a citizen youth. A male slave is always part of the drama, and may be instrumental in helping the young man attain his goal. But however pivotal to the plot, the slave can never be the protagonist whose aspirations and fate are the *raison d'être* of the play.

We must turn from the plot paradigm to the typology of roles in order to learn more about the Greeks' attitude to slavery. A heterogeneous collection of new and traditional masks became progressively codified during and in the wake of Menander's career. In order to understand the system of masks, we can best start with Pollux's catalogue.

Julius Pollux, an Athenian academic of the second century AD, re-produced in précis form from an unknown source a description of the masks of Hellenistic comedy. These are the masks in the order in which he puts them. Some of the masks – 'Maison', 'Hermon's', and probably 'Lycomedes' – are named after the actors who first used them.

Old (free) men
1   Senior grandfather
2   Second grandfather
3   Principal old man
4   Long-beard
5   Hermon's mask*
6   Wedge-beard
7   Lycomedes' mask
8   Pimp

*Hermon's mask also in a wedge-beard version

Young (free) men
1   Perfect youth
2   Dark youth
3   Curly youth
4   Delicate youth
5   The rustic
6   Wavy-haired soldier
        (dark)
7   Wavy-haired soldier
        (blond)
8   The flatterer
9   The parasite
10 The 'portrait' mask
        (an elegant foreigner)
11 The Sicilian parasite

Male slaves
1   Grandfather slave (manumitted)
2   Principal slave*
3   Slave with receding hair
4   Slave with receding hair:
        curly-haired version
5   'Maison' (native cook)
6   'Tettix' (foreign cook)

*Principal slave also in a
wavy-haired version

Women
(a) *old*
  1 The she-wolf
  2 The fat old woman
  3 The housekeeper

(b) *young*
  1 Articulate woman
  2 Articulate curly woman
  3 The maiden
  4 The concealed maiden
       (hair bound like a bride's)
  5 The concealed maiden
       (with unparted hair)
  6 Greying ex-courtesan
  7 The concubine
  8 The complete courtesan
  9 The nubile courtesan
       (unadorned)
 10 The courtesan bound with
       gold
 11 Courtesan bound with tiara
 12 'The little torch'
       (courtesan with flame-
       like hair-do)
 13 Pretty cropped slave-girl
 14 Brothel slave with
       flattened hair

   The division of masks into categories is of fundamental
importance. Aristotle believed that 'the primary and simplest
elements of the household [were] the relationships of master and
slave, of husband and wife, and of father and children'.[3] These
supposedly natural structures of ruler and ruled generate Pollux's
categories. Both within and between categories, the list is organised
hierarchically: age before youth, free before slave, male before
female.
   There is a polar opposition, therefore, between free and enslaved
males. Some sociologically borderline groups, like slave bankers and
free urban artisans, are excluded from the drama. Free non-citizens

like the 'portrait' mask and the Sicilian parasite are, though subordinated to citizens, bracketed with them in the same category. Cooks, who often payed a rental to their legal owners and functioned as economically independent units, along with ex-slaves, are classed with slaves. The division is absolute.

Within the category of female masks, slavery and freedom are not presented as polarities but as the basis of a continuum. While the housekeeper is a slave, the 'she-wolf' may be a free slave-owning brothel-keeper. The taxonomy of younger women passes from the manifest citizens to the type of the 'concealed maiden'. These are girls who, following war, piracy or exposure at birth, have been brought up as slaves or foreign courtesans and are identified in the course of the play as citizen-born. After the concubine (a non-citizen, effectively a common law wife without rights) come the courtesans. Greek courtesans ranged from independent society ladies at one extreme to cheap slave prostitutes at the other, so the category of 'courtesan' is ambiguous in status terms. At the end of the list come the domestic slaves. The logic that dictates a slave/free continuum rather than a polarity is a simple one. Only men could be truly free because only they participated in the democratic process. A woman, like a slave, must always have a *kyrios*, a legal master. She cannot own property because she is conceived legally as property herself.

The plot structures of Hellenistic comedy are related to the system of masks. A free woman can be reared as a slave, a freeman cannot. No surviving Greek comedy (and I must exclude Plautine adaptations from this generalisation) allows a free young man to be mistaken for a slave, nor a slave for a free man.

Masks provide the structural framework for Menander's comedies. It is worth recalling that in his plays all characters speak a uniform Attic Greek, with some linguistic nuancing to suggest character. This is quite unlike the English dramatic tradition, from Shakespeare to *Coronation Street*, where language is the basic marker of social status. In actual Athenian life, a slave might speak very broken Greek or might be born and bred in captivity and therefore speak fluent Greek. A slave cook might be a Sicilian, a native Greek speaker. Conversely, a free peasant or mercenary might have a distinctive local accent. Language is not permitted to complicate or blur the slave/free polarity in Menander's drama, a drama which in so many respects offers the illusion of mirroring Athenian life as it is lived.

To turn now to the naming conventions of the plays – stock names recur for given types of character, and are closely related to the repertory of masks. The list shows a number of Menander's plays in which a stock name is attached to a male slave or young woman mask. In brackets are the number of plays known to me by other Hellenistic authors or by Roman adapters in which the name is also found. (Bear in mind that there is an element of guesswork in this list since most of the material is in fragments.)

Male slaves
Daos (typical Phrygian name) 9 (11)
Getas ('Gete') 6 (2)
Parmenon ('stand-by') 5 (6)
Syros ('Syrian') 4 (7)
Sosias ('security') 4 (5)
Pyrrhias ('fiery' i.e., red-head) 3 (1)
Tibeios (typical Paphlagonian name) 3
Donax ('reed') 2
Dromon ('runner') 1 (5)
Karion ('Carian') 1 (2) – a cook
Sikon ('Sicilian') 1 (1) – a cook
Libys ('Libyan') 1 (1)   – a cook
Spinther ('spark') 1
Onesimos ('helpful') 1
Lydos ('Lydian') 1
Sangarios ('Bithynian') 1
Kerdon ('profit') 1

Young women
Myrrhine ('myrtle') 4 (2) – mature citizen
Plangon ('doll') 4 (1)   – young citizen born
Philoumene ('beloved') 2 (1) – young citizen born
Glykera ('sweet') 2 (1) – courtesan
Chrysis ('golden') 2 (1) – courtesan
Malthake ('soft') 1 (3) – courtesan
Habrotonon ('wormwood') 2 – slave prostitute
Doris ('Carian from Doris') 4 (1) – domestic slave

(Many other female names appear once only.)

While Greek women's names outside the theatre can appear in any status group, women's names in Menander are predictive of status. Many courtesan's names which occur once only may be intended for one-off masks created for a specific play. In accordance with a convention that extends beyond the theatre, women and slaves bear names that characterise their personality, while most free men bear neutral names.

The male slaves bear what are unmistakably slave names. They are forms of ethnic, physical or moral classification, names which in Athenian life served to depersonalise the slave, robbing him of his original foreign name. The most popular mask name, 'Daos', is an indigenous slave name, but was used to signify the universal Phrygian (as 'Paddy' might now be used to signify the Irishman).[4] Comedy markedly simplified the naming conventions of Athenian social life. A real citizen might be called Sosias, but not in comedy. More commonly, a real slave might bear a neutral Greek name – like Moschion or Demeas, two stock citizen names in Menander.[5] Names in Athenian social life probably gave a good indication whether a slave was imported or born into slavery, but comedy obliterates this distinction.

Ethnic designations are relevant to the characterisation of slaves in Menander's comedy. Aristotle followed the Hippocratic tradition in contrasting the intelligence of Asiatics with the *thumos* or 'spirit' of Europeans from the cold north.[6] And thus in Menander Getas from the Danube valley is markedly more aggressive and less sophisticated than Asiatics like Daos and Syros. One Gete applauds the ungovernable polygamy of his race; another accuses a sophisticated Phrygian of effeminacy: punishment mills groan with manly Getes, he claims.[7] Again, Syrians were stereotyped as greedy, so Menander in one play sends a Syrian slave to arbitration to seek possession of some jewellery: the argument turns on greed, and Syros is proved not greedy in this instance.[8]

I shall now examine the visual image of the slave, an image which was reproduced in innumerable performances across the Greek world.

The descriptions in Pollux are frustratingly brief. We can glean, however, the following structural principles:

– old men sport beards, young men are clean shaven (a fashion which came in with Alexander the Great in the 320s BC)

– young men are bronzed, young women are pale (because of their indoor life)
– male slaves are distinguished by red hair (except for the old one who has gone grey, and Tettix who may be an African).

Archaeology provides us with much more information.

As part of the cult of Dionysos, a large number of miniature replicas of comic masks were buried in the cemetery at Lipari, an island-state north of Sicily, during the half century after Menander's death. Though similar masks are found all over the Graeco-Roman world, those of Lipari constitute the best single corpus.[9]

Old men are poorly represented, perhaps because an old man was not the obvious companion for the underworld. There are two mask types, both full of psychological detail. Both have flowing white beards. The young men exist in rich variety. There are nineteen distinct mask types, including three parasite types. All are tanned and beardless. The variations are subtle ones. Since the young man stood at the centre of the comedy, the intense interest in his psychological make-up should not surprise us. Both the young man's mask and the maidens' and courtesans' masks are variations around an aesthetic ideal. There are few major roles for female slaves in Menander, and none of the young female masks can confidently be identified as servile.

There seem to be six distinguishable types of male slave in the masks from Lipari. The number of clear specimens of each type is shown in brackets:

old slave (7)
slave with right eyebrow raised (7)
thick-lipped slave with left brow raised (1)
bald slave (4)
slave with squint (2)
slave with wavy hair (1).

I shall examine the second type which probably corresponds with the 'principal slave' in Pollux's catalogue. (See Fig. 1) The general shape is square rather than oval. The nose is squashed, the eyes bulge. The flesh colour is red. A contemporary physiognomic treatise distinguishes the tan of the lion from the red of the fox.[10] A red complexion is generated by bodily heat, and implies manic movement. Red may also be a racial indicator.

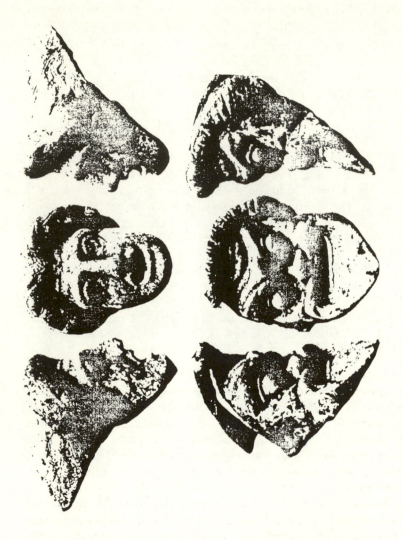

Figure 1:   Young man and slave; miniature terracotta masks from Lipari

All slaves have high arched eyebrows, suggesting for the actor an emotional range which encompasses fear, surprise, mischief, malice. Slaves' faces are not capable of high emotions like soulful romantic love. This slave is distinguished by his asymmetry. Though a raised right brow implies less villainy than a raised left brow, it was a basic physiognomic principle that physical harmony was associated with mental harmony, physical asymmetry implied moral deviance.

The beard has become stylised, fixed in the form of a trumpet. In the comedy of the generation which preceded Menander's, slaves and old free men could not easily be told apart by their masks. In Menander's day the difference was unmistakable. While free old men had flowing hair on their faces, slaves wore a rigid beard–cum–megaphone which fixed their faces in an irremovable grimace.

In many ways this is a surprising face, given the extent to which Greek physiognomy was rooted in ethnographic research, and given the precise ethnic placing of slaves in Menander's texts. The red hair which Pollux attributes to his slaves is equally hard to reconcile with ethnography. I am led to the conclusion that the red hair is a traditional feature of stage slaves, dating back to a period when slaves were presumed to come from the Balkans rather than Asia Minor. The slave mask is plainly not based upon the observation of real slaves but is a purely theatrical construction. In order to make sense of the slave mask, we have to relate it to the logic of the system.

The young man is closest to the ideal type. The perfect young man in Pollux's catalogue is the oldest, and therefore closest to his physical prime in his early thirties. All the masks are conceived as deviations from an ideal physical/psychological type. While subtle deviations are manifested in the young citizens, the slave is conceived as the antithesis of the ideal, and in him all the features of the ideal face are systematically deformed. Thus the Greeks based their visual image of the slave upon the logic of their conceptual system, and not upon observation. For reasons that are plainly sociological, the project of Greek creative artists to reproduce life as they saw it broke down with respect to slaves.

The theatre spectator receives visual and acoustical signals simultaneously. It is therefore essential that we visualise the speaker when we find a slave voicing such sentiments as the following in the theatre:

Don't despise the counsel of a servant – slaves of good character have often proved wiser than their masters. Though fortune may have made the body a slave, the mind still has a free man's character.[11]

We do not know the character of the speaker, but we do know that in Menander slaves often display fine moral qualities. The Greek spectator who witnesses the fine actions and hears the fine sentiments of slaves is for ever reminded by the visual image that these are deviations from the *natural* baseness of the slave.

The slave's sentiments quoted above (probably not from a play of Menander himself as it happens) are worth further comment. Geoffrey de Ste. Croix states that the Aristotelian theory of natural slavery is not prominent after Aristotle's time. The standard Hellenistic, Roman and Christian attitude is precisely as the slave states: that Fortune not Nature makes a man a slave, and that a man's external condition is irrelevant to his inner character.[12] This clearly became the standard *philosophical* position. But I wish to argue in this paper that the Aristotelian view remained inscribed in the conventions of Hellenistic *comedy*, and that this comedy remained for several centuries part of the dominant culture, shaping popular perceptions.

Menander was a subtle dramatist, and I do not wish to imply that his plays were ideological in any crude sense. His dramaturgy was capable of articulating the basic tensions in the Aristotelian position. Nature's intention is not always realised, Aristotle asserts: nature intends the slave to differ from the free man in both body and soul, but in practice one often encounters a slave who has the body or soul of a free man.[13] The basic Aristotelian operation of Menander's comedy is to lay bare nature's intention which in day to day life is commonly obscured. A man and a woman who are naturally meant for each other become free to marry. The ideal type of the free male is defined in relation to the naturally unfree type whose mind and body are corrupted by manual labour and genetic inheritance. But while plot and masks display nature's intention, the particular actions of particular characters in particular situations often run counter to nature's intention. For the audience, the fascination of Menander's comedy lay in seeing how, in subtle ways, characters behaved contrary to type. The audience were encouraged to predict certain patterns of behaviours, and were then entertained by seeing their predictions confounded. The technique of Menander's comedy was to set up a dialectic between life as it 'naturally' is and life as it actually is.

I shall end with a few words about slaves in Plautus. Plautus freely adapted Greek comedies for the entertainment of a Roman audience around the time of the wars against Hannibal. He was an Umbrian by birth and probably worked with immigrant actors. For all their appearance of being adaptations, Plautus' plays are fundamentally Roman in their orientation.

Rome was not a democracy. A Greek democracy can be seen as a tripartite structure: an in-group of citizens, an out-group of non-citizens, and a further out-group of slaves. There were not such rigid lines of demarcation in Roman society. That society can rather be seen as a pyramid built up of a nexus of individual power relationships. (see Table 2)

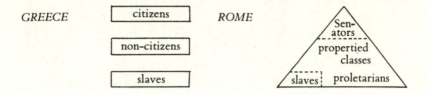

Table 2: In-groups and out-groups in Greek and Roman societies

To be a rich man's slave might be a position of privilege *vis-à-vis* the majority of the population. The ideal of personal freedom in Roman society was not ingrained as it was in citizens of a Greek democracy. There was no clear racial divide between citizens and slaves. Manumitted slaves could become citizens, and find their way into Plautus' audience.

The concern in Plautus' plots is with power rather than citizenship. (see Table 3) The youth may have fallen for a prostitute and

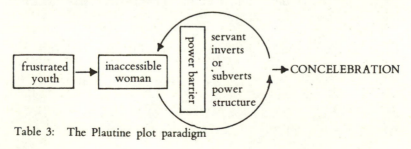

Table 3:   The Plautine plot paradigm

have no interest in marriage. Whether his goal is sex or marriage, either way, he needs money. The obstacle which confronts him is personalised: an authoritarian father, a rich soldier, a wicked slave dealer. This blocking figure is fooled, swindled, or converted to vice, usually through the agency of a family slave. The slave broadly speaking moves to the centre of the drama in Plautus, as he weaves his elaborate and impossible schemes and fantasies. In a sense, the slave becomes the alter ego of the dramatist as he turns himself into the architect of a carnivalesque intrigue.[14]

To give one example: in *The Sisters Bacchis*, freely adapted from Menander, the slave Chrysalus helps his young master to extract cash from his old master so that the young master can sustain his relationship with a courtesan. The climax is a long aria in which the slave compares his ruse with Ulysses' ruse of the Trojan horse. The old master's authority is subverted to the point where he in his turn is seduced into entering the brothel. For all that he is threatened with welts and crucifixion ('not Chrysalus but Crossalus' is a typical pun), Plautus' slave is not modelled on any observed slave. The slave in Menander's original was a Syrian, but Chrysalus has no nationality, no past and no future. He acts without heed to personal interest. We learn nothing of his day-to-day duties. Plautus' slaves are overtly theatrical creations. More than other characters, they banter to the audience and point up the fact that a play is but a play. Chrysalus proclaims how different he is from the Parmenons and Syroses of Greek comedy who (being realistically conceived) steal only trifling sums of money from their masters.[15]

We can learn nothing specific about the condition of Roman slaves from Plautus. The Plautine slave is a kind of algebraic symbol for the underdog in Roman society. Anyone in a relationship of servitude – a son in relation to his father, a conscript in relation to his commanding officer, a poor man or freedman bound in clientage to his patron – all these could relish the triumph of the downtrodden slave and his fantastical inversion of all structures of power.

I will finish with a general observation. We cannot, in either Greece or Rome, look at the stage slave and directly extrapolate any reliable information about slaves in the world outside the theatre. We can, however, look at a given social system at a given point in time, and see how it works as a system, how it succeeds in reproducing itself. We can then look at slavery as part of a self-reproducing system, and at dramatic performance as another element in the same system. By this roundabout means we can put ourselves in a position to understand the complex way in which drama both validated and in some measure challenged the institution of chattel slavery.

Notes

1 Translations of works discussed: the best translation of Plautus' plays is by Paul Nixon in the Loeb parallel text edition (New York/Harvard & London, 1921–38). For Menander, the situation will improve in the next few years. Only volume I of the three-volume Loeb edition (edited and translated by W.G. Arnott) has yet appeared (Harvard and London, 1979). Norma Miller is preparing a new translation for the Penguin Classics series.
2 Ste. Croix (1981), p. 418.
3 *Politics* I. 3 1253b 6–9.
4 Lascu (1969).
5 Treu (1983). For lists of slave names, see also Lauffer (1955/56); Pritchett (1956); Cabanes (1974).
6 *Politics* VII. 6. 1327b. 23–9; Hippocrates *Airs, Waters, Places.*
7 Menander Frag. 547–8 Edmonds = Strabo 296.7; *Aspis* 242–5; cf., MacCary (1969).
8 Polemon cited in *De Physiognomia Liber* 14; Firmicus Mat. *Math.* I. i, I. iv; Menander *Epitrepontes.*
9 Bernabo-Brea (1981).
10 Ps.-Aristotle *Physiognomica* VI. 812a. 15–17.
11 *Select Papyri*, Loeb Edition, ed. D.L. Page (1950), vol. 3, No. 68.
12 *op. cit.*, pp. 417–19.
13 *Politics* I. 2. 1254b. 33 ff.
14 *Bacchides* 649.
15 My interpretation of Plautus draws on Bettini (1982) and on Petrone (1983).

Further reading

On masks, see Bieber (1961) which is accessible and copiously illustrated. The text leaves much to be desired, and the researcher needs to consult Webster (1969). Physiognomic theory is conveniently documented in Evans (1969). On slavery, the best introduction to Greek slavery is Finley (1960); for slavery in the Roman Republic, see Hopkins (1978). On drama as social process, for a general introduction to the subject, I would recommend Williams (1981), Chs. 5 and 6. There are many perceptive observations on the interface between Athenian democracy and its drama in Humphreys (1983), and some good comments on Menander in Davis (1977–78). For Plautus, see Arnott (1970), Ch. 3.

Five

Slavery as a Punishment in Roman Criminal Law

Joan Burdon

This paper will set out to explain how penal slavery could, in Roman law, be considered separately from other punishments of forced labour and to consider whether this continued to be the case. It will also attempt to explain what was involved in a sentence of penal slavery and the status of those on whom such a punishment would have been inflicted.

While most of the evidence cited concerns the period from the first to sixth centuries AD, earlier relevant evidence will be referred to.

Sources

The bulk of the evidence is obtained from legal sources. For convenience, I will list the most important of these now, together with dates of publication and the abbreviations which will, from then on, be used when reference is made to them.

1 *Twelve Tables (TT)*, essentially a code of existing Roman custom published 450–49 BC.
2 *Theodosian Code (CTh)* published in AD 438 and containing all imperial enactments from the time of Constantine (AD 313–37).
3 *Corpus Iuris Civilis* of Justinian. This consists of:
   a) *Digest* or Pandects (*Dig.*), published in AD 533, a most important work, codifying writings of the great Roman jurists, particularly those from the time of the Emperor Hadrian (AD 117–38) to the mid-third century AD when anarchy ended the classical age of Roman law.
   b) *Code of Justinian (CJ)* of which the revised edition of AD 534 is extant. This contains all the imperial enactments from the time of Justinian (AD 527–65).
   c) *Institutes (J. Inst.)* a law book for students (AD 533).
   d) *Novels (J. Nov.)* new Imperial enactments issued by Justinian himself in the twelve years after the publication of the code.

In addition, works of individual jurists are referred to separately. These are the *Institutes* of Gaius (c. AD 160), (*Gaius Inst.*); the

Sententiae of Paulus (*Sent. Pauli*) and the *Regulae* of Ulpian (*Reg. Ulp.*) These latter two jurists were working at the beginning of the third century AD but their work survives in collections probably made no earlier than the end of the third century.

Details on the other primary sources which provide scattered evidence will be given as they occur in the text. Most of them can be read in English in the Loeb Classical Library Series.

Slaves were traditionally a part of Roman society (cf., for example, Dionysius of Halicarnassus *Roman Antiquities*, 2.28 (first century BC); *TT* V.8; VII.3; X.6; XII.2). This continued to be the case throughout the period under discussion.[1] Essentially, slaves were required for their labour. Although owners were never prevented from forcing their slaves to do dangerous work, evidence suggests that this was often only the case when a slave proved difficult or criminal; then his working conditions were likely to become harsher. The geographer, Strabo (c. 64 BC to AD 21) records that criminal provincial slaves were bought up by Roman tax farmers for the mines (*Geography*, 562). The playwright Plautus (ob. 184 BC) mentions that urban slaves were deterred from bad behaviour by the thought of punishment in chains on far-off country estates (*Poenulus*, 827–9; *Pseudolus*, 534; *Persa*, 21ff., etc.). Juvenal, a Roman satirist who died in AD 130, also mentions this (*Satires*, 8.184–5).

But even in the early Republic, forced labour was not only imposed on those who, in Roman law, were of slave status. It is also found employed as a punishment for free men. The *Twelve Tables* (VIII.14) ruled that a free man, clearly guilty of non-violent theft, should be handed over to work for the person from whom he had stolen. A jurist of the second century AD (Gaius, *Inst.* 3.189) remarked that even jurists from the last two centuries of the Republic could not decide whether such a punishment had reduced the criminal to slave status or whether he was forced to labour as a debt bondsman because of an inability to pay a fine. While Gaius infers that those were the only legal options open at the end of the Republic, neither seems likely when considered at the time of the *Twelve Tables*. It is not stated that the thief was reduced to slavery so becoming owned by the person whom he had offended. Yet it is clear that enslavement was a legal penalty for other offences committed by free criminals at this early stage. It was, for example, the prescribed punishment for defaulting debtors (*TT* III). But enslavement did not retain the criminal within the community. He was sold outside, for the aim of enslavement at this time seems to have been to ensure the non-return of the offender. Exile, at that time a voluntary act, could not guarantee the permanent exclusion of one so totally unacceptable.[2]

It is also unlikely that the thief became a debt bondsman, as it is clear that he was assigned to forced labour as an initial punishment, not as an alternative which was enforced only if an offender could not pay a fine. This again contrasts with another example in the *Twelve Tables* (*TT* XII.2) which does make provision for such an alternative when a head of family did not wish to (or could not) pay for damages done by a dependant. In such circumstances, he was at liberty to hand over the offender to the plaintiff for a length of time which was related, presumably, to the extent of damages proved.

By the late Republic, Gaius recorded that the penalty for manifest non-violent theft by a free man had been changed to a fine (*Gaius Inst.*, 3.189). Theft was a crime commonly associated with the poor and it would seem that, while in the earlier Republic the state had been ready to adopt the pusnishment of forced labour as a practical punishment for those unable to pay a fine, the increased political importance of poorer citizens,[3] especially in the last two centuries BC, had resulted in this change of penalty, which, on the face of it, protected them from public humiliation. In fact, the change must have proved more cosmetic than actual, as a poor criminal, with no patron to aid him, would most probably have been forced to labour as a debt bondsman if unable to pay a fine.[4]

From the beginning of the Republic, then, it is clear that forced labour was a traditional Roman method of ensuring that a criminal of low status paid for crime, though such a penalty could have been either an initial or an alternative punishment. In addition, though in Roman eyes slavery and forced labour were closely linked, it does not seem to have been necessary to reduce a free criminal to slave status before such a sentence could be imposed. The enslavement of a free man to ensure his removal from the state was a legal possibility at an early period,[5] though there is no evidence of the actual imposition of such a sentence at that time. Nor is there any evidence of a Roman criminal condemned to slavery and then retained within the state. It is the exclusion policy involved in the reduction to slavery as a punishment which was the important factor.

The policy of casting out those likely to be dangerous to the state had its origins in the early period when crime control was concerned with the protection of a small city state. The sale into slavery recommended in such cases must be seen more as a preventative measure than as a punishment. Cicero, a Roman lawyer of the first century BC, makes it clear that one of the causes of such enslavement was the refusal of a citizen to do military service (Cicero, *Pro Caecina*, 33.96–35.101). The retention of such a person within the community when he had rejected a responsibility which was essential for the freedom of the whole citizen body, was obviously dangerous. Citizens were the state and assumed responsibility for each other. At the same time, it was recognised that, being human, they were bound to err. Non-dangerous offences could be dealt with within the community. The handing over of a non-dangerous offender of low status to a plaintiff for a period of forced labour was judged to be an appropriate way of ensuring that he paid for his crime but was not excluded from society. In theory too, the eyes of a close knit community should have ensured that the plaintiff did not ill-treat the offender.

However, ideals suitable for a small city state were bound to crumble as Rome early adopted a policy of expansion. By the mid-second century BC, she had organised Italy and from then on sought to conquer the Mediterranean. By the end of the first century BC she had succeeded.[6] Consequently, she became more concerned with what used to be the outside world and with the government and control of the empire which she had acquired. This last was achieved by the imposition of order from above, rather than from consultation with the many conquered peoples. Even in Rome, after the victory of Augustus in 27 BC, the power of the state essentially rested with one man, not with the citizen body.[7] By the second century the state, as a separate entity from the citizen body, punished serious offences as crimes rather than allowing private settlement.[8] It is from this period that there is clear evidence of state imposition of forced labour as a punishment in the provinces. The punishment was not only imposed but also supervised through the machinery of the state.

The letters between Pliny the Younger (AD 61–c. 114) when he was governor of Bithynia (AD 111–13) and the Emperor Trajan (AD 98–117) provide the first evidence for established penalties of forced labour in the provinces, (Pliny, *Epistulae* X, 31–2 [public works]; II.11.8; X.58.3 [mines]). None of this evidence presents these penalties as an innovation which in itself needed to be discussed, though it may well be that the use of such penalties first evolved from punishment devised or adopted from local custom by provincial governors, rather than from the tradition of Rome itself.[9] From the time of Hadrian however, there is evidence of imperial intervention aimed at establishing a general pattern of law throughout the empire.[10] The *Corpus Iuris Civilis* reveals that by the early third century, a uniformity of state punishment had emerged. Most importantly, as Peter Garnsey has shown, the pattern indicates a difference in the types of penalty which were judged to be appropriate for those of either high or low status.[11]

Without going into detail, the division in status can roughly be assumed to be between those of wealth and political power and those who were poor and of little political influence. Setting aside the death penalty as imposed on either group, those of high status legally faced only penalties which imposed varying degrees of exile, financial confiscation or a combination of both. On the other hand, those of low status, whether slave or free, were subjected to punishments of forced labour which could be varied in degree of harshness or in length of time. A rescript of Hadrian makes it clear that, even as early as the second century, the two ranges of punishment were not interchangeable (*Dig.*, 48.19.28.13–14). The division into high and low status was more important for decisions on penalties than was the seriousness of crimes committed.[12] Those of low status automatically faced sentences involving payment with the body. Although in AD 212 most free inhabitants of the empire were granted Roman citizenship by the Emperor Antoninus (Geissen Papyrus No. 40, col. I), neither Roman citizenship nor freedom, in themselves, provided protection from sentences of forced labour. Indeed, by the third century, jurists felt able to link together the punishment of slaves and the free of low status (*Dig.* 48.19.10 pr; 48.19.28.11). Other evidence suggests different areas where distinctions between these two groups were becoming blurred.[13]

Throughout Roman history then, poverty and lack of political influence seem to have been closely linked as reasons why those of low status, even if not slaves, could legally be subjected to punishments of forced labour. It is perhaps significant that, in the early Republic, the state allowed the politically uninfluential dependants of a head of family to be handed over to such a punishment as a method of payment of damages (*TT* XII.2), but there is no evidence that such a punishment was judged to be suitable for the head of family himself. When, by the late Republic, it had become politically necessary to provide the free poor with the opportunity of avoiding payment with the body, poverty could still make such a fate likely. In the imperial period, certainly by the second century, there was no attempt by the state even to pretend that any choice was available to those of low status. The third century jurist Ulpian was convinced that 'extraordinary penalties', such as punishments of hard labour or beating, had evolved because poor criminals were unable to pay the traditional Roman penalty of a fine (*Dig.*, 48.19.1.2). However, though the poverty of the criminal must have influenced the choice of penalty, it is worth remembering that those linked together as of low status were by far the majority of the empire and it is unlikely that everyone in this group was destitute. It may, in fact, be better to consider the imposition of forced labour as a policy which the state could, if it had wished, have imposed on all. Evidence shows that the exemption which those of wealth and political usefulness received from such treatment was granted by the state as a privilege.[14]

When, then, was a free low status criminal judged to have deserved a reduction to penal slavery? In addition, did such a reduction alter the conditions in which a criminal found himself, whether he had previously been slave or free? In order to answer these questions, it is necessary first to examine the conditions imposed by sentences of forced labour where the criminal remained free.

It is very odd to find evidence from the beginning of the second century AD which insists that some sentences of forced labour allowed the free criminal to retain his freedom even when such a sentence had been imposed for life. This implies that there were considered to be some advantages to the retention of freedom which are not immediately apparent. The evidence for maintaining the distinction between penal slavery and forced labour as a punishment for free men begins with Hadrian (AD 117–38). He distinguished between two main types of forced labour as a punishment:

1. that of temporary or life sentences to the public works (with which temporary sentencing of free men to the mines was to be

linked), and
2. that of life sentences to the mines (*Dig.*, 48.19.28.6).

His discussion makes it quite clear that no sentence to the public works (or any sentence which could be considered as equivalent) reduced a criminal to slave status. So much was this the case that, in the opinion of one third century jurist, such a punishment could not be considered suitable for slaves as they were not, in the first instance, free (*Dig.*, 48.19.34 pr). Here, however, the legal logic begins to founder and there is more evidence that the line as to what was suitable for slaves and what was suitable for free men was becoming blurred. Another third century jurist cited circumstances when criminal slaves *could* be sentenced to the public works while retaining slave status (*Dig.*, 48.19.10 pr), and at the begining of the fifth century, an imperial decree recommended sentence to the public works as a suitable punishment for slaves caught wearing barbarian clothes in Rome (*CTh*, 14.10.4. AD 416). It is, however, worth reiterating that no sentence to the public works reduced a free man to slavery even when its occasional suitability as a punishment for slaves had been accepted.

Once the division into high or low status had influenced the type of penalty, the degree of punishment was in part related to the seriousness of the crime committed. So, and staying with the low status group, the emphasis was that for lesser crime, free men should be sent to the public works. Even when the erosion of the distinction between slave and free gave rise to instances where slaves were sent to the public works, it is clear that these were only for minor offences. Both the jurist Paulus and the Theodosian code emphasise that the punishment of the public works was appropriate for free men for lesser crime (*Sent. Pauli.*, V.17.2; *CTh*, 9.40.3.15). Most of the sentencing of a free man to the public works seems to have been of a temporary nature, so allowing for the total reacceptance of the criminal by society after he had paid for his misdemeanour (*Sent. Pauli,* V.18.1; *Dig.*, 47.21.2). In the case of slaves however, such a sentence appears to have been for life (*Dig.*, 48.19.10 pr; *CTh.*, 14.10.4).

In addition, evidence suggests that within the group of low status criminals the division into citizen, free man and slave continued to retain some importance, certainly in the third century. This division imposed certain restrictions as to the amount of payment with the body which could legally be demanded from citizen, free man or slave. The possession of citizenship alone was not enough to save a low class criminal guilty of lesser crime from a temporary sentence of forced labour nor from the customary preliminary beating (*Dig.*, 48.19.10 pr). However, deprivation of citizenship seems to have been essential before a free criminal could be stripped of his entire property and sent to labour on the public works for life (*Dig.*, 48.19.17.1).[15] There is no suggestion that, apart from the time factor involved, the conditions of labour on the public works were any more harsh for a life sentence. Though stripped of citizenship, the criminal retained his freedom (*Dig.*, 48.19.28.6). This factor appears to have exempted him from serving his punishment in chains and from receiving the scourging which would have been administered to slaves (*Dig.*, 48.19.10 pr). For slaves, according to the third century jurist Ulpian, had always, in Roman tradition, been subject to harsher punishment than had free men (*Dig.*, 48.19.28.16; cf., *TT.*, VIII.14). Legally, reduction to slavery allowed the total domination of the slave by his master (cf., *Dig.*, 50.17.32). It is, therefore, significant that all criminals, regardless of status, became penal slaves prior to being sentenced to death by the state (*Dig.*, 28.3.6.6; 29.2.25.3; 48.19.12; 48.19.29).

But penal slavery was also a punishment which could be imposed as a life sentence on those of low status, whether originally slave or free, for dangerous offences. Essentially, such a sentence included the labour of the criminal. However, while his lifelong labour could also have been demanded on the public works, his reduction to penal slavery effectively removed the barrier which legally prevented the subjection of a free offender to unlimited ill treatment by the state, even if this removal led to his subsequent death. In general, these lifelong sentences of penal servitude were served in the mines. The descriptions of conditions there, given by both classical and Christian authors (e.g. Strabo, *Geog*, 562; Diodorus III. 12–14; Cyprian, *Letters*, 77–9; Eusebius, *Ecclesiast. Hist*, 8.12.10), indicate that Ulpian was not exaggerating when he equated this type of sentence with the danger of death (*Dig.*, 48.19.28 pr and 1). The equation of penal servitude with extreme ill treatment is apparent from a jurist's discussion on the condition of young, fit men who were legally pronounced penal slaves, but were sent to train for exhibitions in the arena. As, in the interests of a good performance, these persons were not treated so harshly, it was a matter for argument whether they should, in fact, be called penal slaves (*Dig.*, 48.19.8.11).

For penal slaves sent to the mines, the tradition that slaves, in Roman law, could be punished more harshly than free men (*Dig.*, 48.19.28.16) was observed to the letter. A thorough scourging was a preliminary to sentence and ever after the victim could expect to receive the blows of a slave (*Dig.*, 49.14.12). He must often have suffered extreme physical and mental damage but there is no evidence that medical treatment was ever supplied by the state. He was loaded with chains and fetters that ate into his bones (*Dig.*, 48.19.8.6). Chains are, of course, a way of preventing escape, but when used as a part of punishment they had, in Roman eyes, a greater significance. Not only were they associated with slaves, but with dangerous slaves (cf., *Dig.*, 21.1.48.3). The lack of evidence to indicate that any free man serving a sentence on the public works was ever chained (though of course some system of surveillance was used)[16] serves to emphasise further the connection of chains and servile condition.

It is clear that, as a group, penal slaves were not regarded in the same light as ordinary slaves. Evidence of efforts to define their condition and disabilities begins with the Emperor Antoninus Pius (AD 138–61). The penal slave belonged to no one, certainly not to the emperor, or to the fisc, or to his previous owner if he had had one (*Dig.*, 34.8.3 pr; 49.14.12).[17] The punishment was, in fact, not reserved for men. We know, for example, of a woman sent to the salt mines in Britain (*Dig.* 49.15.6).[18] Several possibilities will be discussed as to why definitions were considered necessary.

If the term '... e of the punishment' is considered as applied to the entire group of such criminals, whether originally slave or free, the emphasis that they did not belong to the emperor may have stemmed from a strong desire on the part of the wealthy imperial slaves (who often occupied such positions of power that they were able to influence the making of law itself)[19] to be disassociated absolutely from such a group.

More importantly perhaps, the emphasis may have been made with reference to the *treatment* of penal slaves. Although Roman law allowed no rights to the slave, from the first century AD, various legislation had attempted, in the interests of state security, to limit the arbitrary ill treatment of slaves by private owners.[20] Pius himself had ruled on this (*Gaius*, 1.53). The insistence that a penal slave belonged to no one but his punishment effectively prevented him from putting forward complaints about the emperor, the state, or indeed, any individual responsible for the supervision of his punishment. Furthermore, the legal fiction that the slave was abused only by his punishment may have been an attempt to deflect any possible accusations of imperial or state ill treatment which might have been made by private owners banned from inflicting arbitrary harm on their own slaves.

In addition, the contrast of limitation of private ill treatment with the unlimited punishment which could legally be imposed on a 'slave of the punishment', should, in theory, have provided non-criminal slaves with some guide as to the limit of the ill treatment which they should have been able to expect. In practice, however, there continued to be no legal ban which restricted masters' ill treatment of slaves, providing that it was claimed to have been administered in the interests of discipline, not as arbitrary cruelty or with intention to kill.

Again, it may have been considered necessary to employ the term 'slave of the punishment' in order to distinguish the condition of criminals who were initially slaves from that in which they found themselves after being sentenced. It may well have been judged essential to deny both a previous owner and the state any right over such a penal slave in order to prevent the owner from claiming for damages inflicted on his property while in the care of the state (cf., *Gaius* 3.210f; *Dig.*, II.3.1; 47.10.25).

It may be possible to advance other arguments as to why the term 'slave of the punishment' was used. What is in no doubt is that many of the arguments and opinions on penal slavery concern themselves with the obligations of a former slave or freedman to his former master (*Sent. Pauli*, 4.8.22(24); *CJ.*, 4.49.4; 9.51.2 and 4). Here, the state shows itself to be much more concerned that a former owner should suffer as little financial loss as possible than worried about the welfare of the penal slave even if the latter had formerly been a free man. For example, time was allowed for a former slave or freedman to settle his obligations to his master or patron before undergoing punishment (*CJ* 9.49.1; *Dig.*, 48.20.7.1). There is, however, no evidence to show that a formerly free man was granted any time to arrange for the future care of his dependants, nor was the respite allowed to the slave or freedman granted for his personal benefit.

Whatever the former condition of the criminal, it was destroyed by a sentence of penal slavery. A former slave, so punished and later pardoned by the emperor, did not revert to the ownership of his former master (*Dig.*, 48.19.8.12). The question of ownership in these circumstances remained obscure until, at the beginning of the third century, the Emperor Caracalla declared that the slave should belong to the fisc (*Dig.*, 40.5.24.5; 48.19.8.12; *CJ* 9.51.8). But even Pius, so adamant that a penal slave belonged to no one but his punishment, had ruled that a child, born to a previously free, female penal slave, belonged to, and therefore could be sold by, the fisc (*Dig.*, 40.5.24.6).

Again, Caracalla clarified this, stating that this was the case only if the child were conceived after sentence, otherwise his family, though not his mother, retained its rights over him (*CJ.*, 9.47.4). In effect then, while the law insisted that penal slaves had no owners save their punishment, anyone who was so forced to work for the state and whose children, conceived and born in such conditions, became state slaves, must realistically have belonged to the state. Certainly the total subjection of penal slaves was achieved through the machinery of the state.[21] Therefore, much of the legal argument on their condition can only be understood in relation to the Roman obsession with property, ownership and the automatic inclusion of slaves as a part of property.[22]

Evidence from the *Digest* shows that penal slaves who had formerly been free, had their property confiscated on sentence. They were not, in fact, alone in this; anyone condemned to a sentence which deprived him of citizenship suffered such a fate (e.g. *Dig.*, 28.1.8.4; 48.20.1 pr; *CJ.*, 9.49.4; *Sent. Pauli.*, 5.12.12). The general legal provisions (which varied from time to time) allowing a share of property to the families of the condemned[23] would have been unlikely to have benefited dependents of low status. In the mid-third century, the Emperor Gordian discounted the likelihood of a penal slave ever having owned much (*CJ*, 9.49.4).

Once condemned a formerly free man lost all his rights over family and household (*Dig.*, 37.14(13).21; 40.1.8; 48.19.2.1; 48.19.29; 49.23.1). A formerly free woman lost the right of relationship over all children, whether conceived before or after sentence (*Dig.*, 48.23.4; *CJ*, 9.47.4). When one partner became a penal slave a marriage was dissolved (*J. Nov.*, 20.8). In Roman law, slaves were always considered to be incapable of making a legal marriage (*Ulp. Reg.*, 5.5; *Sent Pauli*, 2.19.6; *J. Nov.*, 22.9). All guardianship obligations were dissolved by condemnation (*J. Inst.*, 1.22.4). Such condemnation, in fact, rendered the criminal dutiless and no one had any obligations towards him. His plight was considered to be so desperate that he was not allowed to inform in criminal trials because his condition could have encouraged him to make false accusations (*Dig.*, 49.14.18). Legally, it was possible for him to be released from his lifelong sentence only through imperial pardon. There is no way of estimating how frequently these were granted.

If pardoned, a formerly free person could then apply for restitution of property and family rights. (*CJ.*, 9.49.4; 9.51.2.5 and 9) but such a restoration cannot have been simple.[24] We have no evidence of such individuals' attempts to pick up the threads of their lives, most probably because the events in the lives of those of low status were rarely considered as interesting enough to record. But some potential difficulties are self-evident. In particular, family relationships could have been impossible to restore. After dissolution of marriage following condemnation, the partner of a penal slave may well have remarried. In such an event it would have been particularly difficult for a pardoned woman to regain rights over her children. In any event, any child she might have conceived while undergoing sentence remained the property of the state. A former slave, when pardoned, would not have had quite the same problems because he did not formerly possess property or marital rights. But he did not return to his old master, becoming instead the slave of the fisc (*Dig.*, 40.5.24.5; 48.19.8.12; *CJ* 9.51.8).

Sentences to the public works, generally carried out in urban surroundings, adhered to the Roman principle of public punishment, (cf., Appian *Civil Wars* 1.120 for an extreme exmaple). In the case of penal slavery, this does not appear to have been the primary purpose. The aim seems to have been to ensure state control of dangerous criminals of low status. In accordance with Roman tradition, a policy of exclusion was adopted. In early Rome, sale into foreign slavery had been judged an effective means of protecting the state from any dangerous criminal. In the late Republic, the punishment of exile outside Rome was used for this purpose. In the imperial period, although Rome now managed a vast empire, the dangerousness of high-class offenders could still be controlled effectively by lifelong exile. But the protection from the much larger group of low status dangerous criminals was achieved by their removal to mines far away from urban centres (*Dig.*, 48.19.10.1; cf., *Dig.*, 48.19.8.4), where their reduction to penal slavery allowed for their total control through rigid supervision and the harshest type of discipline. This emphasis on total control by the state is evident from the policy which allowed for the ransoming back of any penal slaves who had been captured by barbarians (*Dig.*, 49.15.6), in order to discourage their private resale as ordinary slaves. In addition, the reduction of a criminal to penal slavery allowed the state, if it wished, to impose the final control, the death sentence, on any dangerous criminal. Yet this policy of state control over dangerousness had certain flexibility. Violence was the crime most expected from dangerous criminals of low status and Antoninus Pius made it clear that, when old age or infirmity had rendered such offenders non-violent, it would be safe to release them after ten years had been served (*Dig.*, 48.19.22).[25]

It would seem clear that the state had no anticipation that a penal slave would ever return deterred or reformed by his sentence, though ill treatment may have rendered him incapable of further harm. This contrasts with sentences to the public works, most of which envisaged the eventual return of the offender to the community from which he was never totally excluded. A penal slave was, in essence, a penal slave for life. Because his return to the community was not envisaged, the state was not concerned to limit the degradation, loss of status, bodily ill-treatment and frightful labour conditions which were heaped upon him. As Romans had long acknowledged that constant ill-treatment made ordinary slaves more dangerous (Diodorus, *Hist.* 34),[26] the state must have been aware that extremes of hardship experienced in the mines would have served to render penal slaves more intractable. At the time of Hadrian, it would seem that temporary sentences which sent men to the mines were not encouraged, probably because it was feared that the criminals would have been greatly hardened from such an experience (*Dig.*, 48.19.28.6). Yet by the fourth century, such temporary sentences seem to have become acceptable for free men (*Dig.*, 48.19.23; 48.19.8.8.; *CTh*, 1.5.3). This perhaps indicates two points: 1. that the distinction between conditions of punishment which were acceptable to slave or free of low status were in danger of disappearing altogether, and 2. the effects of such a temporary punishment were not, by this time, expected to debase further the character of low status free men from whom little was expected anyway.

So the original principle which aimed at seeing that those who were to return to the community after punishment should not be degraded totally by the experience was no longer judged to be of great importance.

Despite the fact that the control of the dangerous was the primary aim of penal servitude, the principle that the publicity of the punishment could act as a deterrent to those considering crime was not totally ignored. The awful conditions in the mines were well known and no efforts were made by the state to suppress this knowledge. Christian writers make it plain that chain gangs of penal slaves could be seen making their way to the mines (e.g. Cyprian, *Letters*, 77–9; Eusebius, *De Mart. Pal.*, 7.3–4; 8.1; 8.13). Fettered, tattooed,[27] in rags and with half-shorn heads their condition emphasised that these were no ordinary slaves. Indeed, their appearance defied the Roman tradition that slaves should not normally wear a distinctive dress, designed to prevent slaves from calculating their own numbers as a potentially powerful group (Seneca, *De Clem.* 1.24.1). The sorry sight of penal slaves, by contrast, was intended to emphasise the power of the state to remove and totally degrade criminals. Even pardoned penal slaves retained their tattooed faces, or later, limbs (*CTh* 9.40.2, AD 316), which together with their broken bodies, would have served as a reminder of state control.

By the fourth century AD, many non-criminals of low status were legally tied to their place of origin and to their occupation and, consequently, were unable to operate as a mobile work force.[28] Convict labour of any type could have supplied this state need and have been employed anywhere in the empire. Evidence suggests that only penal slaves were used in this way up to the fourth century.

Ulpian, writing in the third century, clearly shows that they could be moved from province to province to fulfil local needs for a labour force in the mines (*Dig.*, 48.19.8.4; cf. *Dig.*, 48.19.10.1). Eusebius, a Christian writer describing the persecutions of Christians in the early fourth century, tells of the shifting of convicts from the Egyptian mines to Syria (Eusebius, *De Mart. Pal.* 8.1). Likely penal slaves were also reserved for the arena (*Dig.*, 48.19.8.11) and there is evidence of their condemnation to the weaving mills (Lactantius, *De Mort. Pers*, 21.4; Eusebius, *Vis. Const.*, 2.34; *CTh* 4.3.6).

In contrast, criminals sent to the public works seem to have been retained to work within their own urban centres, (Pliny, *Letters*, X.31–2), though from the fourth century there is evidence that shortage of bakers in Rome resulted in the transportation of at least some of these free lesser criminals to Rome, far away from home, and

family life (*CTh*, 9.40.3; 5–7; 14.3.12; 14.17.6). This type of transportation was however traditionally associated with slavery (e.g.
Tacitus, *Annals,* 4.46).

Particularly in the mines then, penal slavery might have been
viewed as supplying an important labour supply. In fact, it seems unlikely that the *economic* use of penal slaves was ever a primary concern
of the state. The mutilations which were, on occasions, inflicted on
penal slaves before they were sent to the mines, cannot have
improved their capacity for work (Eusebius, *De Mart. Pal.*, 7.3–4; 8.1;
8.13). In addition, Eusebius states that the point of sending Christians
to the mines was not because their labour was particularly required,
but simply to add to their sufferings (Eusebius, *Hist. Ecc.*, 8.12.10).
The same principle must have applied equally to non-Christian penal
slaves.

In the early sixth century, Justinian abolished penal slavery, giving
as his reason that he wished to preserve the sanctity of marriage
which was automatically dissolved by reduction to slavery (*J. Nov.*,
22.8 and 9).[29] He did not, however, do away with the penalty of condemnation to the mines for free men, nor suggest that such penalties
should be of only a temporary nature, nor that in future such convicts should be treated more humanely. He pursued a general policy
of freeing slaves as often as possible[30] and it is significant that he did
not appear to distinguish between them and free men of low status
except for the inability of the former to marry. His attitude
concerning employment on public works may also be significant. In
the early imperial period, emperors had been glad to provide work in
the public building projects for the unemployed of Rome,[31] but did
not force them to undertake any kind of employment. In contrast,
Justinian, in the sixth century, did not hesitate to order that the unemployed of Constantinople should be put to work on public projects
to earn their keep (*J. Nov.*, 80.5, AD 539). His abolition of penal
slavery, without any insistence regarding limitation of the degree of
punishment which could henceforth be imposed on free men, gives
an indication that the distinctions as to what was appropriate
punishment for slaves as opposed to free men of low status had
virtually disappeared. This can be taken as the culmination of a
process which was certainly under way in the third century. The
legal necessity of reduction to penal slavery before the worst sorts of
punishment could be imposed had become obsolete. Even amputation
had, by this time, become an acceptable penalty.[32] As for punishments

to the mines, it may be that even lesser criminals were regularly sent there because, at least in Constantinople, Justinian had adopted a policy of employing vagrants on the public works formerly used for their punishment. This, however, is impossible to prove, just as it is impossible to know, through lack of evidence, just how many criminals were punished as penal slaves in the mines at any period up to the time of Justinian's abolition of penal slavery.

Acknowledgment

I am grateful for the advice and criticism given to me by my tutor, Dr M. D. Goodman, during the preparation of this paper.

Notes

1 Hopkins (1978).
2 Jones (1972) p. 14.
3 Cf. Lewis and Reinhold (1966) vol. 1 pp. 89ff for the class struggles of the Roman Republic.
4 Cf. Brunt (1958) p. 168; Frederiksen (1966) p. 129.
5 The ruling that defaulting debtors should either be killed or sold as slaves abroad is found in other early systems, cf. for example, Finley (1965) pp. 159ff.
6 For the expansion of Rome cf. Lewis and Reinhold (1966) vol. 1, Chs. 2 and 4.
7 Lewis and Reinhold (1966) vol. 1, Ch. 5.
8 Jones (1972) Ch. 3 *passim*.
9 It is true that in the first century AD, the Emperors Tiberius and Gaius condemned men of high rank to such penalties (Suetonius, *Tiberius*, 51; *Gaius Caligula*, 27). These events may, however, have been occasioned by an emperor's desire to humiliate personal enemies. As we have seen, by the latter centuries of the Republic forced labour had been discarded as an initial penalty for Roman citizens (Gaius, *Inst.*, 3.189). The fact that Nero, needing labour for his building programme in Rome in the mid-first century AD, sent for convict labour from the provinces, perhaps suggests that such labour was not commonly available in Rome and Italy at that time (Suetonius, *Nero*, 31).
10 Cf., Buckland (1975) p. 10.
11 Garnsey (1970) part II, p. 103f, 'The dual penalty system'.
12 Mommsen (1887–88) pp. 1045ff. gives a list of crimes together with the type of punishment which could be expected according to the status of the individual.

13 E.g., by the third century AD, free tenants were on occasion forced to remain on their farms when debt had reduced them to the state of debt bondsmen, compelled to pay off their debt with bodily labour (*Berlin Papyrus,* No. 7). At the same time, landlords were allowing slaves to take up tenancies on farms as 'quasi-coloni' cf., Ste. Croix (1983) pp. 237–8 and sv. Index 'slave, "quasi-colonus"'.

14 Cf., Garnsey (1970) part 4, Ch. 10, 'Privileged groups.

15 Cf., *CJ*, 9.47.1 which equates a life sentence to the public works for a free low status criminal with deportation for a free criminal of high status.

16 Artemidorus, *Oneirocriticon,* 1.21, indicates that the convict on the public works had a half-shaven head as a distinguishing mark. This is a good way of marking out the criminal from the rest of society while leaving no permanent mark. This method is, therefore, especially applicable for temporary sentencing where the criminal is expected to rejoin the community.

17 Other references to these penal slaves, *Digest,* 28.3.6.6–7; 29.1.13.2; 29.2.25.3; 40.1.8 pr; 40.5.24.6; 48.19.8.8. and 12; 48.19.8.17 pr; *Sententiae Pauli,* 3.6.29.

18 Cf., Birley (1953) pp. 87ff.

19 Cf., Hopkins (1978) pp. 124f. and Ch. IV.

20 Cf., Hopkins (1978) p. 122; Lewis and Reinhold (1966), vol. II, p. 268.

21 There is evidence that some convicts were placed in charge of the military, cf., Eusebius *De. Mart. Pal,* 13; *Corpus Inscriptionum Latinarum,* 3.12069; Cantacuzene (1928) p. 82. There is no way of knowing if this was invariably the case.

22 Cf., Ste. Croix (1981) pp. 328f.

23 Buckland (1908) p. 408; Jones (1964) pp. 421ff.

24 On what exactly should have been restored cf. Buckland (1908) pp. 410f.

25 The fact that in the early fourth century, Maximus did not allow infirm convicts in the mines (many of whom were Christians) to be freed, but killed them instead, can perhaps be taken as an indication that he was aware that physical infirmity would not prevent their continuing Christian teaching if freed; cf., Eusebius, *De. Mart. Pal.,* 13.4–10; *Hist. Ecc.,* 8.13.5. In addition, cf. *De. Mart. Pal.,* 13.1–4 where many Christians who had been released continued to live close to the mines.

26 Hence the imperial legislation aimed at reducing danger from slave revolts by limiting arbitrary cruelty of masters, cf. note 20 above.

27 That the branding referred to in *CTh.,* 9.40.2 was most probably tattooing, cf. Millar (1984) p. 128, note 7. I am grateful to G.E.M. de Ste. Croix for drawing my attention to this paper during the slavery workshop.

28 Cf., Jones (1964) s.v. Index, 'coloni' and 'hereditary service'.

29 For Justinian's views of the sanctity of marriage cf. Bury (1958) vol. II, pp. 408f.

30 Bury (1958) vol. II, pp. 401f.
31 Brunt (1980).
32 Bury (1958) vol. II, p. 415.

Further reading

Very little has been written on this subject. Of the secondary sources referenced above, the following will prove the most helpful: Buckland (1908); Garnsey (1970); Lewis and Reinhold (1966); Millar (1984); Mommsen (1887–88).

Six

Biblical Laws of Slavery: a Comparative Approach

Bernard S. Jackson

Without attempting here any exhaustive examination of the biblical evidence on slavery.[1] I propose to show that the biblical sources (perhaps not accidentally) display two features which are found also in classical antiquity. First, we can distinguish two different paradigms of slavery: captives (and their descendants) and debt-slaves, these paradigms being composed of a number of typical oppositions. Secondly, these oppositions generate a crisis in labelling. Opposition grows to the use of the concept of slavery in relation to debt-slaves. But that is not to say that the institution ceases to exist; it merely continues under a different name. Such a hypothesis makes it necessary for us to distinguish between the rules themselves and their ideological presentation.

A few preliminary words about slavery in classical antiquity may be in order.[2] Moses Finley has presented a typology, 'a spectrum of statuses, with the free citizen at one end and the slave at the other, and with a considerable number of shades of dependence in between'.[3] He enumerates these shades of dependence (progressing from the slave end of the spectrum to the free) as the helot, the debt-bondsman ('who was not a slave although under some conditions he could eventually be sold into slavery abroad'), the conditionally man-umitted slave and the freed man. He proposes this typology for heuristic purposes:

> All six categories rarely, if ever, appeared concurrently
> within the same community, nor were they equal in
> importance or equally significant in all periods of Greek
> history. By and large, the slave proper was the decisive
> figure (to the virtual exclusion of the others) in the econo-
> mically and politically advanced communities; whereas helotage
> and debt bondage were to be found in the more archaic communi-
> ties, whether in Crete or Sparta or Thessaly at an even later date,
> or in Athens in its pre-Solonian period (*ibid.*).

To a degree, even Finley here adopts the later Greek ideology: citizens cannot become slaves at home; slavery is a status of foreigners, the result of war or capture,[4] or sale of those (or their descendants) acquired in that way. Later, however, Finley himself appears to equivocate on the status of debt bondsmen, even while maintaining the basic correlation between slaves and foreigners:

> The impression one gets is clearly that the majority of the slaves were foreigners. In a sense, they were all foreigners. That is to say, it was the rule (apart from debt bondage) that Athenians were never kept as slaves in Athens, or Corinthians in Corinth.[5]

Schlaifer is less reluctant to regard debt bondage as a source of slavery. Citing Plutarch, *Solon* 13.3, he observes that 'Solon prohibited both the use of the body as security and the sale of oneself or one's children in to slavery.'[6] Schlaifer's account is consistent, in this respect, with that of Aristotle, who gives an account of Solon's reform (*Constitution of Athens*, 2.6), and who quotes Solon himself as having described this aspect of the *seisaktheia* (statute for debt relief) in the words: 'And those who suffered the disgrace of slavery here at home, trembling at their masters' whims, I set them free.'[7]

At Rome, it seems that debt-slavery was well recognised in the ancient period, and indeed functioned as a possible incident of the Roman system of patriarchal family authority, called *patria potestas*. This much can be safely inferred from the famous provision of the most ancient code of Roman law (c. 450 BC), of the Twelve Tables, *Si pater filium ter venum duit, a patre filius liber esto*, 'if a father sells his son three times, the son shall be free of the father' (Gaius, *Institutes* I, 132). There must have been a reversion to the original patriarchal family head after each sale. The sale was thus conceived as essentially non-permanent. This is intelligible only in the context of debt-slavery, where the father sells his child either to the creditor directly or to a third party, in order to raise the money to pay the creditor. Such arrangements are fully documented in the ancient Near East, e.g., *Laws of Hammurabi*, 117 (henceforth *LH*), and, as we shall see, in the Bible. Whether there ever existed at Rome a rule requiring the termination of such debt-slavery after a finite period of time (as in both *LH* 117 and the Bible) is not known. It is more likely that the creditor was required to release the debt-slave either at a time agreed *ab initio* (at the outset) with the *pater* (family head), or when the debt had been worked off by the equivalent value of the slave's service. Two of the classical jurists of Roman law later provide an indication that a mechanism may well have existed, in the ancient period, to ensure that the creditor received no more than the economic value of the debt. First, Gaius (second century AD) speaks of release from *mancipium* ('bondage', now conceived as a free but dependent status) by the censor against the wishes of the holder (*Institutes*, I. 140). Secondly, Papinian (third century AD) writes:

> If though a free man handed over in noxal surrender as much has been acquired as the loss he caused, the owner may be forced to manumit that man by the praetor who authorised the noxal surrender (*Collatio*, 2.3).

Noxal surrender was an institution according to which a dependent member of the family (free or slave) who had committed a delict (an offence) could, in some circumstances, be handed over to the victim in lieu of compensation. The status of the person surrendered, like that of the debt-slave (used to work off a contractual obligation) was bondage, *mancipium*. It is reasonable to suppose that the same, or a similar, procedure to ensure release was available also for the debt-slave.

Lévy-Bruhl argues that none of the sources of slavery applied to a Roman citizen in the regal and early Republican periods: all slaves were foreigners, the result (directly or indirectly) of capture. Those categories of servitude which resulted from debt (such as *nexi* = bondsmen, *addicti* = adjudged by the court) were not slaves. Nor were children sold by their *pater familias* (family head) into *mancipium*. They were described, he notes, as *in mancipio* (in bondage) or *in causa mancipii* (in a position of bondage), rather than as themselves *mancipia*.[8] But Lévy-Bruhl is here imposing the Romans' later ideology upon the most ancient period of their history. One can see why later *mancipia* (third century AD) became problematic. The jurist Florentinus provides etymologies for both *servi* (slaves) and *mancipia* (bondsmen/women), clearly regarding them as belonging to the same concept of *servitus* (slavery), which in this passage is opposed to *libertas* (freedom):

> Slaves (*servi*) are so called because commanders generally sell

the people they capture and thereby save (*servare*) them instead of killing them. '*Mancipia*' is derived from the fact that they are captured from the enemy by force of arms (*manu capiantur*).[9]

But despite the alteration of the label, as it applied to free persons sold by their *pater familias*, the perception still remained that their position was comparable to that of slaves. Gaius remarks that all children, male or female, who are in a parent's *potestas* (power) can be mancipated by him in just the same manner as slaves (*Institutes*, I.117), and even goes so far as to explain the fact that persons *in mancipio* are subject to the same forms of manumission as are slaves by remarking that 'they rank as slaves', *quia servorum loco habentur* (*Institutes* I. 138).

The different procedures and terminology applied in the sources to those termed *nexi* (bondsmen) or *addicti* (ajudged by the court) results from a difference in the status they enjoyed before enslavement, not a different valuation of their status once rendered debt-slaves. Whereas those who entered *mancipium* had previously been dependents, *alieni iuris* (i.e., subject to *patria potestas*), different rules were provided by the *Twelve Tables* for debtors who were themselves heads of household, but who preferred that exaction of the debt should be against their own person, rather than against the person of one of their dependants. Naturally, the procedure here differed. This was no longer a private matter, a sale between two heads of household. It was now the subjection of one head of household to another, and the institutions of the state were clearly involved. According to the writer Aulus Gellius, quoting and interpreting the *Twelve Tables*, the *praetor* could ultimately assign the debtor to the creditor, who was authorised to take him away and keep him bound with rope or fetters. If at the end of sixty days the debt could still not be repaid, the debtor could be sold abroad (*trans Tiberim*) as a permanent slave to a foreigner.[10] It seems to me perverse to call the debtor anything other than a slave in the period of sixty days before he was sold abroad: his freedom was restrained in the most elementary manner. It differed from other slavery mainly in its temporary duration. Indeed, the account provided by Livy of the abolition of this institution in the late fourth century BC indicates that a debt-slave might not only be subjected to chains, but might also be liable to unwanted sexual advances and beating.[11]

We may note that the *cause célèbre* which in Livy's narrative (the historical or literary character of which is unimportant for present purposes) led to the abolition of the institution was one where the debtor had apparently anticipated judicial assignment of his person to the creditor, by voluntarily giving himself in bondage to the creditor, and this 'because of a debt he had inherited from his father' (Livy, quoted above). Voluntary self-sale for such reasons is also found in the ancient Near East. We may safely assume that it represents the original context of slavery *iure civili*, according to the classical jurist Marcian (third century AD), who writes:

> Slaves come into our ownership either by civil law or the common law of peoples (*ius gentium*) – by the civil law, if anyone over twenty allows himself to be sold in order to benefit by retaining a share of the purchase price; and by the common law of peoples, those who have been captured in war and those who are the children of our slave women are our slaves.[12]

Classical law, after the abolition of debt-slavery in Rome, understood this situation as that of a free man who sought fraudulently to have himself sold as a slave, knowing that he would then be able to reassert his freedom (if the fraud were not proved). But that is clearly an artificial reinterpretation. Indeed, this text, taken in conjunction with Livy's account of the abolition of debt-slavery, suggests that a free man who sought to pay off his debt in this way (voluntarily, as opposed to the result of a judicial decree) might remain in slavery and work off his debt actually in Rome, without being sold abroad to raise the money.

In short, institutions of debt-slavery existed in ancient Rome. Traces of them remain in the classical sources, even though *mancipium* is reclassified as a form of family dependency, rather than a form of slavery. We may well imagine that it was the infusion into Rome of foreign captives in the imperial wars of the late Republic that prompted this reclassification. For the paradigm forms of slavery are distinguished by the correlation of two oppositions: when the result of war or capture, it is permanent, and applies to an outsider; when the product of debt, it is temporary: hence, the permanent enslavement of a citizen (in the regal and early Republican periods) could only be achieved by selling him abroad. The arrival, in numbers, of foreign slaves in Rome may well have prompted the rejection of these opposed paradigms as species of a single *genus*; indigenous debt-slavery had to be reclassified, to remove the implied comparison.

Biblical law clearly knows of both types, permanent slavery and debt bondage. *Deuteronomy* 20: 10–14 requires the enslavement of the population of a city which surrenders, and the enslavement of the women and children of a city which is defeated (cf., *Numbers* 31: 26). Both narrative sources and the norms of biblical law contemplate self-sale because of poverty[13] and the sale into slavery of children.[14]

The temporal status of debt-slavery is a recurrent theme in biblical literature. Sometimes, its regulation is attributed to temporal limits imposed by divine law, though the sources differ as to the period. *Deuteronomy* 15: 12, imposes a maximum limit of six years. *Leviticus* 25: 40, allows service until the arrival of the jubilee year, fixed by the calendar to occur every fifty years. Elsewhere, we find references to individual acts of relief instigated by the temporal authority of the time, such action being more akin to the Greek *seisaktheia* (debt-relief) and the Old Babylonian *misharum* (economic ordinance). The *deror* (act of release) proclaimed by King Zedekiah (*Jeremiah* 34) is particularly important in this regard.

The typology of slavery is particularly important for our understanding of the provisions of the 'Covenant Code' (*Exodus* 21–2), generally considered to be the earliest of the biblical 'legal' collections. It commences with the following two paragraphs, here rendered according to the Revised Standard Version:

(2) When you buy a Hebrew (*ivri*) slave, he shall serve six years, and in the seventh he shall go out free, for nothing.
(3) If he comes in single, he shall go out single; if he comes in married, then his wife shall go out with him.
(4) If his master gives him a wife and she bears him sons or daughters, the wife and her children shall be her master's and he shall go out alone.
(5) But if the slave plainly says, 'I love my master, my wife, and my children; I will not go out free',
(6) Then his master shall bring him to God, and he shall bring him to the door or the doorpost; and his master shall bore his ear through with an awl; and he shall service him for life.

(7) When a man sells his daughter as a slave, she shall not go out as the male slaves do.

(8) If she does not please her master, who had designated her for himself, then he shall let her be redeemed; he shall have no right to sell her to a foreign people, since he has dealt faithlessly with her.

(9) If he designated her for his son, he shall deal with her as with a daughter.

(10) If he takes another wife to himself, he shall not diminish her food, her clothing, or her marital rights.

(11) And if he does not do these three things for her, she shall go out for nothing, without payment of money (*Exodus* 21: 2–11).

The Hewbrew word *ivri* ('Hebrew') has been the subject of considerable scholarly discussion. As against the traditional interpretation (represented by the present translation) which takes it to be a 'gentilic', there are those who see it as a reference to an inferior social class, comparable to the *habiru* of the Akkadian documents and cognate designations found also in Ugaritic and Egyptian sources (Cassuto, 1967, p. 265). Such *habiru* were often foreign, but not necessarily so. But it seems clear that later biblical writers viewed these provisions of *Exodus* as referring to debt-slavery. That is the context understood by Jeremiah, in his account of the *deror* of Zedekiah, where he complains of the lack of observance of this particular law, requiring release *ex lege* of the debt-slave after six years. It is similarly implied by Deuteronomy, which recapitulates the six-year rule (15: 12). And it is in precisely this kind of context that Hammurabi prescribes a release in the fourth year for the wife, son or daughter sold or delivered into slavery in order to pay a debt (*LH* 117).

There is also internal evidence from this passage to support the conclusion that we are here dealing with debt slavery. The second paragraph, dealing with the sale of a daughter, speaks of a man selling his daughter; financial pressure on the father is clearly the context. But verse 7 goes on with the clearest possible cross-reference to the first paragraph, instead of stating the same or a comparable rule independently. This supports the community of context between the two paragraphs, and thus speaks for the conclusion that the acquisition of the male slave is also for the payment of debt. We should not be misled, in this regard, by the difference between the two verbs used to introduce the cases, *kanah* ('acquire') in the case of the male-slave, *makhar* ('sell') in the case of the female. Debt-slavery might arise either as a result of a voluntary agreement between the parties, or from unilateral action on the part of the creditor. The latter form, sometimes described as 'distress', is found in the Laws of Eshnunna (c.1900 BC, Eshnunna being the Mesopotamian city state where they were found),[15] the Laws of Hammurabi (1700 BC Babylon) and elsewhere. There is, in fact, reason to suspect that the word *ivri* is not original in the present text. The context was certainly debt-slavery, but the ethnic association quite normally correlated with this form of slavery was not an issue at this time. In the later biblical rules on slavery, particularly *Deuteronomy* 15, it was to become so.

A second problem with this text, over which scholarly opinion has been much divided, concerns the apparent difference between male and female slaves resulting from the collocation of these two paragraphs. It would appear that there is one form of slavery (temporary) for males, while there is quite another form – involving a permanent sexual relationship – for women. This was perceived as a problem as early as the first recapitulation of these laws, in *Deuteronomy* 15. There, the first paragraph is explicitly extended to cover a Hebrew male or female slave, and the second paragraph of the Covenant Code, providing for a permanent relationship, is taken (*Deuteronomy* 15: 17) to be a special case of voluntary extension of slavery (as here provided in *Exodus*, 21: 5–6). Indeed, the evidence from both other biblical sources and from the ancient Near East shows that women were used at least as commonly as debt-slaves (temporary debt-slaves) as were men. So why should the Covenant Code have appeared to make such a distinction? Could it not have made the matter clear by having the first paragraph explicitly cover both male and female? I suggest that there is a good reason for the present formulation. It is only by limiting the first paragraph to the case of a male debt-slave that the draftsman is in a position to contrast the sexual/familial aspects of the matter. Verse 4 requires the debt-slave to abandon the woman his master has provided, and any children he has fathered by her. This provides a clue to the structural relationship between the two passages. It indicates that a male debt-slave may be used for sexual services – effectively, to breed permanent slaves for his master – without interference with his status. Sexual services are no different from other services in this respect. The second paragraph gives us the opposite side of the coin. A woman debt-slave can only be used for sexual services if her status is thereby changed. Sexual activity alters the status of the woman debt-slave but not that of the male. (Interestingly, *Deuteronomy* extends this humanitarian perception to the case of the woman captive, *Deuteronomy*, 21: 10–14.) If the master wants the female slave as a breeding member of his household, he can only have her on a permanent basis. He then has to regularise her status. He can do so in two ways, either by taking her for himself, or for his son. In the latter case, we are told that she must be treated as a daughter (21: 9). Where he takes her himself, he cannot thereafter arbitrarily dispose of her by a foreign sale. Indeed, verse 8 is widely interpreted as banning disposal outside the family. The complaint of Rachel and Leah against their father, Laban, uses similar terminology: 'Are we not regarded by him as foreigners (*nokhri'ot*)? For he has sold us (*mekharanu*), and he has been using up the money given for us' (*Genesis* 31: 15).

The formulation of this text of *Exodus* is also significant in relation to procedures of emancipation. It is noticeable that only in the case of a slave who wishes voluntarily to remain in slavery is there any ceremony required. Release in the seventh year, according to this text, is automatic, and is marked by no formality whatsoever. It is, by implication, simply a reversion to the man's normal status. What is exceptional, and therefore requires due signification to the community, is the choice to remain in bondage.[16] Whether the complete absence of any formality to mark the end of the period of debt-slavery corresponded to reality may, in fact, be doubted. The formulation of the comparable rule in the Laws of Hammurabi (117) has been viewed as implying some official adjudication or participation.[17] But clearly, the author wishes – perhaps by a selective presentation (the technique which, as we have seen, structures the relationship between the two paragraphs) – to stress the difference in kind between the two changes of status, and to emphasise that the conversion of debt-slavery into permanent slavery is far more significant than the termination *ex lege* of debt-slavery. We may note that the choice of ceremony is by no means arbitrary. The ear of the slave is pierced with an awl. The ear is the source of hearing, and is thus thought of as the source of obedience. *Shama* ('to hear') is the standard term for 'to obey'. Similarly, in the Laws of Hammurabi

(282), the punishment for a rebellious slave, one who rejects the authority of his master, is to have his ear cut off – a 'mirroring' punishment.

The typology of slavery must also be taken into account in the interpretation of a number of provisions of the Covenant Code relating to injuries (fatal and non-fatal) inflicted by the master on the slave. *Exodus* 21: 20–1 provides:

> When a man strikes his slave, male or female, with a rod
> and the slave dies under his hand, he shall be punished. But
> if the slave survives a day or two, he is not to be punished;
> for the slave is his money (Revised Standard Version).

The distinction between immediate death and death after a day or two is not sufficiently explained in terms of a crude test of causation; the previous paragraph, dealing with fatal injuries to a free man, implies that if the injured party dies while on his sick bed, before such time as he 'rises again and walks abroad with his staff', the man who struck him is regarded as having caused his death (*Exodus* 21: 18–19). Some such crude test of causation is required also in the case of the slave, but here the line is clearly drawn more favourably to the master. As Daube has argued,[18] the master's right to discipline his slave is here being regulated, albeit in a somewhat arbitrary fashion. That the master-slave relationship is a distinguishing feature of this norm may be seen from the concluding motive clause: 'For he is his money.' But in reality that motive goes too far. If the slave were fully equated with property, there should be *no* liability even when the slave did die under the master's hand, i.e., where he did *not* survive even for a day or two. That, indeed, was the situation in early Roman law.

The motive clause is suspicious; it is quite uncharacteristic of the drafting of the Covenant Code. I regard it as an addition to the original text. And it is clearly relevant to the typology of slavery. Only someone who considered this to be a case of permanent slavery could have been responsible for this motive clause. But it is most doubtful that permanent slavery was contemplated by the original author. The provision makes much more sense if we regard it as applicable to debt-slavery. The comparative evidence strongly supports this view. The ancient Near Eastern collections do not regulate assaults committed by a master on his own slaves; they only deal with assaults on the slaves of others. Some commentators have seen this as evidence of the higher moral standard of biblical, as compared with ancient Near Eastern, law.[19] But in fact, the ancient Near Eastern collections *do* regulate assaults by a master on his debt-slave. What has confused the issue is the fact that the Covenant Code unselfconsciously uses the terminology 'slave' (*eved, amah*) in the context of debt-slavery as well as in the context of permanent slavery, while the ancient Near Eastern collections (anticipating the tendency observed in classical antiquity) reserved different terminology for the debt-slave. The rules analogous to *Exodus* 21: 20–1, are Laws of Eshnunna 23–4 and Laws of Hammurabi 115–16. The latter draws a distinction between the natural death of a person distrained for debt in the house of his creditor, and a death due to blows or ill treatment. In the latter case, the sanctions are severe. If the creditor has seized a son of the debtor, who has died in such circumstances, the son of the creditor shall be put to death.

There is also internal evidence within the Covenant Code to suggest that the rules protecting the slave from assault by his master refer to debt-slavery. *Exodus* 21: 26–7 provides:

> Where a man strikes the eye of his slave, male or female, and destroys it, he shall let the slave go free for the eye's sake. If he knocks out the tooth of his slave, male or female, he shall let the slave go free for the tooth's sake (Revised Standard Version).

Once again, the same terminology of *eved* and *amah* is used as in the opening paragraphs of the collection. Moreover, there is here a further terminological link. These verses say that the slave thus injured shall go out 'free' – *lahofshi*, a relatively rare term, but one used also in verse 2 of the chapter. We can hardly imagine a permanent slave, a captive in war, being released because his master has knocked his tooth out. That is not to say that we should regard the 'slave', wherever mentioned in the Covenant Code, as exclusively referring to the debt-slave. As may be seen from the motive-clause attached to verse 21, a contrary view was expressed even within the biblical period. The solution to this problem requires close attention to the literary history of the collection as a whole. Suffice it here to note that there is one other rule, dealing with the case of a slave killed by a goring ox (*Exodus* 21: 32), where the slave does appear to be treated as money, and by inference may be a permanent slave, rather than a debt-slave.[20]

One further paragraph of the Covenant Code deserves our attention in this context. There is a paragraph on theft, which, as rearranged by the Revised Standard Version, commences as follows (*Exodus* 22:1):

> If a man steals an ox or a sheep, and kills it or sells it, he shall pay five oxen for an ox, and four sheep for a sheep.
> He shall make restitution; if he has nothing, then he shall be sold for his theft.

But this translation is misleading in two respects. The phrase 'for his theft', translating the Hebrew word *bignevato*, should properly be rendered 'in exchange for the stolen animal'; the same noun, *genevah*, unambiguously has this concrete meaning in the next verse.[21] Secondly, the verb rendered 'he shall be sold' may equally mean 'he shall be handed over' (i.e., to the victim of the theft). Once again, we may ask: what form of slavery is here envisaged? It *could* be penal, depriving the thief permanently of his freedom – even though this may appear irrational, if he suffers such a penalty only if he does not have the means to make the necessary compensation. The Laws of Hammurabi, paragraph 8, take that irrationality a stage further, in prescribing the death penalty for the thief who has not the means to pay. Roman criminal law also came to use slavery as a form of punishment for certain crimes. Alternatively, and far more logically, the enslavement may here be regarded as designed to work off a debt, much as the Roman *mancipium* encompassed both debt-slavery and noxal surrender. What seems to me to speak in favour of an interpretation of this provision in terms of debt-slavery is twofold. First, this is the natural inference to draw, given the location of this rule in a collection which has the rules of temporary slavery at its head. Second, the laws of theft – as I argue at some length in a forthcoming study – themselves rest upon a typology of offenders as insiders or outsiders. The typical thief is an insider, as opposed to the brigand, who is an outsider.[22] That the thief is an insider is demonstrated, in theological terms, by the prohibition of theft in the Decalogue – regarded by the compilers of the Bible as the text of the very covenant which defined membership of the community. It is the same deep structural opposition between insider and outside that is

transformed in the context of the typology of slavery into a
distinction between the debt-slave and the slave captured in war, and
which is transformed in the context of offences against property into
that between the thief and the brigand. The Covenant Code, more
than any other of the biblical legal collections, is exclusively
concerned with insiders. The action of the thief is the action of an
insider; we may expect the sanctions applied to him to maintain that
status.

The Covenant Code does not treat the labelling of the debt-slave
as a slave as at all problematic. This was not the case, however, with
some of the later biblical sources. The reclassification which we
observe is not universal: at the very least, the complaint of the people
at the time of Nehemiah can be expressed in the terminology of *eved*
('slave'):

> Now our flesh is as the flesh of our brethren, our children
> are as their children; yet we are forcing our sons and our
> daughters to be slaves, and some of our daughters have
> already been enslaved; but it is not in our power to help it,
> for other men have our fields and our vineyards (*Nehemiah*
> 5: 5).

Contrast with this the reclassification effected by a priestly writer, as
found in *Leviticus*:

> And if your brother becomes poor beside you, and sells himself to
> you, you shall not make him serve as a slave [*avodat eved*]: he shall
> be with you as a hired servant and as a sojourner. He shall serve
> with you until the year of the jubilee; then he shall go out from
> you, he and his children with him, and go back to his own family,
> and return to the possession of his fathers. For they are my
> servants [literally, 'slaves', *avaday*], whom I brought out of the land
> of Egypt; they shall not be sold as slaves. You shall not rule over
> him with harshness, but shall fear your God. As for your male and
> female slaves [*ve'avdekha va'amatakha*] whom you may have: you
> may buy male and female slaves from among the nations that are
> round about you. You may also buy from among the strangers
> who sojourn with you and their families that are with you, who
> have been born in your land; and they may be your property. You
> may bequeath them to your sons after you, to inherit as a

possession for ever; you may make slaves of them, but over your brethren the people of Israel you shall not rule, one over another, with harshness (*Leviticus* 25: 39–46, Revised Standard Version).

The insider/outsider opposition is here made explicit. Not only may insiders only be debt-slaves, subject at most to temporary servitude; their status is now equated to that of a hired servant or a resident alien. The terms *eved* and *amah*, used of the debt-slave in the Covenant Code, are now appropriated for permanent slavery, which is now restricted to outsiders (though including, for this purpose, resident aliens who are so purchased). But purchase is unlikely to have been the original source of such slavery; in most cases, the slave purchased from foreigners will himself have been acquired in warfare, or will have been a descendant of such captives.

The reclassification, and its integration into an explicit typology of slavery, could not be more clear. But we may note that the version of the Covenant Code rules which is provided by *Deuteronomy* 15: 12–18 adopts the same ideology, but expresses it through silence. If we compare the versions in *Exodus* and *Deuteronomy* in the light of the problematic revealed by *Leviticus*, we find one striking fact: *Deuteronomy* avoids using the noun *eved* ('slave') in contexts where *Exodus* uses it, and reserves its use for the status of the debt-slave who has opted voluntarily to become a permanent slave, once the ceremony with the awl has been performed (verse 17). That contrasts markedly with the text in *Exodus*, where the term is used of that slave at the time he seeks the change of status from debt-slave to permanent slave, and before that change has been effected (*Exodus* 21:5). Similarly, whereas *Exodus* commences by describing the debt-slave as *eved* ('When you acquire a Hebrew slave'), *Deuteronomy* prefers: 'If your brother, a Hebrew man, or a Hebrew woman, is sold to you'. Certainly, the verb *avad* is used to express the obligation to serve the master for six years. Nevertheless, a crucial change of label has been effected.

What was it that caused this reclassification to take place? If one could be more certain regarding the dating of the various components which make up the Covenant Code, one might possibly hypothesise an historical development comparable to that at Rome, namely that it was the new experience of captives taken in war (a theme certainly of interest to *Deuteronomy*) which prompted the greater self-consciousness regarding the labelling of the debt-slave.

Unfortunately, the present state of our knowledge is not sufficient to justify argument in this direction. (On the contrary, it might in fact be more reasonable to argue from the lack of self-consciousness regarding the labelling of the debt-slave for a particularly early date (or remote community) for the provenance of the slave-laws of the Covenant Code.) More promising, perhaps, is the possibility of literary influence. Wisdom elements, including sensitivity to foreign concepts and terminology, have been noted as a particularly important feature of the drafting of *Deuteronomy*;[23] but attention to theological and cultic concerns has, perhaps, retarded the development of scholarly interest in the same problem as regards the priestly sources (within which *Leviticus* 25, noted above, is to be found). The most obvious source of literary influence will have been the ancient Near Eastern collections, particularly the Laws of Hammurabi, copies of which were widely disseminated in the ancient Near East for at least a millenium after the original composition. We have noted that Hammurabi also avoids labelling the debt-slave with the same terminology (*wardum*) as is applied to permanent slavery. However, I myself would not exclude the possibility of reciprocal influence between the ancient Near East and classical antiquity. In particular, Solon's *seisaktheia* comes as no surprise to students of oriental kingship. We thus have a range of possibilities from which to choose: internal influences, external influences, or some combination of the two. Beyond that, in the present state of our knowledge, it is impossible to conjecture.

Notes

1 See Cardellini (1981).
2 Most of the Greek and Roman sources referred to are translated in the Loeb Classical Library. See especially *Remains of Old Latin* (ed.) E.H. Warmington (1935) for the Roman *Twelve Tables*. The *Institutes* of Gaius are translated by F. de Zalueta (Clarendon Press, 1946–53), and a full English translation of the main source of Roman juristic writings, the *Digest* of Justinian, has recently been published in English by the University of Pennsylvania Press, edited by Alan Watson (1985). For the ancient Near Eastern sources, see J.B. Pritchard (ed.), *Ancient Near Eastern Sources Relating to the Old Testament* (Princeton University Press, 1969, 3rd ed.).
3 Finley (1959), p. 147.
4 As in the Homeric poems. See Westermann (1955), p. 2.

5 Finley, *op. cit.*, p. 153.
6 Schlaifer (1936), p. 178.
7 *Constitution of Athens* 12.4; see Wiedemann (1981), p. 38.
8 Lévy-Bruhl (1934), pp. 16–19; repr. 1960. pp. 152–5.
9 *Digest* 1.5.4; Wiedemann (1981), p. 15.
10 *Attic Nights* 20.1.41–6; Wiedemann, *op. cit.*, p. 39.
11 Livy 8.28; Wiedemann, *op. cit.*, p. 41.
12 *Digest* 1.5.5.1; Wiedemann, *op. cit.*, p. 23.
13 See, for example, *Leviticus* 25:39.
14 *Nehemiah* 5:5; cf., Falk (1964), p. 118.
15 LE 22–4; cf., Jackson and Watkins (1984).
16 Cf., Piattelli (1984), p. 1236.
17 Lewy (1958), p. 27 note 58.
18 Daube (1961), p. 249.
19 For example, Paul (1970), pp. 69, 78.
20 Cf., Cardellini (1981), pp. 266f.
21 Cf., Jackson (1972), pp. 140–3.
22 Cf., Jackson (1970).
23 See Weinfeld (1972).

Further reading

For slave systems of classical antiquity, see Buchland (1908), Westermann (1955) and the work by Wiedemann (1981) cited throughout this paper. For Near Eastern and biblical slavery, see Cardellini (1981), Mendelsohn (1949) and Phillips (1984).

Seven

Debt Bondage in Latin America
Alan Knight

Though Latin America contained bastions of chattel slavery in Cuba and Brazil, forms of unfree labour which were not chattel slavery were more widespread during both the colonial period (c.1500–1820) and the national period (post-1820). These included forced labour drafts (the Peruvian *mita*, New Spain's *repartimiento de indios* and *coatequitl*); prison labour (*presidios* and *obrajes*); and, above all, debt-peonage. Comparative studies of the latter institution (which are rare) stress the central importance of Latin America, not least Mexico. And national studies, past and relatively present, give a picture of Mexico as a nation of peonage and poverty which, according to a polemical account of 1908, included 750,000 chattel slaves and 5 million debt peons.[1] However, as a recent debate has shown, the nature of Latin American debt peonage is highly contentious.[2] Was it *de facto* slavery, debt being a device to create a class of slaves long after formal slavery had been abolished? Or was debt simply the result of cash advances, made in order to secure a basically proletarian labour force? In other words was the debt-peon a surrogate slave or surrogate proletarian? The question is by no means academic. It presumably made a difference to the endebted individual, in ways which will be suggested. Such subjective differences would have affected the quality, productivity and control of labour. Furthermore, landlords, in opting for a debt-peonage system, made decisions which carried major implications for economic development. In simple terms, the choice of a *de facto* servile system placed a premium on extra-economic coercion. Possibly this inhibited productivity. Certainly it meant that landlord competition in the market depended heavily on extra-economic factors (e.g., political and physical controls) rather than on relative economic efficiency in the free market. It made more sense to invest in, say, political bribes or a plantation police force, than in a steam plough. Profits accrued according to economically irrational principles – and more so in a society where *de facto* slave labour was dragooned within the society itself, by classic extra-economic coercion, rather than being imported through an international slave market. In this respect, Latin American slave systems (in Brazil and Cuba) adhered more faithfully to market practices (pressures to modernise, equalisation of the rate of profit) than their debt-peon equivalents; and it is no coincidence that erstwhile chattel slave societies (Cuba and, *a fortiori*, São Paulo in Brazil) made a more successful transition to agrarian capitalism in the wake of abolition than did predominantly debt-peon societies (compare Yucatán, Guatemala).

The mere fact of debt, which is the overt feature of debt peonage, may thus create an illusory similitude among forms of labour which differ radically in respect of subjective conditions/perceptions and objective social implications. Given the ambiguous nature of debt, I shall begin by suggesting two theoretical viewpoints which afford an organising scheme to make sense of these wide disparities. The aim, which may be of relevance beyond Latin America or Mexico, is to break up the 'broad spectrum of unfreedom' into constituent parts.[3] Both are of Marxist provenance, but one is of a more common-sense, empirical kind, the other more rigorously theoretical; as such, they are complementary rather than antithetical.

In seeking to clarify the old debate over the character of New World slavery (that is, the supposed differences between Latin Catholic and Anglo-Saxon Protestant slavery) Genovese put forward three main criteria: (i) 'day-to-day living conditions' (food, clothing, housing, hours worked); (ii) 'conditions of life' (cultural, religious, familial rights/opportunities); and (iii) 'access to freedom and citizenship'.[4] Thus, North American slaves might have enjoyed superior material conditions compared with, say, their Brazilian counterparts, but the latter enjoyed somewhat greater access to freedom. Such geographic comparisons have chronological equivalents: with the growth of sugar production, Cuban slaves experienced greater control, regimentation and exploitation (hence, notwithstanding Cuba's 'Latin', Catholic heritage, a derogation of rights ii. and iii.). In the 1860s, however, the interdiction of the slave trade 'forced some proprietors to take better care of their slaves and to promote their well being and comfort' (i.e., to improve i.).[5] In the Mexican case which I shall consider, peons – including peons (broadly defined) in the same region and the same period – sometimes experienced quite different treatment, which is amenable to analysis according to these 'Genovese criteria'.

A second conceptualisation may be derived from grand theory. Here, however, grand theory is often misinterpreted, and some preliminary clarification is necessary. It is a commonplace that Marx's and Engels' observations on pre-capitalist epochs rest on far less thorough study than Marx's description and analysis of capitalism.[6] Partly because of this deficiency, discussions of pre- (or non-) capitalist social formations have often been bedevilled by theoretical confusion and polemic (consider, for examples, debates about the transition from feudalism to capitalism; the feudal or capitalist character of colonial Latin America; the validity and application of the concept of an Asiatic mode of production). Two particular controversies central to these debates are also central to the specific question of slavery and unfree labour. First, there is the question of whether modes of production should be defined 'at the level of production' (for which, roughly speaking, the key criteria are to be found in the labour system); or 'at the level of circulation' (the key criteria being market relations and profit-maximisation). The categorisation of 'New World' slavery is, obviously, a litmus test of these respective definitions; however, Marx's own categorisation is ambiguous and, within the terms of this debate, inconclusive.[7] Secondly, the very definition of 'free' as against 'unfree' labour begs a range of questions. The classic 'free wage labourer' (proletarian) embodies at least three related attributes: (i) he is 'free' from direct compulsion ('extra-economic coercion'); (ii) he lacks ownership of the means of production; and as a result (iii) he 'freely' negotiates the sale of his labour power. It is no easy thing, however, to derive a mirror-image 'unfree' worker from these attributes; on the contrary, the reverse theorising of unfree from free labour is as problematical as the reverse theorising of 'pre-capitalist' social formations from capitalist.

Fortunately, a recent theoretical study sheds light on the problem. According to Gerry Cohen, Marx's concept of the 'social mode (of production)' embraced three dimensions, namely, 'its purpose, the form of the producer's surplus labour, and the means of exploiting producers (or mode of exploitation)'.[8] 'Purpose' is straightforward: it relates to the familiar distinction between production for use and production for exchange (and exchange, Cohen rightly argues, should be seen as a continuum, ranging from barter through profit-maximisation without capital accumulation to profit-maximisation serving capital accumulation). This is relevant to the present discussion, but uncontentious. The second and third dimensions (form of surplus labour and mode of exploitation) are also important, but more problematic since, as Cohen correctly says, they have been regularly and misleadingly conflated. In fact, the form of surplus labour ('the form in which surplus labour is extracted', e.g., by means of the cash nexus; by labour rent; by the sharecropper's surrender of a portion of the crop) must be conceptually distinguished from 'the mode of exploitation, or *the means whereby the producer is made to perform surplus labour* (whatever may be the form of the surplus)'.[9] In this last respect, the conventional distinction is between economic pressure (which compels a proletarian to enter the cash nexus) and 'extra-economic coercion', that is, the compulsion of force and/or ideology. Many (most?) theorists – as well as those few historians who have engaged in such exercises – have collapsed together the 'form of surplus labour' and the 'mode of exploitation': that is, they have assumed either a necessary *theoretical* identity between the two, or a given, *historical* identity. Pre- or non-capitalist relations of production – whose pre- or non-capitalist character is determined by the extraction of surplus from subordinate classes who are not free wage labourers – are assumed to depend on extra-economic coercion.[10]

Thus, Cohen summarises the 'standard historical liaisons' ('standard', that is, according to conventional opinion) in these terms: 'extra-economic mode of exploitation with surplus not in the form of value, and exploitation mediated by labour contract with surplus in value form'.[11] But, not only are alternative liaisons theoretically possible, as Cohen shows; they are also historically significant, and they figure among the examples presented in this paper. For it will be argued that the broad category of 'debt-peonage' included such apparent anomalies – or illicit liaisons – as coerced wage labourers (that is, workers whose 'mode of exploitation' is coercive, but whose surplus labour is extracted at least formally via the cash nexus) and voluntary serfs (that is, workers whose 'mode of exploitation' is economic – the market – but whose surplus labour is realised in direct forms, such as labour rent).[12]

These concepts help elucidate the character and dynamics of unfree labour in nineteenth-century Latin America, especially Mexico. And the notion of dynamics is important, since the history of this subject is the history not of a slowly dissolving colonial legacy, but rather of a spurt of change and innovation, chiefly in the last third of the nineteenth century. Then, precisely as a result of economic development, forms of unfree labour were dramatically extended and strengthened, at a time when formal chattel slavery was on the wane in Brazil and Cuba. Then, parts of southern Mexico, Guatemala and Peru underwent a kind of second serfdom, induced by global market demand for agricultural goods.[13] This is not, however, to give priority to external processes, or to reduce Latin American (under) development to some simple dependent reflex. On the contrary, it is vital to give full attention (as Brenner has stressed, in an analogous case) to the 'particular, historically developed class structures through which these processes actually worked themselves out and through which their fundamental character was actually determined'.[14]

This, in turn, requires an analysis that is both diachronic and regional, that encompasses variations over time and space. Since, however, I am subject to a salutary editorial discipline, I shall attempt only to present some broad conclusions. I suggest that three types of debt peonage existed in nineteenth-century Mexico (and, more tentatively, I would apply the same typology to Latin America as a whole). All shared the element of debt, hence their superficial kinship. But they differed radically in respect of their characters (which, as stated above, are amenable to the Genovese and Cohen criteria) and of their impact on rural society. Thus, instead of being lumped together as a generic category – debt-peonage – they should be 'split' into three distinct types.

In type (1) debt peons were really wage labourers, often temporary wage labourers, whose debts were advances (*anticipos*) designed to attract workers to commercial plantations, and to pay their interim subsistence or transport costs. Advances were particularly used to winkle subsistence peasants out of (usually mountain) villages and get them on to the plantation during planting and harvesting. Debt was an incentive; it operated within a voluntarist, emergent free wage labour system; it did not denote *de facto* slavery. At the outset, elements of coercion were sometimes present but, as type (1) sucessfully evolved, these became superfluous and counter-productive. Debt thus figured as an important instrument for the fashioning of a rural proletariat, and its achievements were permanent. From a theoretical perspective, this form of debt peonage may be viewed as a variant of free wage labour, with surplus labour extracted via the cash nexus and the market supplying the mode of exploitation (that is, the pressures inducing peasants to become proletarians). If, in this respect, it is theoretically uncontentious, it should be of particular interest to that growing band of historians who are concerned with the creation of proletariats and the inculcation of the time and work discipline of (in this case, rural) capitalism.[15] From the point of view of Genovese's criteria (of which the third, access to freedom, is in this case irrelevant), it is sufficient to show that the conditions of work and remuneration were sufficient to attract workers by means of the advance.

Plenty of cases of such voluntaristic labour supply can be cited. In most of northern Mexico, for example, where, in conditions of labour shortage, landlords were obliged to attract labour by cash incentives (here, attempts to revive an older, coercive peonage foundered: wage labour was an ancient feature of north Mexican society, mines competed with commercial estates, like the Laguna cotton plantations, and the proximity of the US made coercive recruitment and control impossible). During the Revolution (1910–20), in a striking re-enactment of the North American experience, progressive northern proconsuls imposed their free labour principles upon the slavocrat south. Even the latter, the bastion of the old plantocracy, contained important pockets of free labour. The classic example was coastal Chiapas, where the coffee planters of Soconusco induced an annual seasonal flow of 10,000 workers from the sierra.[16] Here, as in Peru (where the coastal sugar interests pioneered a similar *enganche* system) initial coercion declined over time: by 1910 it was clear that Indian labourers trekked down to Soconusco or Lambayeque because they wanted the wages, which were higher than elsewhere. And, by thus 'raiding the cash economy',[17] Indian villagers recycled resources to the sierra, where they could be devoted to land acquisition and improvement. The villagers' voluntaristic commitment to seasonal migration was therefore comprehensible (and, for once, the much over-worked 'articulation of modes of production' may be usefully and appropriately applied).

Switching the focus, however, we may ask why the planters preferred to rely on cash incentives rather than extra-economic coercion – as, for example, the equivalent planters of coastal Guatemala did.[18] It was not a question of crops, or of the supposed superiority of free wage labour for the exploitation of, say, coffee or tobacco as against sugar or cotton. Cheek-by-jowl, the coffee estates

of Guatemala were coercive, those of Soconusco voluntarist
(tobacco, likewise, was produced by *de facto* slaves in Mexico's Valle
Nacional, and by seasonal migrants nearby at San Andrés Tuxtla). In
the Soconusco case, German planters, realising healthy profits
through the boom years of the 1890s, operated amid an indigenous
Mexican landlord class wedded to servile debt peonage. Unable to
compete on the political level ('here', a German observed, 'the
planter possesses no effective means to bring back the endebted
workers who have deserted') the Germans logically bid up wages. In
the recurrent debates about debt peonage and its economic rights and
wrongs Soconusco stood for free labour, while the Mexican landlords
of the sierra justified peonage.[19] Finally, the Germans partly solved
their labour problems by attracting workers from neighbouring
Guatemala: across national boundaries extra-economic coercion was
at a discount, while cash incentives were effective. We may
generalise that quasi-proletarian peonage developed – in Soconusco
or Peru – where relatively profitable and highly capitalised
plantations used their economic power to undercut more traditional
landlords still reliant on political muscle.

The second form of peonage (type 2) may be termed 'traditional'.
It enjoyed the longest history even if, under late nineteenth-century
commercial pressures, it underwent certain changes. Debt peonage,
conventionally defined, had flourished in colonial Mexico. But, as
recent scholarship stresses, debts were often more of an inducement
than a bond; they tended to be slight (three weeks wages or less);
hence they cannot be seen 'as a controlling and universal hacienda
technique'.[20] Rather, peons' debts were items in a labour contract of a
customary kind over which both parties haggled to secure advantage.
When population growth tipped the balance in favour of employers
during the eighteenth century, landlords sought to curtail debts, not
necessarily with peon approval. Furthermore, the status of resident
peons, ostensibly tied to the estate by debt, was often enviable:

> to Indian workers the hacienda offered solutions to economic
> conditions not to be found elsewhere. As monetary values
> came to occupy a large role in Indian society...the hacienda
> offered a regular or irregular income. To Indians who had
> lost their lands [largely, of course, to haciendas] the hacienda
> provided a dwelling and a means of livelihood.[21]

Similar conclusions have been drawn from nineteenth-century haciendas in north-central San Luis, Querétaro and Zacatecas; debts were few, management made few attempts to ratchet them up, and the relatively secure standard of living of the resident 'debt' peons was the principal factor tying them to the estate.[22] These were, in effect, 'voluntary' peons in the same sense that proletarians are 'voluntary' wage labourers. Debts figured as perks more than as bonds. Thus, the historic liaison is dissolved: these peons remained on the hacienda not because they were bound or coerced but because market pressures encouraged them (the mode of exploitation was economic); but they yielded surplus labour in a variety of ways, many involving kind (sharecropping) or labour rent. The latter form, indeed, was prevalent not only in Mexico, but, even more clearly, in Andean America, where the haciendas of Bolivia and the Peruvian altiplano operated on classically manorial lines, permitting peasants to farm plots or tend herds in return for regular labour on the limited demesne or in the big house.

The impact of the market, greatly enhanced in the later nineteenth century and coinciding with population growth, had paradoxical consequences. Profits rose and real wages fell (in Mexico from the 1890s). Debts declined in importance as they had a century before in roughly comparable circumstances. The labour market favoured the buyer, and landlords – especially in densely populated central Mexico – had less need of debts to attract and retain workers. On the sugar plantations of Morelos the landlord's chief sanction against the permanent peons was the threat of expulsion from the estate. Such resident workers (*realeños* in Morelos, *peones acasillados* throughout Mexico, *colonos* in the Andean region) often represented a privileged stratum, partially insulated from the vicissitudes of the market (an increasingly hostile arena) and thus better off than the day labourers (*jornaleros*), temporary workers (*eventuales*) and casual migrants. Resident peons tended to be docile: they were 'docile, obedient and submissive' folk, who played little part in major rebellions like Yucatán's Caste War or the peasant insurrections of the Revolution.[23] Some planters, like the ironically named Péons of Yucatán, maintained a degree of paternalist authority which befitted their old, colonial lineage, and which shored up the system. Not only did the resident peons of Yucatán rarely rebel, they even proved racalcitrant to the radical, emancipationist appeals of northern carpet-baggers. When debts were declared abolished, some peons refused to recognise the new dispensation. Elsewhere, progressive landlords who sought to eliminate debts and institute a form of pure wage labour were stymied by their own workers, who continued to run up debts by demanding advances against future pay and to solicit (and get) payment in food rations in place of cash. Rationalisation of the estate, which at a time of falling real wages the landlords favoured, was thus successfully resisted by peons who defended their interests by cleaving to an archaic peonage.[24] And what happened in Mexico during the Porfirian boom (1876–1911) was repeated a generation or so later in parts of the Peruvian sierra where similarly progressive, often pastoral, landlords faced the dogged opposition of shepherds who clung to earlier feudal rights and obligations. As one landlord – 'the greatest Peruvian entrepreneur, capable of holding his own in the mining industry against the American companies' – found to his chagrin, the rationalisation of estate farming, and the elimination of debts and other feudal relics, was well-nigh impossible. And 'it was not the landlords' class consciousness and prestige which demanded the persistence of the system but, on the contrary, it was the resistance on the part of the peasants which made it difficult to change it to a system of wage-labour (or share-cropping or cash-tenancy), which could have been far more respectable and very possibly more profitable'.[25]

Of course, *peon/colono* defence of debt and other feudal abuses/ privileges was far from invariable. Counter-examples – the Cochabamba valley of Bolivia or La Convención in Peru – can easily be cited, in which peasants struggled to throw them off, as the English rebels of 1381 had. The key difference derived from the market's impact: where peasants could directly and profitably participate in the market, feudal restraints were irksome; where the market benefited only plantation production (Mexican sugar, maguey and henequen) or where resident peons could play the market from within hacienda confines (Peruvian shepherds), resident peons, debts notwithstanding, clung to their niches within the estate. These niches may not have been much, but they were better than what was on offer in the 'broad and alien world' outside.

So far, I have argued that ostensible debt peonage concealed a surrogate proletariat in the first instance, and a species of customary, resident peasantry in the second. Though surplus labour was realised in different forms in these two cases, the mode of exploitation was similar, and economic. Hence these cannot be termed servile relations. And, practically speaking, the voluntaristic character of these relationships gave them great durability. Wage labour, of course, increased apace, assisted by the device of monetary advances, while traditional peonage lasted through centuries of colonial and national rule. Hence its theoretically anomalous character cannot be written off in terms of its being a transitional phenomenon. But there was a third form of peonage which, despite strenuous denials and slippery evasions, was unmistakably servile and coercive, representing a new and calculating response to enhanced market demand in the later nineteenth century, and reproducing aspects of chattel slavery despite the prior, formal abolition of slavery. Indeed, since this new, servile peonage displayed few mitigating paternalistic features, it probably outdid formal chattel slavery in oppression (measured according to Genovese's criteria i (and ii) and thus more closely approximated to Elkins' famous concentration camp analogy than the North American slave system which Elkins had in mind.[26] Examples include southern Mexico (parts of Veracruz, Yacatán, Tabasco and Chiapas), the coastal plantations of Peru in the 1860s and 1870s (during the heyday of Chinese coolie labour, and before the regular migrations from the sierra had been contrived), the Peruvian Amazon during the rubber boom of the 1890s, and the Guatemalan coffee plantations.

In each case, a fresh powerful market demand impinged upon underpopulated territory where traditional estates were weak, and where indigenous populations, if they existed, were resistant to plantation labour, partly because they retained the means of production in their own hands, partly because plantation work itself was particularly unpleasant, unhealthy and thus unpopular. Here a vicious circle set in: if labourers could only be dragooned on to Guatemalan coffee estates, and kept there by coercion, conditions hardly favoured the development of voluntaristic incentives. On the contrary, the more peons fled the barracoons, the more they had to be policed and punished; hence the more the system had to rely on further dragooning. This would help explain the markedly divergent development of the (coercive) Guatemalan and the (voluntaristic) Soconusco coffee zones, notwithstanding their contiguity.[27] At a certain point, therefore, particular circumstances determined a cumulative development of either free wage labour or a coercive system. For it should be noted that the classic scenario for servile labour systems, as sketched by Domar or Chirot, does not radically differ from scenarios which have produced free wage labour (but not traditional peonage), that is, market demand, scarce labour, free land, and a powerful landlord class. Certainly these elements figured in the regions of servile peonage just mentioned; but they also figured in northern Mexico and the Argentine pampas, where free labour was the outcome.[28]

So, why coercion? Why were Chinese coolies conned by a contract system into subjecting themselves to *de facto* slavery (if they survived the Pacific version of the Middle Passage)? Why did the rubber companies of the Putumayo institute a labour system of un-paralleled brutality?[29] Why did southern Mexican planters (in Yucatán's henequen zone, in the lumber camps of Chiapas/Tabasco, and in the tobacco fields of the Valle Nacional) rely on the ruthless exploitation of duped debt peons (for whom debts *did* furnish the excuse for bondage), of deported prisoners, of indentured Koreans (the equivalents of Peru's Chinese), and of Yaqui Indian prisoners-of-war?[30] It is unlikely that a common explanation can embrace all these cases. Three sets of considerations, however, are relevant. The first is economic. Coerced labour was clearly chosen because it seemed to pay dividends, at least in the short-term (and some of these operations, such as the Putumayo rubber industry, were distinctly short-term, get-rich-quick, predatory undertakings).[31] Yucatecan planters supplemented their traditional peon labour force with deportees and Yaquis because they were cheap (much cheaper than traditional peons) and expendable. In each case, too, market signals were powerful, if volatile. Producers faced short-lived booms and feared recurrent busts. They could not rely on long-term investment – including investment in a free wage labour force, possibly of immigrant origin – as the Argentine *estancieros* could. Conversely, labour was recalcitrant. Indigenous populations, where they existed, were insufficient or (more often) inept, that is, they displayed all the fecklessness of 'lazy natives' who shunned hard work. The Chinanteco Indians would not work in the Valle Nacional (*their* Valle Nacional), so debt peons and deportees had to be brought in. On the remote Putumayo, foremen could be imported (e.g., from the West Indies) but a labour force had to be created from among the Amazon Indians by whatever horrific means were necessary. Similarly, the Indians of Chiapas had to be swindled and snared to supply labour for the notorious *monterías*, as the novels of B. Traven describe.[32] But the fact was the natives were lazy for entirely comprehensible reasons.

For in these cases the familiar resistance of subsistence peasants to capitalist time and work discipline was exacerbated by particular circumstances: backbreaking work, in foul conditions, under ruthless supervision, most starkly represented by the guano islands off Peru's coast.[33] Furthermore, guano, timber, henequen, rubber and Peruvian sugar were all products which, unlike cereals or cotton, were subject to no seasonal cycles, hence could be exploited fifty-two weeks of the year. They were therefore unsuitable for the kind of seasonal, migratory labour which characterised many commercial haciendas.[34] Modes could not easily articulate; commercial production demanded a fixed, regimented labour force. From these intrinsic disincentives the vicious circle of coercion labour shortage further coercion, stemmed.

A second consideration is, roughly speaking, political. If, in economic terms, products like guano, rubber and timber were uniquely suited to slave-driving (in certain respects their exploitation resembled mining as much as agriculture), they also tended to be located in remote, inaccessible sites: islands, tropical forests, high sierras. Production thus proceeded in relative autonomy, often in self-governing camps where the company ruled and the mores of the frontier prevailed. Traders on the Putumayo spoke of 'my Indians' and 'my river' and did what they liked with both; the Peruvian authorities (when they were not hand-in-glove) were powerless: 'established usage was far stronger than the law'.[35] The authorities similarly connived at company abuses in Mexico's Valle Nacional (somewhat less so in populous Yucatán, where oppressive planters occasionally faced court cases). And, we may note, a comparable combination of year-round exploitation and frontier justice gave the turpentine camps of the American South – where peonage still flourished after 1900 – their peculiar and brutal character.[36] Thus, it was not just a question of coercive peonage correlating with a politically powerful landlord class as Domar and Chirot suggest. Such a class, dominating Argentina, relied on wage labour and displayed a certain aristocratic legalism. Rather, it was the existence of semi-autonomous pockets, controlled by companies who scarcely acknowledged the national political regime, which allowed abuses to grow unchecked and unreported. The classic case, of course, was King Leopold's Congo.

Thirdly, along with the economic and political factors, was a psychological trait, the inheritance of history. If peonage in the United

States represented the 'shadow of slavery' in the south, so too, in Latin American, peonage of the extreme coercive kind carried on from chattel slavery. In Peru, plans to import Chinese coolies began (1849) as the abolition of slavery loomed (1854). Cuban planters similarly looked to Chinese or Yucateco contract labour to offset the inexorable decline of slavery after the 1850s. Landlords raised on coercive methods thus found it hard to relinquish them. Significantly, the worst slave-drivers of the Valle Nacional, or among Yucatán's *nouveaux riches*, were Spanish immigrants, some of whom were fresh from Cuba.[37] This psychological factor should not be exaggerated: the São Paulo slavocrats made a rapid, decisive break with servile labour in the 1880s and, both here and in Cuba, post-abolition plantations soon evolved highly successful (that is, highly profitable) voluntaristic labour systems, based on wage labour and tenancy. But considerations of market, production and labour supply strongly favoured such a transition. In the cases of servile peonage cited here, on the other hand, these considerations differed: they created economic circumstances in which the *esclavista* mentality (a mentality lacking the paternalist and aristocratic veneer of Genovese's southern planters) was not transformed but rather was given a new lease of life.

It might, however, be better to say, a stay of execution. For while voluntaristic and traditional peonage both displayed vigour and longevity (the second especially), coercive peonage was short-lived, at least in the cases mentioned. Depending on pure extra-economic coercion, lacking the institutional legitimacy of other peonages, it was vulnerable to attack, though attack from outside rather than from below. In the Putumayo, as in the Congo, international pressure was brought to bear, as it had been against an earlier generation of slavers. More important, Peru's rubber markets collapsed, just as her guano markets had in the past. In the United States and Mexico, domestic reformers inveighed against the abuses of peonage and, in Mexico's case, the triumph of the northern revolution brought to power a new elite hostile to the pretensions of the plantocracy. While that elite found the dismantling of traditional peonage problematic (since it involved sundering old allegiances which had a basis in peon economic interest), the elimination of coercive peonage was a more straightforward political act. Luis Felipe Dominguez marched through the *monterías*, liberating bonded workers; Salvador Alvarado, claiming to have emancipated 100,000 peons in Yucatán, certainly initiated the system's demise.[38] And with the collapse of the old regime the Spanish planters quit the Valle Nacional and the Chinantecos recovered their patrimony. A visitor who returned to the site in 1928:

> cantered back through the long valley in the morning coolness [and] recalled it as of fifteen years before. Then the slaves would have been at work for hours, making every inch of ground productive. Now much land was idle. Here and there white-pyjamaed Indians were gardening – for their own use, clearly. In the river Indian boys were splashing ... Whatever else the agrarian revolution failed to do it has wiped out the horrors of *hacienda* slavery, which reached their culmination in the valley called 'national'.[39]

Thus, while the proletarian and traditional forms of peonage (types 1 and 2) survived with vigour, the first sanctioned by the expanding rationale and morality of the market, the second underpinned (especially in the Andean highlands) by more archaic interests and practices, the extreme, coercive form (classic debt peonage, type 3) proved vulnerable to reform, revolution, and its own precarious reliance on crude physical controls. If, in Cuba and coastal Peru, coercive peonage at least assisted in the transition from chattel slavery to emergent free wage labour, elsewhere (southern Mexico, Amazonian Peru) it was created *de novo*, in particular and brutal circumstances, and in response to powerful though fluctuating market demand. It did not create a potential proletariat: arguably it destroyed one.[40] Dependent on crude coercion, and lacking the local legitimacy of alternative peonages, it could be annihilated by political action, once action was taken within its remote enclaves. In default of such action, it continued, as it continues today.[41]

Notes

1 Kloosterboer (1960); Simpson (1937), p. 39; Turner (1911), pp. 110–11.
2 Bauer (1979).
3 See Kolchin (1977–78), p. 472.
4 In Genovese and Foner (eds) (1969b), pp. 202–10.
5 Knight (1970) p. 75, quoting the planter Cristóbal Madán.
6 Hobsbawm, 'Introduction' in Marx (1964), p. 20.

7 Cf., Laclau (1977), pp. 43–50, and Genovese and Genovese (1983), pp. 3–25 for a fair sample of views, insights, and confusions.

8 Cohen (1978), pp. 79–83.

9 *ibid.*, p. 82 (my italics).

10 Or 'coercive sanction': Hilton in Hilton *et al.* (1978), p. 38. Similar assumptions are made by Hindess and Hirst (1975), Anderson (1974), and Barratt Brown (1984), which schematically makes the point, p. 197.

11 Cohen, *op. cit.*, p. 83.

12 Behind all this, lurking within the 'mode of exploitation', are additional factors, which cannot be elucidated here: they are the factors – economic on the one hand, violent or ideological on the other – which induce workers to enter upon subordinate relations and thus yield up a surplus. Though this distinction is clear in many cases (compare, say, Ford car-workers and galley-slaves), it can also appear blurred, especially where the state deploys its power not to compel labour directly (corvée), but rather to tax or dispossess peasantries, thus forcing them to enter the labour market as wage-labourers, sharecroppers, etc. In extreme cases (e.g., colonial states in Southern Africa; late nineteenth-century Guatemala) the role of the state is so evident that it would be hard to classify this as a purely economic mode of exploitation. On the other hand, if extra-economic coercion is too readily admitted (wherever, for example, peasantries undergo proletarianisation), this basic distinction, underlying an entire corpus of theory, crumbles away. I know of no satisfactory discussion of this problem which (I am uncomfortably aware) hovers in the background of this argument.

13 The Guatemalan case, which particularly raises the problem mentioned in note 12, is ably discussed by McCreery (1983).

14 Brenner (1977), p. 91.

15 Thompson (1967) was probably seminal in this regard.

16 Benjamin (1981), pp. 88–9.

17 Scott (1976), p. 212; on Peru, Blanchard (1979).

18 After schemes for European immigration failed: McCreery (1976).

19 Karl Kaerger, quoted in Katz (1980), p. 81; Benjamin, *op. cit.*, p. 73.

20 Gibson (1964), p. 254.

21 *Ibid.*, p. 255.

22 Tutino (1979); Cross (1978).

23 Navarro (1968–69), p. 23, quoting a Spanish consular view; Knight (1986), vol. I, pp. 85–9.

24 Bellingeri (1976).

25 Alier (1977), p. 42–6.

26 Elkins (1959).

27 Cf., Benjamin and McCreery, *op. cit.*

28 Domar (1970); Chirot (1974–75).

29 Casement to Grey, 17 March 1911, Anti-Slavery Society Papers, MS. Brit. Emp. G317, Rhodes House, Oxford.
30 Turner, *op. cit.*; Navarro (1977–78).
31 Within a decade of starting up, Putumayo rubber production began to decline, ruthless exploitation of the forest and its inhabitants having 'gravely imperilled the financial prospects of the enterprise': Casement to Grey, *op. cit.*
32 *The Government, The Carreta, March to the Monteñas, The Rebellion of the Hanged.*
33 Stewart (1951), pp. 95–8.
34 In the case of Peruvian sugar, the subsequent development of seasonal migration patterns, from sierra to coast, was determined more by the exigencies of the sierra labour supply than those of the coastal climate.
35 Casement to Grey, *op. cit.*
36 Daniel (1972).
37 Turner, *op. cit.*, p. 132; Joseph (1982), pp. 103–4.
39 Gruening (1928), pp. 139–40.
40 Physically, by sometimes decimating the population; structurally, by inhibiting the development of genuine free wage labour, since proletarianisation and *de facto* enslavement could hardly proceed happily in tandem.
41 Not least in the Amazon basin once again; Ennew (1981), pp. 52–3.

Further reading

Benjamin (April–June 1981); Collier (1968); Inglis (1973), part III; Spenser (1984), and Wells (1984).

Eight

Slaves and Peasants in Buganda
Michael Twaddle

> There is possibly some danger that 'slavery' will become as
> all-embracing an explanation of political relations as we can
> explain in no other way in pre-colonial Africa as 'petty
> bourgeoisie' has become in colonial and post-colonial Africa
> – the kinless outsiders ... whose plasticity of class-conscious-
> ness makes them capable of just about anything.[1]

It is embarrassing to present a paper about slavery in Buganda to any
audience of scholars nowadays. The embarrassment concerns not so
much the embarrassment of the subject itself, nor really the
difficulties any researcher will encounter when asking elderly people
in one of the former interlacustrine kingdoms in East Africa whether
they are or their relatives were once slaves[2] but rather the sheer lack
of attention paid to it recently by researchers. If elsewhere in Africa
it is true to say that 'the study of slavery ... has been transformed
from a neglected subject to one of the most fashionable'[3], in Buganda
it is still a neglected subject. Thus, in Paul Lovejoy's recent and very
interesting continental survey, *Transformations in Slavery: a History of
Slavery in Africa* (Cambridge University Press, 1983) there is no
reference to Buganda at all. At the very outset of this paper, it is
worth asking why.

Scholarly caution and the difficulties of undertaking any kind of
research in Idi Amin's Uganda aside, historians have tended to treat
the East African slave trade as a less crucial stimulant of change in
the Buganda kingdom than the introduction of various kinds of Islam
and Christianity during the nineteenth century. They have also paid
much more attention to considering the seismic political changes set
in motion by the overthrow of Kabaka Mwanga II in 1888 and the
arrival of British chartered company officials shortly afterwards than
to analysing earlier – and subsequent – socio-economic changes
associated with the East African slave trade. And, in a sense, the very
stress upon slavery in colonialist rhetoric at the time predisposed both

Imperial British East Africa Company officials and most subsequent historians to minimise the significance of domestic slavery during these momentous developments.

Frederick Lugard made sure he had a foot in both camps. 'Those in England who, amid the engagements and pleasures of their social positions, find time to champion the cause of the slave, understand so little of the real state of the case', exclaimed Lugard in his massive personal apologia, *The Rise of our East African Empire* (1893). In particular Lugard was concerned to underline

> one great crucial point as regards domestic slavery ... whether the slaves in question are *aliens*, acquired and imported and retained as slaves by a people with whom they have nothing in common – no community of language, customs and prejudices – or whether they are 'sons of the soil' of the same race as the masters, and merely merit the term 'slaves' because their chief has an absolute right over them, and because they are compelled to work, not for any fixed wage, but for contingent and equally definite advantages, and form, in fact, but the lowest grade in the social scale. In the first place, there is an *a priori* probability that the slave will be more harshly treated and more readily sold; in the second case the probabilities are the reverse (Lugard (1893), pp. 169–70).

The assumption that domestic slavery in Buganda amongst other places in Africa was more benign than chattel slavery in the Americas because of its absorptionist potentialities, is an assumption which links Lugard to the whole company of African slavery scholarship assembled by Suzanne Miers and Igor Kopytoff in *Slavery in Africa: Historical and Anthropological Perspectives* (University of Wisconsin Press, 1977).

Lucy Mair also gave support to it in her fine ethnography of the Buganda people after nearly forty years of British colonial rule, *An African People in the Twentieth Century* (1934). There she reported how before the British protectorate 'In a chief's household there would be ... a considerable number of slaves. Even a peasant might have slaves attached to him, although his whole household was on a smaller scale.' These slaves would have been 'almost entirely captives in war

– women and boys, the men having been killed' (a point also stressed by the Ganda vernacular chronicler, Sir Apolo Kagwa[4]). Certain duties, it is true, were specifically allotted to slaves, but, for

> the greater part, they shared in the ordinary life of the household, were described by the head as 'his children', and a stranger would not be aware that they were slaves unless this was expressly explained to him. Captured women were taken at once as wives, and except that they had no relative to go to in case of ill treatment or their husband's death their different status ceased to have much importance. Girls might be married into their master's family or might marry other slaves; the latter on marriage set up their own houses, described themselves as members of their master's clan, and observed its practices. They differed from 'free men' in that they could not leave him and that they could not inherit from a real member of the clan.[5]

As a working ethnography of Buganda during the early British protectorate these remarks seem unexceptionable, but as a comprehensive guide to pre-British conditions they require adjustment. For, as Frederick Cooper has pointed out, the 'emphasis on the integrative nature of slavery' in many anthropological accounts compiled during colonial times 'may largely reflect the fact that with the removal of its coercive and exploitative dimensions – and above all its means of reproduction – the social dimension is all that is left'.[6] More of this point shortly.

Sociologically, as displayed in the symposium on *The King's Men* edited by L. A. Fallers in 1964, Buganda before the British colonial takeover is presented as a royal despotism characterised by substantial internal social mobility as well as maximum mobilisation for external predation: a 'brigand state' in which relations between peasants and masters were subsumed within more important ties between peasant and chief and, most importantly of all, between kabaka or king and everybody else. So influential has this view been within the wider scholarly community that, in his otherwise highly intelligent survey of the problem of slavery in African studies, Frederick Cooper apparently takes Fallers' stress upon pre-colonial Buganda having been characterised by 'a continuum of dyadic relationships – between superior and inferior ... with slaves performing no distinct functions and not constituting a specific status group' as the starting-point for his remarks about Buganda, rather than as the principal *problem* for any student of slavery in nineteenth-century Buganda.[7]

To summarise thus far, neglect of the implications of slavery for Buganda during the nineteenth century may be said to have been amongst other things a byproduct of the *historiographical tendency* to treat the Muslim and Christian disturbances of the 1888–92 period in excessively religious terms, and a *sociological consequence* of undue stress upon the development of the Buganda kingdom as a royal despotism without significant social distinctions within the peasantry or between slaves and peasants. On this view chiefs were frequently divided into intricate orders of clan and administrative chiefs, which successive kings endeavoured to play off against one another, while peasants were 'the undistinguished ordinary people who were *not* something else' and the lives of slaves were 'not very different from the lives of ordinary peasants, except that they were affected by the lack of kinsmen'.[8]

Here I shall suggest otherwise, and am indebted to E. M. K. Mulira, both for his own researches into Ganda slavery summarised in *Economic Development and Tribal Change* (1954) and for his personal comments and helpfulness at a time of some considerable political uncertainty when I was revisiting Uganda during 1981.

To start with, Mulira makes plain that there *were* significant difference amongst slaves and between slaves and peasants in pre-colonial Buganda. As his contribution to Audrey Richards' symposium makes clear,

> Peasants were rewarded for valour in battle by the present of slaves by the lord or chief for whom they had fought. They could be given slaves by relatives who had been promoted to the rank of chiefs, and they could inherit slaves from their fathers. There were the *abanyage* (those pillaged or stolen in war); as well as the *abagule* (those bought). All these came into the category of *abenvumu* or true slaves, that is to say people not free in any sense.

In addition there were people 'given into slavery, usually in lieu of debts' and also sons of rich peasants and chiefs were presented to chiefly households in order to work as servants (*abasige*). 'All these different classes of dependents in a household were classed as *abaddu* (male servants) or *abazana* (female servants) whether they were slave or free-born'.[9]

Mulira also points out that both peasants and chiefs frequently passed slaves off as their own children when presenting *abasige* to a superior, and for this reason 'the child from another tribe who attracted attention and served his lord faithfully was likely to reach a court office, more likely, some say, than a Ganda boy who had a strong allegiance to his own family which might run counter to the service demanded by his lord'. 'Ganda society,' comments Mulira, 'was always a very mobile one. Promotion depended on the personal favour of chiefs and king'.[10] As a result even slaves could reach the top positions in the royal palace by skilfully cultivating the art of being deferential to their superiors. From another point of view, to be sure, the slave who gets to the top may be seen as the exception that proves the rule – as well as providing his or her chiefly or royal master with the ultimate sanctions of death or sale abroad in order to ensure complete loyalty.

Subsequent sociological studies of pre-colonial Buganda culminating in *The King's Men* (1964) went on to suggest that the old kingdom was characterised by internal mobility wholly unusual in the interlacustrine area of East Africa, and that the comparative absence of status groups was intimately related to the growth of despotic royal power. Both propositions nowadays look distinctly tatty. Such sociological and historical work as has been done in depth since 1964 mostly suggests that slavery was fairly common in the whole interlacustrine area during the nineteenth century but that, if anything, escape from slavery was more rather than less difficult in Buganda than in neighbouring kingdoms like Bunyoro. John Nyakatura, for example, reports similar kinds of slavery and statuses between slavery and freedom existing in Bunyoro for several centuries prior to the British colonial entry into what is nowadays the modern state of Uganda: pawns, captives, and people bought with cowrie shells or by barter. He suggests ways of escape from slavery for chattel slaves which seem markedly more liberal than standard Ganda practice during the nineteenth century.[11] Other lake kingdoms in East Africa probably had not dissimilar systems of slavery, as further research by the present writer into the tiny kingdom of Koki at this time has indicated.

The Christian missionaries who settled in Buganda for extended periods during the 1870s and 1880s described the old kingdom at the height of its pre-colonial powers. Slaves were used widely in house-hold production by the free population, peasant as well as chiefly. Robert Ashe, one of the more reliable missionary observers of Buganda during the last years in power of Kabaka Mutesa I and the first years of his successor, Mwanga II, tells us that most of the peasants 'own two or three slaves' and 'even the poorest peasant will at least have one little slave-boy to grace his presence' when travelling about the country.[12] Slaves were also employed extensively at the palace, as porters and cultivators of the ubiquitous banana for the court population, as well as working as administrative orderlies for all kinds of palace functionaries. There were also an enormous number of women slaves in the royal harem. Suna II, who ruled towards the end of the first half of the nineteenth century, is remembered by one vernacular chronicler as having been 'excessively interested in women', having had 18,000 *bazana* in addition to the 148 wives and 2,000 'reserve wives' also listed in *Mpiza za Baganda*.[13] By contrast, Mutesa I (1856–84) is reported by the same chronicler to have had only half this number of 'reserve wives' and 17,000 *bazana*.

This slave population was undoubtedly ancient although it only reached its greatest size in the century immediately preceding the British colonial takeover, when the old kingdom itself reached its maximum territorial extent. The old kingdom did benefit from continuous plantain production throughout the year and also a comparatively fertile situation along the northern shores of Lake Victoria in which, as Christopher Wrigley has suggested, one woman was able to feed possibly ten men and thus release men for state pursuits.[14]

But comparable situations existed eastwards amongst the much smaller principalities of Busoga, and yet further eastwards where (as far as I know) there were not states at all during the nineteenth century. One woman might *grow* enough food for four, perhaps even for ten men in a non-famine year, but the perishability of the banana plantain required a monstrously large regiment of women and child slaves to *move* it into the palace area of pre-colonial Buganda on a daily basis.

Ganda slavery as such was not therefore the creation of the East African slave trade. Indeed, slaves do not seem to have been one of the first or most important items of trade with merchants from either Zanzibar or Khartoum. Ivory was first and foremost their objective, according to both Emin Pasha and the early Christian missionaries in Buganda, and slaves were only traded substantially at a comparatively late date when the British crackdown on the slave trade at Zanzibar and the East African coast generally pushed the coastal supply system inland as far as Buganda,[15] and when Baganda chiefs' demands for guns and cloth led them to overcome earlier predilections for employing slaves in ways other than items of external exchange. The result of the slave trade was clearly an increase in the number of raids against smaller neighbouring states and stateless societies in the interlacustrine area, to such an extent that the first European missionaries in Buganda had great difficulty in deciding how far the horrors of the slave trade were attributable to indigenous slavery, how far direct products of the trade with the East African coast.

Christian missionaries were themselves divided over other aspects of Ganda slavery too. Simply to get followers both the Church Missionary Society and the White Fathers initially had to purchase slaves, the CMS mostly as personal retainers, the White Fathers both for their orphanage and as servants. A number of the first Ganda Christians slaughtered by Mwanga II in the persecutions of 1885–86 which were accompanied by some of the most profound and moving declarations of spiritual commitment by the victim, were therefore slaves. Missionaries of both denominations despaired for a time of Christianity ever making more than a few converts in such a bloodthirsty country. The White Fathers actually withdrew from Buganda for several years during the mid-1880s, and the CMS nearly departed too on several occasions. On the CMS side only Alexander Mackay stayed, arguing that only British imperial suppression of the slave trade would save both Buganda and Christianity. Mackay's figure of 2,000 slaves exported annually from Buganda in 1888–89 has been widely quoted by historians from Lugard onwards,[16] but it was probably just an estimate not unaffected by Felkin's earlier figure of 1,000 per annum.[17]

Slavery was also a difficult matter for European missionaries to come to terms with once several of their converts in the king's bodyguard dramatically seized control of the Ganda political system and, in October 1889, brought Christianity to political power in Buganda: Arab and Muslim chiefs of course should be instantly deprived of *their* slaves whenever possible, but Christian chiefs' slaves were another matter. Publicly both the CMS and the White Fathers were vigorously opposed to both slavery and the slave trade: privately it was a rather different matter. Lugard, too, as we have seen, had his doubts about the advisability of instantly abolishing a system 'advantageous in the prevention of idleness, and the enforcing of respect for rank, which alone enables the government of a semi-savage country to be carried on'.[18] But with the declaration of the British protectorate over Buganda in 1893–94 slave-taking was no longer allowed even to Christian chiefs, and thereafter only existing slaves were officially allowed to remain within Christian chiefs' enclosures both by missionaries and by protectorate officials. Nevertheless, even well into the 1900s slavery is mentioned as a matter of considerable importance as regards social control of followers in a wide variety of sources, missionary as well as vernacular.

Was such slavery therefore really oppressive? Once deprived of the means of reproduction through external raiding of slaves from neighbouring societies, and the sanctions of death and mutilation drastically modified, the status of slavery (*obuddu*) in Buganda did tend to slide remorselessly into the immediately adjacent social category of peasant cultivation occupied by people called *bakopi*. When British protectorate officials thrust their enormously burdensome labour obligations onto a peasantry so recently deprived of access to new sources of slaves through external warfare, there was inevitable resentment and in 1897 actual rebellion throughout the country. Many chiefs too rebelled at this time in company with Mwanga II against the imposition of the British protectorate, and gave as one of their reasons for revolt to both CMS and White Fathers their loss of substantial slave followings. Burdensome as the mid-1890s were for many Baganda experiencing the first pangs of British protection, these years were nothing as compared to the period between Mwanga's rebellion and the First World War, when British labour demands upon the Ganda peasantry probably exceeded anything suffered even at the height of Mutesa I's powers.[19] Things only began to get better for the peasantry when cotton-growing got under way in Buganda seriously during the First World War and afterwards, and as the first generation of British-supported chiefs died out and Ganda chiefship became, in Lucy Mair's words, a matter of 'merit coupled with education'.[20]

Before the British protectorate, it is difficult to say precisely how oppressive the system of slavery in Buganda really was. The evidence is mostly secondary and anecdotal, but Robert Walker (another of the more reliable CMS missionary reporters of nineteenth-century Buganda) relates how

One night when I was living at Mika's island he came and
told me that a canoe full of slaves had put in for the night
on his island.

I advised him to go and capture the lot. In a little time I heard
him assembling his men, and with them he went down and
secured the canoe and the people. All of them were brought up to
me that I might take down their stories and then send the account
of them up to the Kaitikiro [chief minister of Buganda]. There
were 8 slaves 2 women, 2 girls, 4 small children.

After interviewing them, Walker says that they 'did not seem to be
very unhappy: perhaps their lives had not been very bright before
and they thought the changes might be for the better'.[21]

This particular letter of Walker's was not one to be published
subsequently in a CMS missionary magazine, but it fits in with a
sizeable amount of similar anecdotal evidence from the same period.
Admittedly, this period was one of considerable disruption, but
lacking kinship ties, slaves were more likely to suffer death and
mutilation in Buganda during the 1880s than was the free population,
and household agriculture was not necessarily less arduous than plantation work elsewhere. Admittedly, that was one of Lugard's per-
sistent themes in his writings about differences between African and
West Indian slave systems, and it was also one of the things stressed by
Frederick Cooper in his work on East African plantation slavery. 'In
reality, slave owners had no choice but to establish relations of
reciprocity with their slaves' there as 'they lacked the instruments of
coercion to control them in the same manner as the slaveowners of
Jamaica', writes Cooper. 'The people of planter origin whom I interviewed perceived the behaviour of slave owners to have been based
on benevolence, not reciprocity. And benevolence was a
consequence of being Muslim'.[22]

It is also interesting that Ibrahim Soghayroun sees the slavery
practised by the Nubian soldiers recruited by Lugard to support
British power in Uganda amonst other things as an aid to the spread
of Islam rather than as an obstacle to its further advance. Perhaps
Muslims *were* nicer to their slaves than Christians in Buganda.[23] At
any rate John Roscoe expressly links the coming of the East African
slave trade there with a *decrease* in violence against slaves. 'The king
ceased to send people to death at the slaughter-places, and sent
thousands of slaves to the Coast instead'.[24]

In other ways, the slave trade *increased* violence by stepping up predation both inside and outside Buganda.

Outside Buganda, the slave trade stimulated raids for ivory as well as women in order to pay for the increased supplies of cloth and guns desired by Ganda chiefs in order to build up their followings during the 1870s and 1880s. Of course, not all of these raids were successful. There was one especially humiliating defeat of a Ganda plundering expedition at the hands of the Jopadhola people of eastern Uganda at the very end of Mutesa's reign. In Mwanga's first years there was an even more humiliating defeat at the hands of the Banyoro, much more formidable a force during the 1880s than ever before. Increasingly, therefore, Mwanga turned to his own people for both ivory (organising specialist bands of elephant hunters for the purpose, armed with guns) and slaves. It is probably with reference to these years that Apolo Kagwa writes of royal agents seizing *bazana* from peasant freemen within Buganda as well as the more customary captives from outside.

One of the problems of Kabaka Kalema's short attempt to establish an Islamic state in Buganda after the fall of Mwanga II (1888–90), is why ordinary people proved so resistant to his rule. (Granted Mwanga's predations, one might expect them to have been in favour, initially at least, of anybody who came after Mwanga!) Elsewhere I have argued that the very attempt to create an Islamic state aroused opposition because of its assault upon Ganda custom and traditional religion, and because of pragmatic appreciation of the likely success of lightning attacks upon the Muslims by young bloods like Semei Kakungulu.[25] But clearly increased slave-taking by any Ganda king from the Ganda peasantry, Muslim or otherwise, would inevitably have incurred peasant opposition, and from Banyoro sources we know that this was precisely what Kalema also indulged in during his brief reign as Kabaka of Buganda.[26] By the time vernacular chronical-histories came to be composed about these tumultuous years, 'peasantry versus chiefs' had become an accepted part of Ganda social and political life during the twentieth century. But earlier things had been different.

Slavery therefore deserves much more careful scrutiny in Buganda than it has hitherto received. Even with the highly inadequate numerical evidence presently in our possession, it is clear that slavery was an important institution in pre-colonial Buganda both before and after the period of Arab coastal trade in the middle decades of the nineteenth century. Imports of guns and cloth introduced new strains into the old kingdom, not only through increased inter-kingdom warfare in the East African interior, but also by further undermining royal control over both external resources and internal gift-exchange and facilitating the rise of new men like Semei Kakungulu able to attract both followers and slaves in greater numbers than customary before.

We must be careful not to make slaves explain too much of these developments, but thus far historians have not made them explain nearly enough of the crisis of the nineteenth-century Ganda state and its reconstruction under British colonial rule.

Acknowledgement

I am most grateful to the British Academy and Hayter Fund for travel funds enabling me to revisit Uganda in 1981 and add slavery to other interests in the area, and also to colleagues at Makerere University who were helpful at a very difficult time for them.

Notes

1 Lonsdale (1981), p. 23.
2 See Uzoigwe (1972), p. 446.
3 Cooper (1979), p. 103.
4 Kagwa (1952), p. 156.
5 Mair (1934), pp. 31–3.
6 Cooper, *op. cit.*, p. 111.
7 *ibid.*, p. 123.
8 Perlman (1970), pp. 137, 140.
9 Mulira summarised by Richards (1954), pp. 170–1.
10 *idem.*
11 Nyakatura (1970), pp. 37–8.
12 Ashe (1889), pp. 96, 291.
13 Kagwa (1934), p. 51.
14 Wrigley (1964), p. 18.
15 Tosh (1970); Cooper (1977), p. 125 note 40; Iliffe (1979), Ch. 3.
16 See Holmes (1971), p. 484; Beachey (1976), p. 194; Marissal (1978), p. 231.
   For a good discussion of more general statistics regarding the East
   African slave trade, see Martin and Ryan (1977).
17 Felkin (1885–86), p. 746.
18 Lugard (1893), p. 171.
19 See Twaddle (in press).

20 Mair, *op. cit.*, p. 170.
21 Walker to Miss Sibley, 11 April 1891: CMS Archives, London, Acc. 88/F2/1–2.
22 Cooper (1981), p. 288.
23 Soghayroun (1981), p. 31.
24 Roscoe (1911), p. 229.
25 Twaddle (1972).
26 See Nyakutura (1973), p. 144.

Further reading

Lovejoy (1983) is the best introductory survey. Miers and Kopytoff (1977) was a pioneering symposium of considerable importance, but has been criticised by Cooper (1979) and also more generally by Finley (1980), pp. 69–70, 164. A successor volume, provisionally entitled *The End of Slavery in Africa* is shortly also to be published by the University of Wisconsin Press, eds S. Miers and R. Roberts: this will contain a chapter on 'The ending of slavery in Buganda' by the present writer, which elaborates further several themes in the present paper.

Nine

Perceptions from an African Slaving Frontier[1]

Wendy James

The traveller Henry Salt talked with various slaves at the court of a *ras* (high noble) at Chelicut in Tigre, northern Ethiopia, in 1810. Among them was Oma-zéna, who like the others was simply described as 'Shangalla' or 'Shankalla', a variant of an Amharic word applied to a whole range of peripheral peoples with the overtones of the American English 'nigger' – and since 1974 banned in Ethiopia. The use of the term was formerly associated with theories of 'natural slavery' indigenous to old Ethiopian civilisation, which thus bracketed together the darker-skinned peoples fringing the plateau heartland of the country to the west and south-west. In itself it signifies no particular cultural or linguistic group. But from the linguistic information Salt collected we know that Oma-zéna was from the Gumuz-speaking people of the upper Blue Nile, and he himself named his section as Dizzela. He gave a somewhat lyrical account of his people, mentioning the lack of priests and rulers, the fact that all men were regarded as equals, and that hunting was a favourite and fruitful sport. Oma-zéna remembered also the delightful music of the lyre, and 'seemed quite exhilarated at the bare recollection of its harmony'. However, his people were continually engaged in war with the highland Agow of the region, who 'frequently invade the country for the express purpose of procuring slaves'.[2]

We know something of Oma-zéna and his natal society at that time only because he had been separated from it, and as an otherwise anonymous slave had his existence redefined as a part of the social and political history of the Ethiopian state. Ironically, only as a result of that initial alienation did he have the chance to become a part of the documented historical record; of the society he came from, official history tells us almost nothing. However, the inner history of peoples like the Gumuz is still accessible to the present-day fieldworker. It is my experience from field research in the Sudan and Ethiopia that not only the consciously transmitted oral tradition of such peoples but also their patterns of social and cultural practice, indeed their very categories of understanding the world today, are in part the legacy of those former slaving systems which they have in some sense survived. The modern study of social and cultural life among peoples like the Gumuz, from whom Oma-zéna was abducted in the late eighteenth century, should be an integral part of the historical study of these slaving systems. The experience and knowledge of such societies can not only throw light on slavery and the slave-trade but are also in themselves a part of the wider history of these systems.

The overwhelming majority of writings on slavery, whether empirical or theoretical in focus, have been biased in the sense that they have taken as their main field the *slave-holding* society, and their main angle of view the perspective of the owners, or as is sometimes expressed, the hosts of the slave. The status, rights, 'personhood' and so on of the slave are discussed in terms of the categories of the holding society. But this society, whether an agricultural village or a military state, represents almost by definition a structure of power sufficiently strong to impose unilateral definitions upon the jural and moral aspects of slavery, as it imposes control upon the productive and reproductive potential of the slave's body. It is true that a large corpus of studies has been devoted to the social history of slave societies themselves in the New World, but even here the slave point of view is necessarily encompassed by the wider structures which have created the slave community in the first place. In the field of African slavery studies, where one might expect to find a variety of other approaches, it is unfortunately still very common to discover that analysis of indigenous patterns of slavery also take the slave-holding society as their point of reference.

The arguments for dispensing with a universal definition of slavery put forward by Miers and Kopytoff in the introduction to their collection of studies on African systems rest entirely upon the subtle gradations of status and assimilation (or 'reduction of marginality') open to the slave within the holding society.[3] That original 'deracination' which is entailed in even the most benign forms of later assimilation elsewhere, lucidly illuminated in Claude Meillassoux' work,[4] figures nowhere in the bland discussion of Miers and Kopytoff, who see what they enclose in inverted commas as 'slavery' (even the trans-Atlantic variety) as being everywhere rather like kinship. I would suggest that the view from the territorial frontiers, from those slave-raided areas of Africa in particular which have seen the 'deracination' at first hand, can supply a complementary, even a truer view of the nature of slavery. Slavery must be seen from the outside as well as the inside of the slaving system, for the system itself entails a predatory relationship with the world beyond.

Of course it has often been pointed out that individual slaves are perceived as strangers, even foreigners, by the society which holds them.[5] But the implications of this internal distinction are not often pursued through to the wider external relations which have produced it. The presence of a slave in a holding society surely tells us something of the relationship between that society and the community from which the slave or one of his or her forebears was uprooted. This event may perhaps have been arbitrary, almost accidental, a random event. But far more likely, especially on an old frontier like that of the Sudan-Ethiopian border, it took place in the context of an enduring, even institutional relationship of unequal power, in which the weaker, through supplying slaves, contributed to the maintenance of the stronger. Jack Goody in a recent collection has recognised and named this relationship clearly. A general practice of slavery

> involves external as well as internal inequality, an unequal balance of power between peoples ... it has been especially common where states existed side by side with zones inhabited by 'uncontrolled', stateless or tribal peoples, whom they could raid for human booty without fear of reprisals.[6]

He explains further:

> All slave-holding societies required victims, only a small number of whom ever came from within. What they needed were victim societies, groups who consisted not of subjects but of outsiders who could be dominated by force.[7]

Philip Burnham's paper in the same volume examines such a relationship, between the Fulbe-conquered state of Ngaoundere in what is now northern Cameroon and the Gbaya people who bordered it. The rise of Ngaoundere in the nineteenth century was linked to its self-perpetuating exploitation of the Gbaya country as a slave reservoir; many of the slaves were passed on in the long-distance trade.[8] Other recent analyses of African cases have suggested that even where slaves were acquired for local use, rather than long-distance trade, the slave population rarely reproduced itself in captivity. Even in biological terms, this seems to have been the case: several papers in the recent collection on *Women and Slavery in Africa* have suggested that the fertility of slave women was low, and that their value was as labourers rather than as mothers.[9] It is already well-known that in African slave-holding societies, including those defined in part by Islamic law, there were many routes to freedom, over time, for the existing captive population, and that for this sociological reason, labour requirements meant that the slave population had to be continually replenished from outside. A variety of factors, sometimes in combination, helped ensure that in these African cases at least, the slave-holding centre was not in itself a 'system': it required a boundary, beyond which it perceived its human reserves, and upon whose exploitation it depended for its own reproduction. However internally secure and benignly assimilative such a holding society, on this model it could never absorb everybody; it would always entail a specification of non-members, non-citizens and non-kin without its limits, and would regard predatory violence against them as in some way legitimate. Such a reservoir of outsiders was a part of the wider pattern which the slaving society entailed and against which it defined its own freedoms, its political coherence, its ethnicity, kinship links and often exclusive religious allegiance. Sean O'Fahey's vivid picture of the Dār Fūr *ghazwa*, or slave-raiding expedition, reminds us of the explicit political symbolism of this relationship: on leaving the actual territory of Dār Fūr on a southern raid, a leader would assume the position of *sultan*, and allocate to other members of the party the titles of the sultan's court.

> The slavers were acting out the triumph of political and military organisation of the Sudanic state over the acephalous societies that were its victims.[10]

The Sudan-Ethiopian border is one of the older political frontier zones in Africa. It has been exploited for slaves, among other things, for many centuries, both from the Nile valley side and from the Ethiopian plateau. These pressures intensified greatly during the nineteenth century, at first on the Sudanese side with the Turko-Egyptian military conquest of 1821 and then on the Ethiopian side following the formation of Menilek's new empire in the 1880s.[11]

Slave raiding actually increased in large areas of south-western Ethiopia during the first two decades of the present century, and of course slave-holding was not officially ended until the 1930s. The direct experience of enslavement and life under slavery is thus well within living memory in Ethiopia and its peripheral regions. For various reasons we can therefore see particularly clearly the features of a well-established slaving frontier, and the view from such a frontier should illuminate our understanding of what is involved in slavery. From this angle, distinctions such as those between the taking of slaves for tribute, taxation, military recruitment, commercial profit or as judicial punishment are somewhat academic (let alone the later discriminations of status within the holding society): what is esentially involved is bodily alienation.

In the case of the Gumuz of Gojjam, James Bruce had already reported slave raiding incursions from the Ethiopian highlands some decades before Salt's account. Interestingly, Bruce tells us (for the 1760s and early 1770s) that some Gumuz families were nevertheless trading with Agow highlanders, and ensuring their mutual security by an exchange of children, who later intermarried with their respective host families.[12] At the time of Oma-zéna's childhood, which would have been about this time, there was then a possibility of kinship and mutual society between 'Shankalla' and Agow. But by the 1880s, the situation was changing. The Dutch traveller Schuver has given us an account of a Gumuz village, Dasifi, to the south of the chiefdom of Gubba, in 1882.[13] Gubba had installed a chief there, alongside the traditional one. The Gubba chief had apparently just put a wife to death for adultery, (something not, as far as I can judge, a traditional punishment) and was going to sell the lover into slavery. The region of this village was subsequently raided several times, both by encroaching Ethiopian military forces and by the chiefs of Gubba itself, because of the demands placed upon them by Addis Ababa. By 1918, the region of Dasifi was finally abandoned, the people mainly having fled to the south and across the Blue Nile, where their descendants may still be found.[14] Today, these people see the protection they were originally offered by the Oromo highlanders in their new province as having been violated by incidents, including slave-raiding, which have taken place since; they have drawn in their horns as a community, and no longer have reciprocal marriage links with highlanders. However, they still maintain contact with the Sudan (to which the old chiefdom of Gubba was tributary), young men often going there as seasonal labourers. A well-travelled man emphasised to me that I should not call the people 'Shankalla': this was a bad term they had only recently been called by the Ethiopians (even though they had come to use it of themselves). When I asked what, therefore, I should call them, he replied: 'Call us Funj' (the name of the royal house of the old Sudanese kingdom of Sennar). And he continued,

> Why do they [the Ethiopians] say Shankalla? The reason is this: because they want to sell these Shankalla people and make them slaves. But we are Funj. We are Sudanese. We are one with them. Those black Sudanese, they are the same as us... The Funj are the people who used to be called *el hurra* [freemen, in Arabic]; now we are not slaves, but Funj and freemen. These Funj are the real freemen, and nobody sold them... We are sons of the eldest [sons of Adam] and that means we are freemen.

Ironically, many of the old nobility of Sennar reached their position through enslavement and subsequent attainment of power, and even formal freedom: but that is another story.[15] Here I would just draw attention to the currency of notions such as *freedom* (interestingly in the Arabic tongue) in the discourse of this peripheral area far from the centres in which slave-holding itself is the context in which freedoms come to be specifically defined. A preference for the Sudanese side of things, by contrast with the Ethiopian, is itself of interest since the old Sudanese systems of slavery did indeed hold far more opportunities for emancipation and advancement than the Ethiopian, though a great deal of research still has to be done here. The Gumuz certainly have participated in the history of the Nile valley states: an interesting detail is that their word for 'warrior' is *jadiya*, quite evidently an internalised form of the Arabic *jihadiyya*, black slave riflemen of the Turko-Egyptian regime in the Sudan, later taken over by the Mahdists. The claim to being the eldest sons of Adam in the text above is an ironic reversal of the explicit morality of the creation story as current in the Ethiopian Orthodox Church. In that context, the 'Shankalla' are the sons of Ham, in the sense of hewers of wood, etc.; but being sons of the firstborn, in Gumuz eyes, can be regarded as a prior claim to land, and is so treated in some myths I have collected.

Let me move on to some of those internal *defensive* features of

Gumuz society today which I have suggested are characteristic of slave-raided areas. In explicit oral representations of the past, they describe how they retreated in successive stages from Gojjam, and withdrew to a region beyond the boundaries of their former Gubba rulers, where they were both physically remote and partially under the protection of the Oromo chiefs. Specific accounts are given by eye-witnesses of the 1918 raid, in which individuals were lost whose names are remembered. However, those very names in at least some cases have been given again, to children born after the event – a symbolic replacement, or patching up of the loss. Although communities were fragmented and have been reassembled in various ways, the idiom of kinship has been very broadly applied, often in a consciously metaphorical way, to give the appearance of continuity and make clear the moral cohesion of what was a disrupted series of communities.

Among the Gumuz, there is a strong sense that 'we do not enslave ourselves'. Few chiefs or leaders are able to build up much authority; strong leaders are feared as they may be co-opted by higher powers, and start to 'eat their own people'. An 'acephalous' front is consciously maintained and evasive tactics employed in relation to highland authorities. There are many limitations on commerce and other transactions. Ironically, like Miers and Kopytoff, though for different reasons, the Gumuz see marriage by bridewealth payment as being like selling a woman into slavery. Among themselves, they practise a form of mutual exchange like that which Bruce recorded between Gumuz and Agow two hundred years ago, and regarded as a means of ensuring security in the face of slave raiding. They see their marriage system as a series of exchanges of sisters between groups, which safeguards the future of each woman and her children. Women themselves prefer this security to the uncertain and arbitrary power which they associate with a husband who has 'bought' them for mere goods. We recall here the political agent of Gubba who in 1882 had his wife put to death and the adulterer sold. That wife must presumably have been either enslaved or paid for: she did not have the security of exchange marriage. Adultery today could lead to beating, fighting and hence death, but not as a judicial punishment; the pledging of a sister was an insurance against bad treatment of a wife. The wider context of slave-raiding in the old days was almost certainly one of the greater demand for women slaves (the central theme of the new collection *Women and Slavery in Africa*[16]) and this would seem to lend even more point to marriage practices like those of the Gumuz and some of their neighbours. It is also pertinent to note that the other main part of the continent where marriage is by the direct exchange of sisters or daughters is the middle belt of West Africa.[17]

Some of my informants have spelled out connections between their marriage practice and the slave raiding past. They see themselves as poor in a material sense today, while the highlanders are perceived as rich because they had slaves to do the work for them. Because of their poverty, the Gumuz say, they do not have money to pay bridewealth. One man said when I asked about bridewealth:

> The Oromo! They have done it from long ago. We
> Shankalla, we cannot give money ... we don't have cattle to
> farm with. The Oromo have plenty of money. We
> Shankalla, we hoe with our hands, hacking the ground...
> The Oromo even long ago, had plenty. The slaves used to
> do the ploughing, and now the Oromo pay 200 [Ethiopian]
> dollars bridewealth, even 600 dollars.

In fact the valley people seemed more prosperous than the highland peasants were, at least in the mid-1970s. They practised moreover a system of currency circulation among themselves which was over-valued by comparison with highland money; they preferred 'hard' 50 cent coins to paper money, and reckoned three (instead of two) to a dollar. This system, known as the 'Shankalla dollar' to local highland merchants, naturally deterred them from creaming off the produce of the valley too cheaply. Like the endogamous circulation of women in marriage, this system appeared to play a defensive role in relation to the threat of outside penetration.

The lowland Gumuz today show signs of having reabsorbed many people into their ranks. I know of a case where for example a woman was bought back out of slavery. This was mentioned to me as a case where the Gumuz had paid bridewealth in marriage, as the Oromo do! This woman's offspring had subsequently been absorbed into the exchange system. In other cases, male returnees (even at the present day) may be found 'sisters' to exchange so that they may settle and found a family. A man cannot 'enter the society' by settling and marrying with bridewealth. A kin link of some kind has to be established before marriage; and I believe that this has been done for a considerable number of escaped and freed slaves. In the case of women, if we are to believe Oma-zéna's reported account, a captive woman could be adopted as a sister and then exchanged for a wife.[18]

Analogous modes of transforming strangers into members of an egalitarian community and erasing differences of origin are found elsewhere in the border region. For example the Uduk on the Sudan side are a people who have reconstituted their community since the turn of the century.[19] Among them there are many short matrilines which are thought to have originated from a stranger, typically a girl wandering in the bush without kin and without succour. This fondling figure is termed *cinkina/*. Such a *cinkina/* is protected, adopted, and brought up to be married within the community, and her distinct origin is glossed over very quickly. The relationship between her protectors and her own descendants is termed 'blood-friendship', as are other alliances which follow from the saving of life; and many of these come to be regarded as 'real' blood kinship. What might seem to us an unequal relation of clientage is regarded by the Uduk as a happy occasion for the extension of kinship, and the remaking of a disrupted community.

However, to be a *cinkina/* outside the community is a different matter. Such a human being has merely a bodily, not a social existence. The same term is used of those in the past captured as slaves, and also for the domestic servants of today (though not agricultural labourers). A *cinkina/*, helpless and without a network of kin, is in a sense human material, liable to become the tool of others. A *cinkina/* is a *thing*, the Uduk say, like an animal, and not a person.

It is widely assumed that the notion of autonomous personhood is a sophisticated invention, and that the clear distinction between a commodity and the persons who exchange it is a modern achievement. The contrast is drawn with pre-capitalist or archaic forms of society in which persons and the products of their labour were inseparable in their interrelation.[20] It is true that in benign and prosperous times, it would not be possible to identify a sphere of the production and exchange of commodities as such, that is goods for an impersonal market, among the Gumuz or the Uduk. But the unrestrained extension of political and market demands into this region, from two great centres of state formation whose power structure has depended partly upon systematic slaving at the periphery, has sharpened the perceptions of the indigenous people. Distinctions between persons and things, persons and animals, freedom and captivity, commerce and gift-exchange, are made both in explicit discourse and also through imagery and symbolism. Not only have these people witnessed what can be the human cost of the quest for valuables such as gold and ivory, but seen at first hand, and reflected upon, what it is for human beings to be forcibly appropriated and in a tangible bodily sense turned into commodities themselves. The immediacy of their perception reminds us of what is truly entailed in slavery and is a salutary complement to the finer points of platonic moral debate over the relationship between the slave and the society which comes to incorporate him or her. This debate takes for granted the power relations not only within the holding society but also those which reach beyond it to the non-citizens of its periphery.

The writings of Michel Foucault have drawn our eyes away from the defining centres of official discourse, down the hierarchies and through the institutional pathways, to the immediacy of the practical workings of power upon ordinary persons. In provincial clinics, in small prisons, in the very privacy of erotic experience, the workings of medicine, the law, or official sexual morality have their most direct expression as aspects of the extending power-network of society upon the person.[21] Following Foucault's vision, we may suggest that in the case of slavery too, it is at the far extremities that the nature of the power relations involved can be seen most directly. Those who have evaded or escaped the tentacles of the system, or who have otherwise managed to survive on its margins, can see its distinctive features more accurately than those who control or theorise about its workings from the centre. At the farthest territorial limits of the old slaving systems, we can still seek that 'subjugated knowledge'[22] which has seen the physical loss of freedom and the bodily alienation of persons. In these peripheral zones the truths of this remembered experience may well have survived better than among the ragbag of captives and their descendants brought together in the reconstituted slave communities of a distant land. The communities of the marginal regions may not only remember those acts of disruption and bodily alienation, which Meillassoux has reminded us are at the beginning of every slave's story, but they may also have built a moral world around these memories.

An image which is for me as graphic and telling a picture of slavery as one could find anywhere occurs in the account which Salt gives us of the conversation with the old slave Oma-zéna. When his own people were fortunate enough to acquire male slaves in war, no fancy words disguised their situation: 'When the Dizzela take any prisoners', he said, 'they tie their legs, and employ them either in making cloth or manfacturing iron; and, if incapable of work, they kill them.'[23] Whether this was literally true, or merely a piece of wishful thinking on the part of Oma-zéna himself after many years as a slave in highland Ethiopia (though admittedly under more comfortable circumstances) we do not know. In either case, however, this evocative picture of a human being deprived of physical freedom and made an instrument of work under threat of death sums up what would, I think, be generally agreed to be the essence of slavery; it is almost a visual icon of that state, and would be recognised as such across the world. Tied legs; forced labour; no protector: Oma-zéna put it very clearly, and he knew what he was talking about.

Notes

1 This paper draws on field research in Ethiopia, supported by the SSRC in London, carried out as a visiting scholar of the Institute of Ethiopian Studies in Addis Ababa University during 1974 and 1975. In the field I was assisted by Mr Gali Sambato. Previous work in the Sudan was supported by the University of Khartoum.
2 Salt (1967), pp. 378–81.
3 Miers and Kopytoff (1977), pp. 3–81.
4 Meillassoux (1975), especially the Introduction.
5 See, for example, Lévy-Bruhl (1960); Finley (1968); Patterson (1982).
6 Goody (1980), p. 24.
7 *ibid.*, p. 31.
8 Burnham (1980), *passim.*
9 Robertson and Klein (1983).
10 O'Fahey (1973), p. 33.
11 For the Sudan, see D. H. Johnson's paper in this volume. For Ethiopia, see Donham and James (1986), especially Chs. 1, 5 and 8.
12 Bruce (1804), vol. 5, pp. 399–402.
13 Schuver (1883), p. 80.
14 James (1986) gives a fuller account of this community than is possible here.
15 James (1977).
16 Robertson and Klein, *op. cit.*
17 James (1975).
18 Salt, *op. cit.*, p. 379.

19 James (1979).
20 A classic study, for example, is that of Mauss (1954).
21 Foucault (1972), and other works.
22 *ibid.*
23 Salt, *op. cit.*, p. 380.

Further reading

Of the works cited above, see especially James (1977) and (1979), and the collections of Watson (1980b), Meillassoux (1975), Robertson and Klein (1983), and in particular Donham and James (1986). Additional to these, see Lovejoy (1981), vol. 6ff.

Ten

Sudanese Military Slavery from the Eighteenth to the Twentieth Century

Douglas H. Johnson

The idea of a slave soldier seems strange to us today. If, as Mao claimed, power comes from the barrel of a gun, then the holder of that gun must have some power. A slave with a rifle seems a contradiction in terms. Yet even in recent times there have been not only slave soldiers, but also slave armies. The very remoteness of the idea of military slavery from modern political thinking and modern concepts of slavery may be one reason why analyses of slave armies concentrate on their remote origins or treat them as early stages in political or social evolution.[1] Military slavery has not been treated as an institution of long endurance and continuity which is crucial to the understanding of political relations of dependency and marginality within the regions where it was practised. African historians still tend to treat it as only one of many possible fates for the individual slave.

It is perhaps the variety of times and places where slave soldiers have appeared which inhibits a clear focus on the continuity and character of the institution itself. For this reason I will examine only one example of military slavery, but the most extensive and important example in modern African history. I will look at Sudanese military slavery as it developed in the Nile valley in what is now the Republic of the Sudan, and trace how it radiated from there into parts of East Africa and the Central Sudan during the eighteenth, nineteenth, and twentieth centuries. I will try to suggest some reasons why it underwent a vigorous expansion, as an institution, just at that point when military slavery was disappearing in most of the Muslim world. I will also try to demonstrate how a comprehensive study of Sudanese military slavery can contribute to our understanding of African slavery in general, and of the political and social structures and relations which were established in many countries during the colonial period. The points I shall raise should therefore be seen as points of departure for further investigation, and suggestions of what such a study might reveal, rather than firm conclusions.

Outline of Sudanese military slavery[2]

Military slavery was a well-established institution in many Islamic societies prior to the eighteenth century, though the Napoleonic wars were the beginning of the end of military slavery in the Ottoman empire. By the end of the eighteenth century, prior to the Turco-Egyptian conquest of the Sudan, the two great eastern Sudanese kingdoms of Sinnar and Dar Fur both had standing armies of slave soldiers and carried out continual raids against neighbouring stateless peoples to maintain these bodies of permanent soldiers. With the Turco-Egyptian conquest of the Sudan, beginning in 1820, large numbers of Sudanese African slaves were enrolled in the Egyptian army, and while these slave regiments did not constitute a majority of what became the modern Egyptian army, they were the main force in Egyptian imperial expansion in the Sudan and East Africa and were sent to fight in other imperial ventures in Greece, Turkey and Mexico.

In the 1850s private slave armies under the command of a variety of ivory and slave merchants began to appear in the Southern Sudan, where they ruled Bahr al-Ghazal and conquered Dar Fur. Slave soldiers from these armies and the Egyptian army subsequently became the nucleus of the Mahdist army from 1882 to 1898. Other slave armies, sometimes led by slave soldiers themselves, played a significant role in the creation and revival of the states of Bornu, Dar Kuti, Dar Banda, Dar Masalit and Dar Fur in the 1880s and 1890s.

Sudanese slave soldiers in the Egyptian army were also stationed along the frontier first to contain, and then to overthrow, the Mahdist state. They were recruited into the European commercial companies operating in East Africa in the 1890s and were used by both Britain and Germany in the conquest of their East African possessions. The Anglo-Egyptian army continued to recruit and use slave soldiers in the first quarter of this century. Even with the eventual demise of military slavery in the Sudan, ex-slave soldiers and ex-slave soldier communities gave service to the colonial governments of the Sudan, Uganda and Kenya, and were the nucleus around which nascent urban centres grew in the Southern Sudan and northern Uganda.

Families of professional soldiers, descended from these slave soldiers, played an important role in colonial and post-colonial armies.

Given the spread and endurance of Sudanese military slavery, it is surprising that the institution itself has been consistently ignored by African historians. Contemporary colonial sources masked the existence of slave soldiers behind a number of euphemisms, and modern historians of Egypt, the Sudan and Tanzania have been reluctant to probe behind this veil. Both the geographical spread of Sudanese military slavery and the sensitivity of the subject in the Sudan and in other African countries have inhibited a comprehensive study and an appreciation of the importance of this institution in the formation of colonial states.

That the institution is important should be evident, I hope, from the brief summary I have just given. That it is difficult to study is a product not just of the sensitivity of the subject, but of the very ambiguity of the character of military slavery, an ambiguity which has been revealed in recent studies of the origin of Islamic military slavery.

Character of military slavery

In analysing the character of military slavery we come up against a number of problems of comparison which obscure the nature of the institution. The army is the closest institution to slavery in modern nations, and during part of the period we are concerned with European armies shared many traits with military slavery. Violence, abduction and the threat of force have all been used in recruitment in nineteenth- and twentieth-century armies. As late as the mid-nineteenth century Britain's 'volunteer' soldiers were 'enlisted for life'. Flogging and even branding were used as forms of punishment in the British army as late as the last half of the nineteenth century. Thus we cannot say that violence of recruitment, exposure to extreme physical punishment, or the loss of personal freedom alone define the character of military slavery.

Daniel Pipes, in his study of the origins of Islamic military slavery, has identified three essential characteristics of military slavery: the systematic acquisition of slaves for the army, specific military training (usually starting young), and a lifetime of professional soldiering. Military slaves are state property, owned by the government or the state, not by individual masters, and they are employed as instruments of state-craft. Pipes has also identified an ambiguity in the personal status of the military slave. A slave soldier has greater access to power and potential for freedom than other slaves; there is the possibility for individuals to leave slavery even if they continue as soldiers. But whatever the fate of individuals, continuity of slave status is maintained by the military units owned by and in the service of the state.[3]

There are two points arising out of Pipes' study which I would like to expand on as characteristic of Sudanese military slavery: the importance of patronage and the ambiguous status of the slave soldier.

The existence of a patron, usually expressed in the symbol of the head of state, is crucial for the existence of organised bodies of slave soldiers. The patron may dispose of units of slave soldiers, transferring them permanently or temporarily to other sovereigns. Thus the Egyptian viceroys lent slave battalions to the Ottoman Sultan and Maximilian of Mexico and sold an entire battalion of Sudanese soldiers to Germany to put down the Bushiri rising. Slave soldiers can also, as a body, transfer allegiance from one patron to another, as they regularly did in the 1880s and 1890s, alternating service between the Egyptian government, the Mahdist state, the Masalit sultanate, or the Imperial British East Africa Company. The genealogies of many retired officers now living in Omdurman are expressive of this flexibility, for they trace their professional descent not through one army, but many.[4]

In other cases independent bodies of slave soldiers maintained a fictional allegiance to a patron head or patron state. The slave cavalry of the Hamaj 'regents' in Sinnar were nominally in the service of the Funj sultan. Rabih Fadlallah pledged nominal allegiance to the Mahdi and the Mahdist state, while Sanusi Ahmad Abbakar asserted a family link with the ruling family of Wadai as well as allegiance to Rabih. Even after military slavery was replaced by more conventional and regionally oriented recruiting in colonial states, ex-slave soldier communities could continue to claim a special relationship to the colonial government, as the Nubis of Uganda and Kenya did when in 1940 they objected to the colonial government's plan to include them in tribal poll-taxes, putting them on par with the peoples they had helped the colonial governments to conquer.[5]

A close identification with the state did not mean consistent loyalty. Slave soldier revolts were common throughout the history of

Sudanese military slavery. Such revolts, however, often contained an element of a transfer of allegiance to a new leader, or to an older, supplanted leader. The first major slave soldier revolt in the Turco-Egyptian Sudan in 1844 appears to have been linked to army support for the governor-general, Ahmad Pasha, in his rumoured confrontation with the Viceroy of Egypt. The last Sudanese mutiny, in 1924, was ostensibly a reaffirmation of loyalty to the King of Egypt against his British controllers.

This close identification with the state and state power was the source of the slave soldier's ambiguous status as a slave. To be a professional soldier conferred a slave status (even if the soldier was not born a slave), but it did not necessarily mean permanent slave status. The exact quality of a soldier's liberty, however, is, at least with the information currently available, difficult to assess. Muhammad Ali manumitted his personal Turkish mamelukes when he appointed them as officers in his *nizam al-jadid*, but there does not seem to have been any form of official manumission for slave soldiers in Sinnar, Dar Fur, Egypt or the Mahdist state. 'Never think of yourself, we are all the servants of his Highness the Khedive', one Sudanese officer used to tell new soldiers in the 1890s.[6] He himself had been a slave paid in tribute to the Egyptian government by the Baggara Arabs. In the Mahdist state the sale of male slaves was strictly controlled by the government and was considered the personal monopoly of the Khalifa Abdallahi. Slave Commanders achieved high positions of power, but the Khalifa could still dispose of them at will. One commander of the army, Al-Zaki Tamal, was starved to death at the Khalifa's orders.

Persons from non-slave segments of society who joined slave armies seem to have lost something of their free status taking on that of the slave soldier. This was the case of free Masalit who joined the Egyptian army and then the Masalit sultan's own *jihadiyya*. Many free Ja'ali and Danaqla also found themselves in a form of bondage in the armed merchant companies in the Southern Sudan. Dispossessed from their lands along the Nile, they often joined trading companies in Khartoum, only to fall into debt to the companies while serving in the armed camps of the south. Continued indebtedness required continued service with the companies, and many failed to return home with the wealth they hoped would redeem them.

Slave soldiers in the Turco-Egyptian army were usually maintained in government service throughout their lives. 'Soldiers were not allowed to retire but just worked and served until they dropped', one such veteran recalled: 'When no longer fit for active service, they were put on to light work such as looking after the officers' gardens.'[7] Occasionally, whole battalions were discharged in apparent freedom, as was done for financial reasons in the Sudan in 1880, but the soldiers so dismissed 'needed a master' and joined the Mahdi.[8] After the reconquest soldiers retired from the Anglo-Egyptian army were usually settled in military colonies where they continued to serve the government as irregular policemen, wood-cutters for the steamer service, night watchmen at government resthouses, cooks, etc., very much in the style of light work for old soldiers in Turco-Egyptian times. The children of these veterans continued to perform the same services, and the *malakias* of Southern Sudanese towns provided the necessary labourers for a variety of government jobs throughout the Condominium period. While individuals led independent lives, these *malakia* communities continued to be associated with the activities of the government and the state. Similar services were provided by Nubi communities in Uganda.

The slave soldier's ambiguous liberty in relation to the state throughout his life was passed on to his descendants. It is an ambiguity frequently expressed in ethnic terms and is almost a defining characteristic of slave-soldier communities in the past as well as today. It is an ambiguity which is a product of their acquisition by the state and the uses to which they were put. It is to that use we now turn.

Political role and political relations

The armies of the eighteenth- and nineteenth-century eastern Sudanic states were organised around a core of slaves who were often armed with the most advanced, and therefore most expensive, imported weapons for the period and region. The rulers of Sinnar owned not only the soldiers but the horses and armour with which they were equipped. The Egyptian government owned both the firearms and the soldiers who used them. It became axiomatic in warfare that captured slave soldiers brought their weapons with them to the service of their new sovereign. Weapons and soldiers went together. The states and the private trading companies (whether Zubayr al-Rahma's or Sir William MacKinnon's) tried to control the supply and acquisition of both weapons and soldiers in order to maintain their own armies.

In using these permanent armies to establish centralised power, the state also had to use that power to maintain its army. The acquisition of slaves for the army was systematic. The kingdoms of Sinnar and Dar Fur had their hinterlands of enslaveable peoples from which they regularly extracted slaves, often as tribute. This was a factor in the structuring of political relationships between centres of power in the Sudan and areas of refuge from that power. Those who tried to avoid state power found refuge in the hills of the Ethiopian border, the Nuba mountains and the lands of the Southern Sudan. As the states pursued these fugitives the areas of refuge also became areas of supply. The expansion of state power and state control into new lands was often a by product of tribute demands or slave-raiding to maintain the army. Certainly the two were interrelated, and slave-raiding could be undertaken as a means of extending political control. The Dar Fur sultanate periodically reproduced its court structure in slave raids into western Bahr al-Ghazal. Alternatively it granted immunity from raids in return for tribute in slaves.[9] Muhammad Ali conquered the Sudan in order to obtain slaves for his army. Once conquered, his Sudanese subjects were required to provide slaves as tribute, and a tax in slaves for the army continued into the 1870s.

The numbers of slaves required were such that the occasional war captive or kidnap victim was insufficient to meet the demand. This forced an alliance between a number of nomadic Arab peoples and the Egyptian government, the Egyptian army and its nomad allies mounted joint raids into the African heartlands of the Sudan in order to obtain slaves first for the army, and only secondarily for trade or domestic use. This was the beginning of massive slave-raiding in the Sudan which, coupled with changes in taxation and land tenure introduced by the Turco-Egyptian regime in the north, produced an upsurge in domestic slavery and expanded slave ownership beyond the ruling elite. Eventually the supply for both state and domestic needs was being met through the organised activities of concessionaire companies operating in the south. This was the beginning of the great racial antagonism which continues to divide Arab and African Sudanese.[10]

The patterns of raiding followed those initially established by the eastern Sudanic kingdoms, replicating their notions of enslaveable peoples. The Ethiopian border lands and the Nuba hills (the slave reservoir areas for Sinnar) and the lands along the Bahr al-Arab (the hunting grounds of Dar Fur) became the first sources of slaves for the army. The areas so attacked were areas that had a long history of dependency on the periphery of state systems. It was this combination of marginality and dependency which made them ideal suppliers of 'martial races'.

It is in the nature of the martial race syndrome that initial dependency is used to foster both martial traits and allegiance to new masters. Martial groups are brought into a new state system because they are both culturally and politically distinct from the majority of the population. They are vulnerable because of that distinctness, and also because they are frequently held in contempt by both the state elite and other ethnic groups. Once brought into armies both their ethnic and martial distinctiveness are encouraged and exaggerated, giving them a 'vehicle for gaining respect, legitimacy and protection in the larger social order of which they are now, albeit reluctantly, a part'.[11] Thus it was that the peoples of the slave frontier of the Sudan, with their different languages and cultures, became part of a 'martial race' which was identified and maintained as such by a succession of different (and even competing) states.

The slave soldier's distinctiveness from the populace he helped to control was fostered not just in ethnic terms, but in the roles he was given to perform. A product of oppression, he helped to oppress. The slave cavalry of Sinnar, the nineteenth-century rifle-armed *jihadiyya*, the Anglo-Egyptian soldier or policeman were all tax-collectors. In the expansion of conquest states bands of slave soldiers were frequently stationed on the frontiers of pacified countries, poised at areas destined for conquest but still free. Their presence and their activities helped to undermine the stability and independence of neighbouring territories. Thus Sudanese soldiers were stationed on the border between Buganda and Bunyoro and given licence to pillage the country, taking captives (mainly women and children) for their own use.[12] Slave soldiers confronted each other across the Egyptian/Mahdist frontier. There was also the prolonged use of Sudanese soldiers in the southern Sudan in the early twentieth century, at a time when military units in the already pacified northern Sudan were being replaced by a locally recruited gendarmerie.

The need to maintain the strength of Sudanese military slave units continued in Egypt after the official abolition of the slave trade (1854), and in the Sudan after the reconquest (1898). One problem was the continued flexibility of a slave soldier's allegiance, and his ability to transfer from one army to the next. Desertions both ways were frequent during the Mahdist wars; the Khalifa tried desperately to prevent the export of male African slaves to Egypt where they were almost inevitably recruited into the army. In Egypt, along the frontier, British commanders adopted the methods of their Turco-Egyptian predecessors and Mahdists opponents to control the movements of their own soldiers: Sudanese in the army were branded to facilitate the indentification of deserters.[13] In post-conquest Sudan the Anglo-Egyptian government encouraged the enlistment of sons of soldiers, but they also spread the net wide to include any unattached 'servant' – the official euphemism for slave.[14]

Ironically, the need to maintain the 'black battalions' may have prolonged resistance to pacification in the Southern Sudan, where most of the black soldiers were obtained. The lack of volunteers among Southern Sudanese drove the government to measures of recruitment that were scarcely distinguishable from those adopted by the Turco-Egyptian regime. Southern Sudanese tribes engaged in 'offences against the government' had war captives 'enlisted' into the army 'as hostages for the future behaviour of the rest of the tribe'. Runaway 'servants' in the north were also enlisted, as were southern Sudanese convicted of various crimes ranging from murder to membership of secret societies.[15] The needs of what was still essentially a slave army affected the political relations between the state and it subjects.

Occupation and administration required a different type of colonial army from that demanded by conquest and pacification. Forced enlistment, as needed to replace slave soldiers, interfered with administration once pacification was achieved. In the Sudan and Uganda there was also the fear that the Muslim faith of the slave soldiers would undermine their loyalty to the colonial government. For these reasons the institution of military slavery disappeared. But the descendants of slave soldiers continued to regard the army as their chosen profession. Large numbers of Sudanese were enlisted into the King's African Rifles in Uganda and Kenya even after World War II, often through special schools set up for the training of the sons of soldiers as technicians and non-commissioned officers. In the Sudan there are still families of professional soldiers descended from slave soldiers who provide an important continuity in the Sudanese army.

Continuity of slave soldier communities: the 'Nubi' factor

The abolition of slavery and the introduction of new forms of recruitment did not disperse military slave communities but transformed them into ethnically ambiguous groups. The source of this ethnic ambiguity is found in the regional relationships which were a part of the political structure of Sudanese military slavery, something which could be called 'the Nubi factor' both because of its antiquity and its recent continuation.

The name Nubia dates from ancient Egyptian times and referred to that southern 'hunting preserve for human and animal game' up river from Egypt.[16] It had no geographical or ethnic precision, so it was as a general term that it entered pre-Islamic Arabic. That part of upper Egypt and the northern Sudan which is now called Nubia is known in Arabic as *Bilad an-Nuba*, the land of the Nuba,[17] similar in structure, and probably in meaning, to *Bilad as-Sudan*, the land of the blacks. It was one part of Africa which was a source of slaves – the 'Nubi', or Nubians – and Nubi slaves are mentioned in very early Muslim manuscripts.[18] It was, then, a term which came to denote enslaveable peoples.

The frontier of enslaveable people shifted with political events, and the definition of who was enslaveable altered along with who was enslaving. Muslim Egypt fixed its own enslaveable frontier with Christian Nubia by the Baqt treaty of AD 652, imposing an annual tribute of 360 slaves. This treaty was in force for some six hundred years, and in so far as Nubia had to raid other peoples for slaves to fulfil its terms, it forced a southern shift of the definition of enslaveable peoples.[19] Thus the later kingdom of Sinnar, created by a 'Nubian renaissance', had its own *bilad an-Nuba* from which it took slaves. The 'Nuba' who were captured and brought into Sinnar (and settled around the capital as slave soldiers) came from Fazughli in the Ethiopian foothills, as well as Jabal Dayr and Taqali in what are known as the Nuba hills.[20] The 'Nuba' of Sinnar thus included peoples not now assimilated by that ethnic label.

It is in the nature of such ethnic frontiers and labels defining slavery that they will define who is free as much as who is slave. The free/slave-north/south divide, which characterised the definition of *bilad an-Nuba*, can be found right across the eastern and central Sudanic belt, representing a 'nexus of ideas, religion, ethnicity', which expressed the series of relationships existing between the 'free north' and the 'slave south'.[21] Because these frontiers moved, drawing in various peoples in various ways, the precise status of those who were called 'Funj' and 'Hamaj', 'Fur' and 'Fartit', 'Nubi' or 'Nuba', cannot be assumed to be entirely clear.[22] This ambiguity is frequently most acute in leaders of slave soldiers who achieve a power or autonomy of their own. See for instance the confusion over the slave or 'noble' origin of Muhammad Abu Likaylik, the leader of the Hamaj coup against the Funj sultan in 1762; the slave, Hamaj ('commoner'), or Funj ('aristocratic') origin of Rabih Fadlallah; or the ethnic and national ambiguity of Idi Amin's parentage and birth.

To understand how this ethnic ambiguity was maintained, we must recognise that non-combatants formed the majority of any Sudanese military slave community. If soldiers always came with their weapons when transferring from one service to another, they also usually came with their wives, children or dependants, including their own slaves. The importance of maintaining 'a familial structure compatible with army life' has been a consistent feature in the organisation of 'martial races' elsewhere,[23] and the slave soldier communities were perpetuated through their dependants. This is strikingly demonstrated when we look at the statistics of combatants to non-combatants among the Sudanese troops in Uganda in the 1890s.

Of the original group of Emin Pasha's troops who joined Lugard in 1891, only 800 were soldiers while 9,000 were camp followers (men, women and children). By the middle of 1892 there were 1,000 Sudanese soldiers enlisted with the Imperial British East Africa Company, bringing with them 10,000 women and children.[24] Of these children some were gun-boys, that is boys who were either slaves or sons of soldiers attached to a soldier-patron as his gun-bearer, learning the art of war. Ultimately, they became soldiers themselves. But even allowing for this, there is a consistent 10:1 to 12:1 non-combatant to combatant ratio in the figures. These figures were perhaps peculiar to the conditions of Equatoria and northern Uganda at that time, but they do force us to recognise that soldiers, as such, were a minority in the military slave system, a point that has yet to be made in studies of military slaves elsewhere. We must conclude from these figures that the specific character of individual military slave communities was derived, not from the soldiers themselves, or even from their profession, but from the people brought into the community to serve the soldiers in various ways.

This conclusion is consistent with descriptions of the structure of the armed camps of the southern Sudan, army garrisons throughout the Sudan in the late nineteenth century, and the Ugandan Sudanese communities at the beginning of this. All had a nucleus of armed men, families and personal slaves within a fortification, plus client peoples – often refugees from slave raids – outside the fortifications, cultivating and rearing animals for the garrison's use in return for protection. These persons frequently moved with the soldiers, but in some cases the non-combatant community provided a local continuity for shifting garrisons. During the Turco-Egyptian period in the Sudan, battalions transferring from one garrison to another often left their wives and families behind, taking over the wives of the garrison they were relieving. Wholesale marriages between incoming, conquering Sudanese battalions and liberated female slaves or the wives of defeated slave garrisons were also a regular feature of Sudanese military life, especially during the campaigns of the Reconquest (1896–98).

Throughout the late nineteenth century there was a continuity in the sites and personnel of army camps in many parts of the Sudan which spanned the changes in political regimes. Any continuity in the population of the small towns which grew out of these garrisons would generally have been provided by the women, rather than the soldiers, since the women were the most long term and stable residents. The predominance of civilians even within the military system helps to explain the vigorous survival of ex-slave soldier communities today. The ethnic variety of the civilian population drawn into the military slavery system, often deliberately in order to foster links between a garrison and the local community, reinforced the ethnic ambiguity not only of the slave-soldier communities, but of the small urban centres derived from them. In Southern Sudanese and northern Ugandan towns it is possible for rural people to 'become Nubi' by settling in the town, just as it is possible for them to cease to be Nubi by leaving it.[25] The ethnic origin of ancestral soldiers continues to be remembered internally,[26] as do maternal family ties and languages. Alternate ethnic affiliations can thus be activated at various times, and the passing in and out of 'Nubiness' becomes a kind of refuge that some are able to exploit; a continuation of the original ambiguity of the old *bilad an-Nuba* frontier and the slave soldier's status.

The process of 'Nubi-isation' in modern Uganda has its roots in the slave-raiding and *zariba* system of the nineteenth-century Southern Sudan. It provided 'a channel for emancipation, social mobility, and honour through Islam and military service' in the midst of the social chaos it produced.[27] It was, however, the continuation of a longer process which spread up the Nile valley, into the Sudanic belt as the frontier of enslaveable peoples changed. It continues to have an international dimension. Just as refugees from the Sudanese civil war of the 1960s and 1970s 'became Nubi' by going to Uganda and becoming enmeshed in the military system there, so many of these and other Ugandan 'Nubis' have been able to integrate themselves into Sudanese society by reactivating other ethnic ties upon fleeing to the Southern Sudan after the fall of Amin in 1979. Even more recently they have been able to return to Uganda as soldiers and as 'Nubis', apparently bringing more southern Sudanese with them. The Nubi factor not only has a long history in Sudanese military slavery, it has become an entrenched part of Southern Sudanese and Ugandan political life.

Conclusion: comparisons and contrasts

The study of the institution of Sudanese military slavery is important for what it reveals of enduring patterns in social and political relations along the Nile valley and beyond. Military slavery may have been an innovation of Islamic societies, but the moveable enslaveable frontier of *bilad an-Nuba* is pre-Islamic. What, then, can Sudanese military slavery tell us about the history of slavery in Africa? In the first place we must make a distinction between the *institution* of military slavery and the slave soldier. Individual slaves who may be made into soldiers do not constitute an institution of military slavery, with its systematic acquisition of slaves for an army and the resultant pattern of political relationships of regional and ethnic subordination imposed by the state. The two must not be studied together as if they automatically and always represent the same form of slavery. This distinction can be demonstrated by contrasting Sudanese military slavery with West African colonial army recruitment. Both Britain and France incorporated slaves and ex-slaves into their colonial armies in West Africa. In this case a person's existing servile status and political vulnerability made him eligible for recruitment: he became a soldier because he was a slave. In

Sudanese military slavery the reverse was the case. The slave soldier became a slave by being a soldier.

Sudanese slave soldiers came from communities originally outside the state which became vulnerable through state activities. This is the key to understanding the nature of military slavery, and here we can be helped in our analysis by drawing on a study of state power and ethnic soldiers which has focused on the 'impact of the *state* – the autonomous structure of public authority – on ethnic boundaries and ethnic saliency'. It is the state that creates martial races. Martial races typically come from regions on the periphery of the state at the time when they are first organised for military service. Their ethnic identities are defined by their relationship to the state.[28]

Ethnic stratification within and in relation to the state thus becomes a central element in understanding Sudanese military slavery (and perhaps Islamic military slavery in general). This point has already been stressed in a discussion of ethnic labels as political categories for the kingdom of Sinnar.[29] We find it also in studies of the *Abid al-Bukhari* in seventeenth- and eighteenth-century Morocco, where ethnicity, rather than legal status, became the ultimate criterion for recruitment into a new slave army.[30] Because of the importance of state activity in defining social stratification, it is not possible to accept the proposal recently put forward by Lovejoy that Muslim traders merely keyed themselves into an existing network of African war captives, convicted criminals, and debtors in obtaining slaves.[31] The Baqt treaty imposed a structured relationship for the extraction of slaves which was instrumental in creating the regular system of slave raiding that fed Sudanese military slavery. Military slavery, we must remember, is almost exclusively an Islamic institution. Islam thus transferred the very character of slavery and slave-raiding throughout the Nile valley, and the institution of military slavery was both the vehicle and the product of that transformation.

Notes

1 Ayalon (1979); Crone (1980); Pipes (1981). See also Weber (1964), pp. 342–3, 347, 350, 381.
2 Space does not permit full references, but the following provide much of the information on which this article draws: Hill (1959); Holt (1970); O'Fahey and Spaulding (1974); O'Fahey (1980); Spaulding (1982 and

1985); Kapteijns (1985); Soghayroun (1981); Hallam (1977); Warburg (1981).

3 Pipes (1981), pp. 5–23.

4 Interviews at the Retired Officers Club, Omdurman, 5 March 1980.

5 National Records Office, Khartoum [NRO] Equatoria 2/39/137.

6 Machell (1896), p. 31.

7 Bredin (1961), p. 39.

8 Machell (1896), p. 484.

9 O'Fahey (1982), p. 83.

10 Spaulding (1982); Johnson (1982).

11 Enloe (1980), pp. 27, 30–1.

12 Cf., Ternan diaries, Mss. Afr. r. 128, Rhodes House, Oxford.

13 Cf., NRO Cairint 1/23/116–8, '1888–98 Disciplinary and Military Courts, Frontier', and NRO Cairint 1/25/127, '1888–89 Organisation of Sudanese Battalions, Egyptian Army'.

14 *Reports on the Finance, Administration and Condition of the Sudan, 1913*, vol. 2, p. 86, and note 15 below.

15 L.O. Stack to the Governor, Upper Nile Province, 15 December 1913, Southern Records Office, Juba, UNP SCR 34/1. Fergusson to Governor Wau, 16.09.21, and D.C. Rumbek to Governor Wau, 11.01.22, NRO BGP 1/3/14.

16 Adams (1977), p. 1.

17 Cowan (1976), p. 1008.

18 Pipes (1980), pp. 89–90.

19 Adams (1977), pp. 451–3.

20 Bruce (1790), vol. 4, p. 419.

21 O'Fahey (1982), p. 77.

22 James (1977), pp. 95–133; O'Fahey, 1982.

23 Enloe (1980), p. 29

24 *Intelligence Report, Egypt*, 3 (June 1892), Appendix A, 'Relating to the arrival in Cairo of refugees from Equatoria...', pp. 4–12. Soghayroun (1981), pp. 28–9 gives the figures as 670 soldiers out of a total 8200 persons.

25 Soghayroun (1981), pp. 21 and 46; field research, Juba, 1982.

26 Meldon (1908), p. 128; interviews with retired officers in Omdurman.

27 Southall (1975), p. 87.

28 Enloe (1980), pp. 12, 26.

29 James (1977).

30 Meyers (1977 and 1983); Batran (1985).

31 Lovejoy (1983), pp. 15–16.

Further reading

Baer (1967); Buckley (1979); Fisher and Fisher (1970); Willis (1985).

Eleven

Mark Twain and the Ideology of Southern Slavery
R. J. Ellis

This paper sets out to explore what has been acknowledged as one principal feature of slavery's relationship to its society in the southern United States – namely the ideological supports to this institution. The centrality of the role played by ideology was most vigorously advanced by Eugene Genovese in the 1960s, in *The Political Economy of Slavery* and since then in subsequent studies, perhaps most notably in his examination of George Fitzhugh.[1] However, Genovese primarily undertook his depiction by specifying ideology's institutional manifestations – a tactic justified by his view of ideology as a hegemonic structure which he labelled 'seigneuralism'. But ideology as a concept has, since the 1960s, come to be recognised as far less homologous than such a label perhaps implies, rendering descriptions of its functioning more difficult, as one seeks to advance beyond Genovese's level of generalisation. My paper's endeavour to make progress, therefore, assumes a specific focus: Mark Twain's treatment of slavery and the Black in *The Adventures of Huckleberry Finn* (henceforth *HF*) and *Life on the Mississippi* (henceforth *LM*).[2] I will regard these two texts as two contrasting windows through which we can view the South's post-bellum ideology in the 1880s. This exercise gains authority from the fact that many historians regard the 1880s as pivotal in the drift from ante-bellum slavery through emancipation and reconstruction towards the widespread establishment of modes of debt peonage in the post-bellum South.

At the centre of the procedures which I shall deploy in this paper are three assumptions about ideology which I have adapted from the theoretical approach of John B. Thompson, as laid out in his book, *Studies in the Theory of Ideology* (henceforth *TI*).[3] Firstly, that since ideology is concerned with meaning – and meanings in our society are primarily conveyed/communicated through language – ideology must on a fundamental level operate through language. Secondly, that insofar as ideology is concerned to sustain and legitimate patterns of domination and control, language – as a socialised (i.e., a conventional) structure, a medium of social action – must to some degree echo ideological formulations in its patterns of signification. If these are not resisted, patterns of domination will be legitimated in a real effect: 'once we recognise that ideology operates through language and that language is a medium of social action we must also acknowledge that ideology is partially constitutive of what, in our societies, "is real"' (*TI* p. 5). Thirdly, that since ideology is concerned with legitimation, it has an explanatory role and this means that it necessarily erects a discourse engaging with political and social reality – which it is concerned to justify and/or conceal. (One must immediately observe that here Thompson is turning away from any neutral presentation of ideology by regarding it as an essential feature of all social practice only insofar as such social practice sets up patterns of domination. Instead he insists upon a more Marxist critical conception of ideology: 'To study ideology is to study the ways in which meaning (signification) . . . is mobilised for the maintenance of relations of domination' (*TI* p. 4).)

My adoption of Thompson's framework, centring on these three features, is not, however, total. I wish, in particular, to hold firmly to the idea that ideology as a domain works to set up normative attitudes to the world, seeking to establish ideas, opinions and beliefs intended to create values and attitudes constituting a consensus view that can set aside or blur contradictions and tensions in the asymmetrical distribution of power within a society. This, of course, may typically function by way of the creation of a 'lack of consensus at points where oppositional attitudes could emerge/cohere' (*TI* p. 4) – for example, by stressing the sanctity of individual opinions – but these still function through the establishment of a field of agreed meanings, set up in language and saturating social discourse.

In this particular instance it seems to be useful to bring to bear two methods used in analysing narrative discourse. The first is the proposition derived from the Russian formalists that literary artists, when undertaking a work of literature, set themselves up *sui generis* in a special relationship with both language and discourse (which, I would add, their narrative mode necessarily defines). The second is F. K. Stanzel's analytic model of narrative, as laid out in his *A Theory of Narrative* (Henceforth *TN*).[4] This approach will, I hope, open up the possibility of exploring the relationship between language and ideology within a text's discourse, since the text's conscious literariness might be held to function as a form of 'internal distanciation' – though I am seeking to use the term here in a more precisely delimited sense than that which seems to exist in Althusser's formulation, bound up as this is with all the problems of distinguishing what might constitute 'authentic art'.[5] Adding Paul Ricoeur's notion of distanciation provides a further sharpening of focus for me here – in particular his notion that this is a product of the inscription of discourse in writing.[6]

I want to refine this Ricourean notion of interiority by proposing that in certain textually constructed conditions this distanciation of discourse is deliberately set up within the text by the mode of narration deployed, and furthermore that the text's consequent self-engagement exposes the way in which 'the production of discourse is at once controlled, selected, organised and redistributed by a certain number of procedures whose role is to ward off its powers and dangers, to gain mastery over its chance events', as Foucault wrote in his 'The Order of Discourse' (henceforth *OD*).[7] This exposure thus crucially reveals that 'discourse is the power to be seized' (*OD*, p. 53). I want to test out these ideas in seeking to define *Huckleberry Finn* and *Life on the Mississippi* as products of the post-bellum South and Twain's return visit to the Mississippi in the period mid-April to late May 1882 – his first sustained revisit to the South since his departure at the beginning of the Civil War, and a return trip that plainly made a deep impression upon him. In both these texts, worked on coevally by Twain, there is a clear engagement – in different ways and to different degrees – with the ideological supports to slavery deployed in the South – supports plainly seeking to legitimate patterns of domination. I will, then, be approaching these two texts by means of the 'discursive analysis of linguistic constructions and the social analysis of the conditions of discursive production' (*TI*, p. 146). I am hoping to demonstrate that the different narrative parameters operative in the semi-autobiographical *Life on the Mississippi* and the fictional *Huckleberry Finn* are revelatory concerning the grip of ideological structures in the southern United States, their linguistic and discursive supports, and the cultural consequences for this society and particularly the Black.

I want to begin by exploring some of the central passages which discuss the situation of the Black in the post-bellum South in *Life on the Mississippi*. These reveal, I believe, that the discourse between text and social reality is deeply ambivalent.

The basic poverty of the Black is plainly recognised:

> Sometimes there was a group of high-water-stained,
> tumbledown cabins, populous with colored folk, and no
> whites visible; with grassless patches of dry ground here and
> there; a few felled trees, with skeleton cattle, mules and
> horses, eating the leaves and gnawing the bark – no other
> food for them in the flood-wasted land. Sometimes there
> was a single lonely landing-cabin; near it the colored family
> that had hailed us; little and big, old and young, roosting on
> the scant pile of household goods (*LM*, pp. 186–7).

Twain also recognises that this poverty is rooted in the Black's
constant debt-status under the economic system of sharecropping:

> Complaint is made that the planter remains grouty toward
> the former slave, since the war; will have nothing but a chill
> business relation with him, no sentiment permitted to intrude;
> will not keep a 'store' himself, and supply the Negro's wants
> and thus protect the Negro's pocket and make him able and
> willing to stay on the place and an advantage to him to do
> it, but lets that privilege to some thrifty Israelite, who
> encourages the thoughtless Negro and wife to buy all sorts
> of things which they could do without – buy on credit at
> big prices, month after month, credit based on the Negro's
> share of the growing crop; and at the end of the season, the
> Negro's share belongs to the Israelite, the Negro is in debt
> besides, is discouraged, dissatisfied, restless, and both he and
> the planter are injured; for he will take the steamboat and
> migrate. (*LM*, pp. 210–11).

Notice here firstly how the text deflects criticism away from the
planters (whose paternalism is assumed by criticising its neglect) and
from the essential economic structures of sharecropping by
introducing a strain of anti-semitism. But also notice how the
discourse distances the autobiographer from this narrative strategy
by the introduction of the impersonal voice: 'Complaint is made' –
the text elides from itself its narrative authority – but with
duplicitous momentariness. This elision is promoted by a series of
narrative lapses possessing a Machereyian significance.[8] For example,
in the passage just quoted, the blame for the Blacks' migrations is
placed upon their debt burdens; but only fourteen pages earlier

Twain had presented these migrations as stemming from individual impulsiveness:

> We were getting down now into the migrating Negro region. These poor people could never travel when they were slaves; so they make up for the privation now. They stay on a plantation till the desire to travel seizes them; then they pack up, hail a steamboat, and clear out. Not for any particular place ... they only want to be moving. The amount of money on hand will answer the rest of the conundrum for them. If it will take them fifty miles, very well; let it be fifty. If not, a shorter flight will do (*LM*, p. 186).

The two passages are irreconcilable, the discourse crucially ambiguous. Textual clarity on this topic is chiefly reserved for clear examples of ante-bellum excess within the system of chattel slavery, for example when dealing with the vicious activities of the slave-hunting Murel gang (*LM*, pp. 178ff.). Exceptionally, more complex passages reveal oblique doubts about slavery, as when describing the hypothetical, arbitrary results of a 'cut-off' change in the meander pattern of the Mississippi before the Civil War:

> A cut-off plays havoc with boundary lines and jurisdictions: for instance, a man is living in the state of Mississippi today, a cut-off occurs tonight, and tomorrow the man finds himself and his land over on the other side of the river, within the boundaries and subject to the laws of the state of Louisiana! Such a thing, happening in the upper river in the old times, could have transferred a slave from Missouri to Illinois and made a free man of him (*LM*, pp. 14–15).

But when treating with the contemporary conditions, prevailing in the early 1880s, the text's ambivalence is structured by its narrative voice. The treatment of the paternalistic Calhoun Land Company plantation experiment is here instructive. Colonel Calhoun's system is first viewed as a means of preventing the Negro running inexorably into debt as a sharecropper via the establishment of a low-interest loan system, halting the migration-cycle and securing economic stability:

It is hoped that the Calhoun Company will show, by its humane and protective treatment of its laborers, that its method is the most profitable for both planter and Negro; and it is believed that a general adoption of that method will then follow (*LM*, p. 211).

But this sentiment is swiftly compromised in the paragraph which follows. Here again the narrative structure is complicated, this time by the introduction of a fictional Southern White barkeeper who reflects cynically upon the Calhoun Company's endeavours and their viability. He derides the scheme for failing to take account of the Blacks' inconstancy, and their propensity for being taken in by show rather then intrinsic worth. One thus might regard the barkeeper's comments as a problem in reading: is the barkeeper's cynicism shadowed in the text by an ironic satire upon the man himself? But the narrative is nevertheless presenting the stock Southern White common-sense viewpoint and, unsurprisingly, it is racist in its implications:

And where so many are saying their say, shall not the barkeeper testify? He is thoughtful, observant, never drinks; endeavors to earn his salary, and would earn it if there were custom enough. He says ... 'You give a nigger a plain gill of half-dollar brandy for five cents – will he touch it? No. Ain't size enough to it. But you put a pint of all kinds of worthless rubbish, and heave in some red stuff to make it beautiful ... and he wouldn't put down that glass to go to a circus' (*LM*, p. 211).

This is the voice of ideologically-constructed common sense plain enough. My point is that the text's narrative construction can allow a reading supportive of the barman's racism. This is not to say that one cannot deconstruct this narrative with the advantage of historical hindsight. Then one can reflect that one sees here ideology in operation in the way described by Poulantzas:

Ideology has the precise function of hiding the real contradictions and of reconstituting on an imaginary level a relatively coherent discourse which serves as the horizon of agents' experience.[9]

And it is precisely this ideological process, I would argue, that underpins and enables the development of the reconstituted form of slavery known as debt peonage in the South during this period, as the South drifted towards a segregationist culture that could be regarded as the rule by 1900.[10]

But what I am now doing is importing perspectives into the text to set up my own (interrogative) reading of its discourse with social reality. This is certainly a sustainable procedure, especially given *Life on the Mississippi*'s duplicitous evasion of textual authority ('complaint is made'; 'shall not the barkeeper testify?'), but in a sense what is being revealed is an assumed knowledge of the extant ideology. What I now want to do is contextualise Twain's discourse more closely, in a search for the precise ideological co-ordinates which are operative.

Twain's return visit to the Mississippi river basin in 1882 occurred during a key transition period of the region between the end of the Civil War and the start of the twentieth century. Immediately after the Civil War, despite the North's reconstruction efforts, Southern intellectuals – both organic and traditional – were arguing that slavery could and should continue. Pete Daniels, for example, notes that in 1868 an anonymous article in the *De Bows Review* sought to justify this precise position:

> we do not mean by slavery such as that which has just
> been recently abolished, but some form of subordination of
> the inferior race that shall compel them to labor whilst it
> protects their rights and provides for their wants.[11]

By 1900 this sort of solution had been broadly attained.[12] Indeed, the mid-1880s, when Twain revisited the South, represent something of a mid-point in this process: William Warner, a US senator and former member of the Alabama legislature can be found asserting in 1883:

> to a great extent . . . in the days of slavery, the master was
> the first man to protect his negro – partly of course, from
> motives of self-interest, partly also . . . from a feeling of
> humanity and affection . . . so now, the planter is disposed to
> protect his negro labourer, because it is in his interest to do
> so, and because of his kindly feeling towards him (*MS*, p. 91).

The parallelism in the structure of the two main clauses in this passage are an accurate enough representation in discourse of the way in which ideological elisions were supporting the effective reconstitution of slavery in the South. As Sidney Andrews had drily commented in 1866, in what amounts to a reflection on language's ideological capacities: 'What are names if the thing itself remains?' (*MS*, p. 91).

Precisely. Linguistic signs are arbitrary and conventional (a point to which we shall return) and if the ideology of the South that supported slavery remained intact, unthreatened, undisplaced, then the institution would effectively endure. Thus, even though chattel slavery as an explicit economic institution may have been legally abolished, its ideological preservation had material repercussions. And this is where Twain's *The Adventures of Huckleberry Finn* can be presented as a cultural document of considerable, if oblique, penetration. *Life on the Mississippi*, we have observed, in no sense sets up an internal narrative discourse critical of Southern ideology. Rather, its gaps, lapses and silences define its textual deviousness. In *Huckleberry Finn* the narrative becomes more compellingly interrogative, and this interrogation is structured within the narrative's organisation of its discourse.

On one level, which Stanzel calls the 'surface structure' of the narrative (*TN*, p. 6), the novel plainly becomes a forceful critique of the ante-bellum South and chattel slavery. The book does this by setting up an essential, informing level of irony which has been repeatedly analysed. The book takes, as its thematic core, the developing relationship between a poor White – the young Huckleberry Finn – and a fugitive chattel slave – the Black Jim. Their alliance is plainly potentially highly threatening for the South's hegemonic ideology. *Huckleberry Finn* functions, then, in no small part, as a depiction of the social tensions inherent in this ante-bellum friendship, explored overtly in the first person narrative as Huck debates constantly with himself about the propriety of his actions. Readers have no trouble in understanding that they are required to read these debates with irony, not least because this is heavily underscored. Thus, as Huck builds towards his climatic assertion that he is prepared to 'go to hell' for helping Jim escape, the reader readily understands that this will be the 'hell' of social ostracism, since Huck is breaking one of the most fundamental codes of his community, and of Southern White society as a whole (*HF*, p. 451).

By identifying this obvious level of irony, of course, the reader is being required to dissent from these consensus values of ante-bellum Southern society and is thereby led to side not with Huck's conscious beliefs but with his actions in continuing to assist Jim.

We see, then, that this dissent has been carefully located in the discourse: on an ironic level we are reading through Huck's narrative to an overview of the ideological apparatuses that operate to produce Huck's distorted analysis of his situation. Huck continually resorts to blaming his bringing up, his limited education and his irreligion for his 'bad' actions: school, church and family are thus explicitly located as key supports of ideological rectitude. We can hardly avoid reference to the notion of ideological state apparatuses here to support this discursive analysis.[13] For we understand that hegemony has in a sense been preserved, since Huck always believes his actions have been wrong. Instead he recognises the authority of Tom, to whom he readily cedes primacy at Phelp's Farm, for he sees in Tom qualities he does not possess:

> Here was a boy that was respectable, and well brung up; and had a character to lose; and folks at home that had characters; and he was bright and not leather-headed; and knowing and not ignorant; and not mean, but kind (*HF*, p. 473).

Huck recognises Tom's claim to authority as legitimate and therefore surrenders up the initative; he feels he cannot argue against Tom:

> he [Tom] shut me up and says:
> 'Don't you reckon I know what I'm about?'
> 'Yes.'
> 'Didn't I say I was going to help steal the nigger?'
> 'Yes'
> 'Well then.'
> That's all he said, and that's all I said. It warn't no use to say any more; because when he said he'd do a thing, he always done it. But *I* couldn't make out how he was willing to go into this thing; so I just let go, and never bothered no more about it. If he was bound to have it so, *I* couldn't help it (*HF*, p. 473).

Piere Bourdieu provides a germane gloss on this discourse:

> Language is not only an instrument of communication, or
> even knowledge, but also an instrument of power. One seeks
> not only to be understood but also to be believed, obeyed,
> respected, distinguished. Whence the complete definition of
> competence as right to speak.... Competence implies the
> power to impose reception (*TI*, pp. 46–7).

Huck gives way to Tom; a product, this, of his earlier experiences,
when he had been subjected to what Bourdieu describes as
innumerable language-body disciplines seeking to inculcate a
'habitus':

> Miss Watson would say, 'Don't put your feet up there,
> Huckleberry'; and 'don't scrunch up like that Huckleberry –
> set up straight'; and pretty soon she would say, 'Don't gape
> and stretch like that, Huckleberry, why don't you try to
> behave?' (*HF*, p. 195).

Huck's acts may amount to a rebellion against this inculcation by
fleeing down the river with Jim, but the constant corrections to his
behaviour have led him to cede conscious authority to those in
possession of the dominant 'habitus'. His rationalisations reflect this:

> it warn't no use for me to try to learn to do right; a body
> that don't get *started* right when he's little ain't got no show
> – when the pinch comes there ain't nothing to back him up
> and keep him to his work, and so he gets beat (*HF*, p. 312).

At an ironic level, the text is openly reminding us, as Paul Ricoeur
would, that discourse obtains within a socio-historical world of
determining contextual values.[14]

It is plainly these points of breakdown between Huck's expressed
beliefs and the actions he takes that constitute a main level of the
discourse's ironic critique of ideology. Consciously, Huck has been
interpellated as subject.[15] But the text also plainly establishes
language as a primary domain for such interpellation, by showing us
its arbitrary and conventional nature. By the end of *Huckleberry Finn*,
the reader has come to acquire a deep mistrust of language. A series

of textual linguistic plays has revealed its ideological complicity. Tom's redesignation of the Sunday School outing as 'arabs and elephants' in Chapter 3 provides as innocent introduction to this motif, but it is succeeded by repeated redesignations and renamings fracturing signification: Jim becomes a swamp-fever suffering father, an Arab, a recaptured slave; Huck becomes Sarah Williams, George Peters, George Jackson, an English valet and Tom Sawyer. By the end of the book this jostling of language's significations has become fundamental, particularly in the 'case-knife' exchange in the evasion sequence. Here Huck and Tom, both intent on freeing Jim, are bound to carry out this process according to Tom's half-baked understanding of propriety. Thus the prisoner must be dug out with case-knives, not the available pick-axes. When this proves too difficult, Tom relents and the following exchange occurs:

> 'Gimme a case knife.' [says Tom]
> He had his own by him, but I handed him mine. He flung it down and says: 'Gimme a *case-knife*.'
> I didn't know just what to do – but then I thought. I scratched around amongst the old tools and got a pick-ax and gave it to him and he took it and went to work, and never said a word (*HF*, p. 487).

Now this exchange may simply be received as part of the heavy burlesque upon Tom Sawyer's adherence to sterile romantic conventions constituting his 'principles'. But it is also an integral part of the linguistic play in the book, unsettling our attitudes to language.

Huck and Tom, in this short exhange, have set up a new linguistic convention where the sound-image 'case-knife', as a signifier, assumes a new meaning, the concept 'pick-ax'. The text has thus economically established what Frederic de Saussure advanced in 1916 as a basic attribute of language as a sign system: that the meaning of a word is firstly conventional and secondly arbitrary; there is nothing inherent in a word, or the object that the word conventionally denotes, which link the two together; Huck and Tom's exchange illustrates this plainly enough. The clear implication of their 'case-knife' exchange is that language meanings are socially defined; the text deliberately offers the reader this instruction. But the text goes further yet, by requiring us to enter into an ironic recognition of the way in which language operates as socially constitutive, with meaning regarded as social action dependant on social relations and not derived from natural or inherent properties of words or their referents.[16] The text invites us, in other words, to regard language hermeneutically, as an interpretative domain. The novel does this through its unsettling intimation that language is not to be regarded as innocent, but as bearing inscribed within it patterns of domination and ideological concealment. Huck remains subservient to these patterns, and his struggles to accommodate his friendship with Jim are illustrative of this. Early on, in Chapter 14, Huck is compelled to recognise that Jim had 'an uncommon level head for a nigger'. By Chapter 23, Huck, on hearing Jim grieving over his separation from his family, is moved to say: 'I do believe he cared as much for his people as white folks does for their'n. It don't seem natural but I reckon it's so.' Finally, at the end of the evasion sequence, Huck offers his considered verdict on Jim: 'I knowed he was white inside.' Plainly a pattern is present here, one given definition when we recall that in Chapter 16, when confronting the slave-hunters, Huck had produced the assertion that Jim was white as an awkward lie:

> 'Is your man white or black?'
> I didn't answer up prompt. I tried to but the words
> wouldn't come ... so I just give up trying and up and says:
> 'He's white' (*HF*, p. 310).

This stands in sharp contrast to the final assertion that Huck knew Jim to be 'white inside'. Jim's colour is finally denied by Huck's narrative as he literally makes black out to be white in a climactic linguistic evasion of his act of social delinquency. But a further pattern is also present, for on each occasion a linguistic compromise undercuts Huck's reflection: 'an uncommon level head *for a nigger*' [my emphasis]; 'he cared as much for his people as white folks does for their'n. It don't seem *natural* [my emphasis] but I reckon it's so'; '*I knowed he was white inside* [my emphasis]'. I wish to propose that these linguistic compromises are located at another level, extant not in the overt narrative, but in what I shall term the text's *total discourse*.

The text's overt use of irony in part, it is true, leads us to a questioning of the relations of language, meaning and ideology. But, more fundamentally, this questioning exists not as part of Huck's conscious narrative, nor solely as a surface irony, but rather as an element of the text's total discourse, functioning through the narrative's deep structure (*TN*, p. 5). The text distinctly establishes this 'mediacy of narration' (*TN*, p. 6). in its unconventional opening paragraph:

> You don't know about me, without you have read a book by the name of *The Adventures of Tom Sawyer*, but that ain't no matter. That book was made by Mr Mark Twain and he told the truth mainly. There was things that he stretched, but mainly he told the truth. That is nothing. I never seen anybody but lied, one time or another (*HF*, pp. 193–4).

One can of course read this as a conventional attempt to establish the authenticity of the narrative by establishing the identity of Huck Finn as 'real'. But if this is the intent, it is undercut by the startling strategy of having Huck directly address 'you' and name Mark Twain himself in the text. Thus in one movement the text reveals what it seeks to conceal, that Huck Finn's narrative is made by Mark Twain for the reader. The claimed verisimilitude is shown to be illusory, giving the lie, in the total discourse, to the announced moral prerogative of telling the truth. Thus, from the very start, a mistrust of meaning is set up; not because Huck does not seek to tell the truth in his narrative, but because of the relationship in the text between narrative and discourse.

This interaction is quite crucial. So far I have assembled evidence that Twain in *Huckleberry Finn* has been portraying, as would Ricoeur, Bourdieu and Althusser (each in different ways), ideology as socially and linguistically constitutive. I now wish to establish that this portrait is central to the text's overall import. For Twain's explicit invitation to us at a deep structural level to recognise the text's status as a language-discourse, constraining the 'freedom' of Huck's narrative, causes a relatively uncomplicated and forthright post-emancipation critique of ante-bellum Southern chattel slavery to become definitively engaged with the status of meaning in language and society, setting up a self-referential critique of the relationship of discourse to ideology in the South of the 1880s. This far more radical inquiry is established by the textual foregrounding of the shift from Huck's narrative to the text's total discourse, established in the opening paragraph, and also in the book's prefatory epigram, 'persons attempting to find a moral [in this narrative] ... will be banished' (*HF*, p. 193). We know that Twain himself contradicted this assertion, writing in his *Notebooks* in 1895 that *Huckleberry Finn* was 'a book of mine where a sound heart and a deformed conscience come into collision and conscience suffers a defeat'.

I take it, then, that the opening epigram should be taken the opposite way, like Huck's own moral pronouncements, and wish to view its disclaimer as an instruction to undertake what amounts to a moral exercise: applying the total discourse's critique of ideology's saturation of language and social practice to the text's post-bellum context. This transfer is climactically constituted in the evasion sequence, when Tom plays out his elaborate joke of setting 'a free nigger free'. Here, on the surface narrative level, we see Huck and Jim subjected to an act of symbolic violence in Bourdieu's fullest sense of the phrase. Huck and Jim are forced to operate within the terms of Tom's adventure-narrative, parodic of the discourse of the dominant ideology:

> symbolic violence is never so manifest as in ... the confusion which makes them 'lose their drift,' rendering them incapable of 'finding their words,' as if they had been suddenly dispossessed of their own language (*TI*, p. 58).

Or, as Huck put it, 'Well, I let go all holts then' (*HF*, p. 464), 'It warn't no use to say any more' (*HF*, p. 473). But since Jim has been set free – by, ironically, a linguistic act, Miss Watson's will – Tom's treatment of Jim in the text's total discourse is representative of the values of the dominant, now post-bellum, Southern ideology. Tom's function is unchanged: in both surface structural narrative and deep structural discourse he legitimates a series of ideological polarities in the text:[17] white : black; white gen'lman : nigger; freeman : slave; owner : non-owner; educated : ignorant; participant (e.g., voter) : non-participant (e.g., non-voter). By running away, Jim fractures this pattern, threatening the stability of this dominant ideological discourse. The text draws attention to this by a series of deep-structural ironies. Jim, constituted as non-owner by the ideology, begins to conceive of ownership not only of his children, which he plans to steal, but even of himself: 'Yes – en I's rich now, come to look at it. I owns myself, en I's wuth eight hund'd dollars' (*HF*, p. 246). Huck occupies an ambivalent position here: in his acts, confirming Jim's threats, but in his language and consciousness, preserving the polarities, even when formulating his acts of subversion. He elects to regard the Black Jim as White to restabilise the pattern of polarisation, and proposes not to free Jim but to 'steal' what he describes as 'my nigger' – equated with 'my watermelon' and 'my Sunday school book.' At times of crisis for his conscience he returns consistently to the term 'nigger', and like Aunt Sally, does not regard a 'nigger' as a person when discussing a steamboat accident. Once again, however, it is Tom, in preserving the polarities consistently in both his language and his actions, whether Jim is freeman or slave, who bridges most explicitly between the surface and the deep structures, signifying, in his treatment of Jim, the proposition that the ideology of slavery is intact, and apparently eternal, whether the slave is freed by Miss Watson's will or by emancipation. This irony, however, is not part of the overt irony present in Huck's narrative, but is rather a part of the total discourse's engagement with language and narrative. If the reader remains within Huck's consciousness, for example, it is not simply obvious that Pap Finn's racist fury concerning a 'nigger's' right to vote is a direct comment on the processes of disenfranchisement being pursued in the post-bellum South that Twain had just visited and which this text implies he saw as reconstituting the ante-bellum patterns of ideological polarisation effectively preserving slavery. Nor is the irony simply obvious when Huck and Jim, as 'abolitionists', and hence displaced from the security of the South's ideological (Black/White) polarities, lose their certainty about property: is Jim worth 'eight hund'd dollars'? And are the watermelons they take stolen or borrowed? Huck and Jim's challenge to the South's ideological polarisations undermine the conventional confidence placed in language's stability.

These subversive, interrogative ironies, then, by operating in the text's total discourse rather than Huck's conscious narrative, possess an obliquity functioning quite differently from the ambivalent duplicity of *Life on the Mississippi*. The latter's semi-autobiographical discourse does not set up any textually-marked deep structural level: the critique of the South has to be constructed by the reader in the gaps left by the narrative's ambivalences. Hence the confusion, I think, that allows Twain to be constructed as a racist in some contemporary critical debates.[18] Indeed, because *Life on the Mississippi* lacks Huckleberry Finn's self-referential obliquities, its comparatively mild criticisms of the South were subjected to publisher's censorship.[19] Its narrative directness effectively constrained Twain. Thus I read the stress he places on the value of reviving old Southern friendships, those 'tugboat gossip[s]' (*LM*, p. 275) whom he 'managed to hunt out' (*LM*, p. 287), with extra-textual irony. In *Huckleberry Finn* the critique can become far more comprehensive and damaging, because it is valorised into what is, apparently, simply Huck's ante-bellum narrative. Thus the sub-versive revelation of the contingency of the South's 'eternal' set of ideological polarities need not necessarily be recognised. But the frame provided by the narrative's total textual discourse instructs us how this might be done, and the narrative device of Tom's consistency textually sets up the proposal that Southern ideology in the period 1840 to 1884 possesses a clear continuity. The potential substitution of the term 'debt peonage' for 'slave' in the 'slave: free-man' dyad is implicit in Tom's treatment of the 'freed' Jim. Twain's text leads us to deconstruct the linguistic formulation 'free nigger free': nigger/free, in the pattern of ideological polarisations, remain irreconcilably opposed to one another, as Huck's struggles with language reveal. Thus Pete Daniels' assertion when discussing the position of the Black in the South in the period 1865 to 1900 that 'No label seems to fit' is entirely germaine (*MS*, p. 98). Twain's text demonstrates that no linguistic substitution is *à propos* whilst the ante-bellum ideological polarisations are effectively preserved. Indeed, more ominously, Twain's text goes on to allude to the use of lynching as an instrument of repression in the post-bellum South,[20] by pointing out that Jim is only saved from hanging in the Phelps Farm coda by his economic value:

> The men was very huffy, and some of them wanted to hang Jim for an example to all the other niggers around so they wouldn't be trying to run away, like Jim done and making such a raft of trouble.... But the others said, don't do it, it wouldn't answer at all, he ain't our nigger, and his owner would turn up and make us pay for him sure. So that cooled them down a little (*HF*, p. 529).

I need hardly add that, unknown to the Whites, Jim at this point in the text is free and thus this exchange is charged with deep irony: Jim's lynching would have actually been 'free'.

What I have sought to do, then, in this paper, is propose that the self-referential textual structure of *Huckleberry Finn* sets it as a discourse definitively apart from the mode of *Life on the Mississippi*.

By establishing Huck as an unreliable narrator and then exploring discursively the contribution of the social constitution of language and discourse to this unreliability in a deliberately marked fashion, Twain establishes a revelatory critical analysis of Southern ideology. One could carry on this argument, I should like to suggest, by proposing that such an analysis could be extended to other cases where a novel's 'mediacy' (*TN*, p. 6) is rendered up in the text's total discourse by the interplay between deep and surface narrative structures. Through such a device, I would claim (and here I am extending Stanzel's theory into materialist domaines), a critique of the complicity of language, discourse and ideology can be established by a process of internal distantiation. In *Huckleberry Finn* the interplay between surface and deep narrative structures establishes the vice-like grip of ideology upon the Southern lower classes, functioning through a set of apparently eternal consensus polarisations which structure and inform Huck's narrative discourse, representatively expressing Southern beliefs and values in the nineteenth century. The novel thereby proposes that language is not simply a channel of communication, but possesses specific socio-historical attributes as a medium of power-relationships and dominance. This proposal is necessarily obliquely located as an ironic attribute of the total textual discourse, evading thereby the censorship imposed upon *Life on the Mississippi*, which stands in contrast as necessarily ambivalent.

Huckleberry Finn thus escapes from the compromise Bourdieu describes between 'expressive intent' (that which is to be communicated) and 'censorship' (inherent in the structure of the audience-group for which the communication is formulated (*TI*, p. 57)) by means of its multi-layered ironic structure. This textual strategy itself foregrounds these censorship pressures and their ideological co-ordinates. *Huckleberry Finn*, I claim, thereby reveals what Twain understands to be the structure and constituents of Southern post-bellum ideology. The question remains as to how complete and accurate Twain's portrait of a set of integrated, interactive polarities is as a representation of the mechanisms of the ideological perpetuation of slavery as debt peonage in the South. As to his proposal that the dyad nigger/object : white gen'lman/person constitutes a definitive axis for Southern ideology, I would unhesitatingly agree, and one notices, just as Twain has taught us, that this construct is again a procedure of language – a discourse with reality in itself, and one which ensured that the southern poor remained fragmentedly impotent. As Foucault says, 'discourse is the power to be seized'. Huck and Jim exhibit no such mastery, but drift ever further into the deep South.

Notes

1 See Genovese (1965); *ibid.* (1969); *ibid.* (1971).
2 Mark Twain, *The Adventures of Huckleberry Finn*, 1884, rpt. N.Y., Viking Press, 1946, ed. B. De Voto; *Life on the Mississippi*, 1883, rpt. N.Y., New American Library, 1961.
3 Thompson (1984). My debt to Thompson is substantial.
4 See the concept of literariness as advanced by Jakobsen (1956), pp. 55–8; Stanzel (1984).
5 See Althusser, 'A Letter on Art in Reply to Andre Despre' in Althusser (1971), pp. 221–7.
6 Ricoeur (1981b).
7 Foucault in Young (1981), p. 52.
8 See Macherey (1978).
9 Poulantzas (1975), p. 208.
10 Jones (1983), p. 271.
11 Anon., 'Negro Agrarians', *De Bow's Review* no. 5, Feb 1868, quoted in Daniels (1979), p. 88. In future, all references to this article ('The metamorphosis of slavery') will appear in the main text, in parenthesis, preceded by the initials *MS*.
12 Daniels (1972), pp. 22ff.
13 Althusser, 'Ideology and ideological state apparatuses', in Althusser, *op. cit.*
14 See Ricouer (1981a).
15 Althusser, 'Ideology', *op. cit.*
16 See Volosinov (1973), and the discussion of this by Williams (1977).
17 See Lefort (1978).
18 See Pettit (1974) for a sensible early rebuttal of this idea. Pettit, I believe, however, misreads *Life on the Mississippi* when he suggests that in this text Twain 'lacked the courage' to criticise the South as roundly as he wished (p. 88).
19 For accounts of this, see Cardwell (1973); Kruse (1981).
20 See Ellison (1974), pp. 41ff.

Further reading

In the following suggestions as to further reading, I have chosen to focus on texts which, to a greater or lesser extent, treat with 'discourse analysis' – to the neglect of literary criticism and (traditional) history studies, which to some extent are specified in the footnotes above: Egan (1977); Leitch (1983); Macherey (1978); Stanzel (1984); Thompson (1984); Young (1981).

Twelve

'All Americans Are Part African': Slave Influence on 'White' Values

Mechal Sobel

In the past twenty years, as part of the 'second reconstruction' generated by the civil rights revolution of the 1960s and 1970s, an almost totally new view of slave life and black culture in North America has been formulated. While as late as 1964 sociologist E. Franklin Frazier, himself a black, could reasonably maintain that 'the Negroes were practically stripped of their social heritage' in the slave period, it is now very widely accepted, and richly documented, that blacks adapted myriad aspects of African cultures, together with white ways, into what is now viewed as an Afro-American culture.[1] Recognising the impact of the English language, the Christian religion and white power, the new scholarship has nevertheless become convinced that there was a quasi-African matrix into which white cultural patterns were incorporated and that an Afro-American culture developed with an otherness and a separateness from white culture.[2] Lawrence W. Levine, for example, maintains that those aspects he terms the 'sacred world of the black slaves' created a protected space, 'a world apart which they shared with each other and which remained their own domain, free of control of those who ruled the earth'.[3]

While many aspects of the new interpretation are still in dispute, virtually all analysts see the black and the white cultures of the slave period as crucially different, with most accepting that white culture deeply affected the blacks. However, only the institution of slavery (and not slave culture) is generally seen as having affected the whites. Rhys Isaac, for example, in his recent brilliant analysis of eighteenth-century Virginia accepted that there were then 'two divergent cultures', and essentially analysed one, the white, in isolation from the second.[4]

Eugene Genovese is one of the very few analysts who has been directly concerned with blacks' influence on whites, but his seminal studies of the nineteenth-century South were deeply influenced by his understanding of ruling class hegemony. This led him to believe that blacks could not have influenced whites beyond a certain point, even though the material he chose to consider and his own analyses often seemed to indicate otherwise. He apparently remained convinced that there were two separate cultural worlds, as his titles, 'The World the Slaveholders Made', and 'The World the Slaves Made', suggest.[5]

There is only one area in which black cultural influence has been widely acknowledged, that of music, but this is seen as an anomaly. A few other areas have been investigated. Peter H. Wood has done a fine job of establishing African influence on the techniques of rice growing in South Carolina, and in recent decades there have been a number of analysts ready to explore the influence of blacks on isolated crafts, such as canoe-building, or banjo crafting.[6] Although Melville Herskovitz proposed that blacks had more widely influenced whites, and Gary Nash, Ira Berlin, and others have noted that they believe this to have been true, little research has been devoted to African and Afro-American influence on whites and it is still widely assumed that blacks did not influence white culture to any significant extent.[7]

I would like to suggest that the time has come for a rigorous analysis both of new types of questions which address this issue, and of data from an earlier period. Taken in conjunction, I believe this will bring us to a radically different view of the role of African culture in America. Having achieved a relatively broad picture of nineteenth-century slavery, based on the rich documents extant, the time has come to turn more intensively to the earlier less well documented but very significant history of eighteenth-century African and Afro-American slavery. It is from this period in particular that questions of cultural interaction have the potential to yield new answers, inasmuch as it was then that large numbers of Englishmen and Africans were coming in contact with each other for the first time. An attempt can be made to analyse the whites' culture both before and after the players on this stage changed, and thus the impact of African culture on the Anglo-Americans should be assessable.

For the last decade I have been exploring just these problems, analysing the interaction of African and English, Afro-American and Anglo-American cultures in eighteenth-century Virginia. I have come to a radically different view than that currently held by most analysts.[8] I would like to take this opportunity to outline my interpretation and to suggest some of the problems and possibilities.

By now, based on the work of Philip D. Curtin, Herbert S. Klein, and many others, we have a fairly clear picture of black importation into the South.[9] Large-scale slave purchases in the Chesapeake in the first half of the century, and in the lower South in the second, together with a natural population growth among both whites and blacks, created a new population mix. By 1750 Virginia, the most populous colony, was approximately 45 per cent black and in the South overall some 200,000 whites were living in areas where blacks predominated. In the second half of the century, South Carolina became indeed 'more like a negro country'; by 1750 it was already more than two-thirds black.[10]

In that century the South became a slave society, one in which slave labour provided the basis for its economy.[11] While masters were whites, and most blacks were slaves, the great majority of working whites *worked with blacks*. White slave owners and overseers supervised black labourers, spending their days with them; white indentured servants and apprentices worked with black slaves; white craftsmen worked with black craftsmen; white miners with black miners; white sailors with black sailors. Work became essentially a black domain, and working whites worked in it. For example, in the 1730s Robert 'King' Carter had some 1,000 black slaves and perhaps eight white overseers. At his Great House there were twenty-six skilled workmen, fifteen white and eleven black. All these whites worked in an essentially black world of work.[12]

At mid-century, although there was an elite that owned large numbers of slaves, most slave owners owned less than five slaves. These owners worked along with the blacks in the fields while their wives worked with blacks in and around the houses.[13]

Independent white artisans often owned slaves, and worked with them. The 1782 census in Richmond, Virginia, for example, cites three white carpenters who owned twenty-eight slaves; five white tailors who owned fourteen slaves; two white smiths who owned seven slaves; two silversmiths owning eight slaves; and a tanner with six slaves.[14] The whites were in charge but it was blacks they worked with.

The racial reality of family life changed in this period as well. Many families were, in their daily functioning, biracial. Interaction was at a very broad and often intense level. Family histories became mixed and many whites became highly dependent on black nurturance. Blacks often cared for white infants, children and adults; black and white children played together; interracial sex was not uncommon; many white men maintained long-term relationships with black women and fathered mulatto children; many whites became deeply attached to blacks, and while these were often love/hate relationships, the contacts were generally both intensive and extensive.

Landon Carter's diary (1752–77) provides interesting examples. Carter, one of Virginia's major land and slave owners, who was also active in both local and colony government, knew many of his hundreds of slaves, and had an intense lifelong relationship with several of them. One such individual was Nassau, whose father had been a slave of Landon's father, and whose wife and son were Landon's property as well, and who served Carter as his 'man', waiting on him personally day and night. Landon Carter also trained Nassau as a medical practitioner, and relied on his abilities, although he became jealous of his popularity. Nassau treated both blacks and whites, both often preferring his treatment to that of Carter.

Nassau became an alcoholic and often did not fulfil Carter's requests, occasionally disappearing for a while. Carter publicly threatened to sell Nassau to the West Indies, but his public advertisement of this decision seems to have been directed towards Nassau. Nassau, in response chose to leave Carter, to run away, but he apparently returned. While he was gone Carter maintained 'I have been learning to do without him, and though it has been but very badly yet I can bear it and will.'

When at the outset of the revolution, Governor Dunmore promised runaway slaves their freedom, Nassau apparently sought to join him, and Carter had him publicly outlawed. Nevertheless, by the fall of 1777 Landon's diary indicates Nassau was back again, 'tormenting' him with his old ways.

Carter was certainly the master, and had not only threatened Nassau, but had tied and beaten him. Nevertheless, Landon Carter and Nassau [Carter] were clearly in a family relationship and the owner was deeply dependent on his slave.[15]

The evidence available from almost every other eighteenth-century Southern diary illustrates similar interaction. In the diaries of Byrd, Washington, Fithian, Fairfax and Blodget, blacks are not just 'acted upon', but interact with whites.[16] They were in one family, both in terms of the nature of their interrelationship, and in their own view. As the Rev. John Williams routinely noted in his journal for 23 July 1771, 'I had all my family given up to the Lord by prayer, the children black and white, particularly by laying on of hands'.[17]

For the poor and 'middling' sort, recreation as well as work was generally biracial. Cockfights, human fights, horse races and court-day fairs were attended by a mixed multitude of blacks and whites.[18] Poor whites also had both legal and illegal business relationships with blacks, buying and selling goods and participating in crimes together. 'Middling' whites often rented slaves. For these classes, too, interracial social and sexual contacts were not abnormal.[19]

This is not to suggest that blacks and whites were meeting on an equal basis: masters held almost unlimited power over their slaves, and all whites held power over blacks. But slaves were not simply acted upon. Notwithstanding their legal status as chattels, they were participants in dynamic interrelationships in which they acted upon whites and affected them.

Proximity and interaction can be fairly well documented for most of the population. However the issue of value interpenetration is far more complex than that of demography and folkways. I would like to suggest a very wide-ranging argument that raises many questions, especially given the fact that documentation of eighteenth-century African and lower class English and American culture is very difficult.

English migrants to the colonial South brought with them at least two conflicting world views: The great majority held a neo-medieval view of a world where time was cyclical and tied to agricultural pursuits and magical control; where most movement was slow and work regarded as a burden. Overall, magical powers were respected, magical times and places believed in, and causality was essentially understood as arational. Change was neither anticipated nor welcomed.[20] At the same time, a new world view was developing and was already held by a minority of English migrants, primarily Puritans and some of the wealthier Anglican settlers. These people had come to see time as linear, and believed its proper use could lead to a better future. Time and place were viewed as independent variables and, along with causality, were seen as amenable to rational understanding and rational control.[21]

The values of most African migrants were close to those of the older English world view. In Africa time was also tied to daily work and to the yearly agricultural cycle. It could not be speeded up, or regarded independently. Work was generally the burden of the lower status members of society, including free women and slaves of both sexes, and success brought freedom from labour. Traditions were regarded as permanent (the dead were assumed to continue them in afterlife) and change was not generally welcomed. Causality was assumed to be arational: it was believed that spirit power, wielded by live practitioners, spirits or gods, could bring about virtually anything, including death. Individuals who knew how to contact or manipulate this power were of great importance.[22]

As a result of these basic similarities, African attitudes towards time and work melded with and supported old white ways; African attitudes to magic and arational causality deeply affected whites, again melding with and supporting a quasi-medieval world view. In this context the newer rationalism, in so far as it had come into the South, lost ground and Southerners by and large continued the earlier ethic. At the same time, however, that same ethic, while continuing, was also subtly Africanised. Southerners themselves generally did not recognise the nature of the process that was under way in their homes and workplaces.

George Washington was one of the apparently small number conscious of this culture change, and disturbed by it. Time and again he bemoaned the fact that whites and blacks were in too much contact. He noted that his English overseer, in common with others, 'finding it a little troublesome to instruct the Negroes, and to compel them to practice of *his* modes, he slided into theirs'.[23] Much of Washington's time at home was spent trying to impose his concept of time and work on both his white and black workers, but he recognised that in this he failed.

While changes occurred daily and slowly at work and at home, perhaps the most overt interaction, and the deepest interpenetration of values, took place in the First Great Awakening and in the Southern churches that grew out of it.[24] In the South, revivals began where blacks and whites had been in intimate work and family contact. Poor whites, working and living under similar conditions, and in close contact with blacks, were also often in a similar spiritual state. The poor whites' situation was certainly not the same as the blacks', but they too had generally migrated under duress, had suffered abject poverty, unfree condition, and a high death rate, and they too experienced an extreme lack of social and spiritual nurturance. These were the plebian masses, who rarely visited the churches, and whose spiritual life was enriched by folk belief far more than by the latitudinarian rationalism that influenced some of the elite. However, their world view was becoming incoherent, and the old rituals that had marked birth, marriage and death with drama were no longer potent and were in fact being rapidly abandoned. Children were 'often neglected to be baptised', and they were not generally sent to catechism classes, when these were held. Worship was widely disregarded. Small numbers took the sacrament, which was administered no more than five times a year. Christian marriage practices were often not followed, and death and interment were handled on an *ad hoc* basis with most people being buried in orchards or near houses, and not in hallowed burial grounds. The people were 'sublimely ignorant in the very principles of Religion, and very debauch't in Morals', wrote the Rev. John Lang in 1724.

> I have already with Terror observed some upon a death bed, others on a sick bed though requiring to have the Holy Sacrament of the Supper administer'd; So wofully ignorant, that upon examination and tryall they could not rehearse the Articles of our Christian Faith, nor the Lord's prayer and Commandments, nor give any solid accounts of the nature and use of the holy Sacrament. Others offer to come to the Lord's table on Christmas day, whom I discovered to live in incest as married persons: these are very trying instances and very deplorable blindnesses.[25]

Both blacks and whites responded emotionally and enthusiastically to the new call for commitment and change in lifestyle and values. In Virginia in particular, and in the South more generally, the Great Awakening had an effect on the society as a whole. Beginning in the 1740s, but becoming a mass movement in the last third of the century, 'middling' and poor people, both blacks and whites, took new responsibility for themselves, exerting self-control and a new community control by establishing new norms and policing new behaviour.[26]

In this process it was recognised that black attitudes towards spirit and black readiness and ability to enter ecstatic states played an important role in 'heating up' the atmosphere, helping whites to enter into the ecstasy that brought about 'new births'. 'Black countenances eagerly attentive to every word they heard and some of them washed with tears' played an important role in Samuel Davies' revival in Virginia in the 1740s, and in all the subsequent Southern revivals.[27] Blacks and whites were together in virtually every new Baptist and later Methodist church that grew out of the eighteenth-century excitements. In these churches black testimony, black singing and simply the black presence played a very significant role.[28]

The English missionary, Thomas Rankin, at a Methodist service in Petersburg, Virginia, in 1776 noted that, as usual 'The Chapel was full of white and black, and many were without that could not get in'. The service too was not unusual for this revival period: 'Such power descended that hundreds fell to the ground, and the house seemed to shake with the presence of God'.[29]

Blacks and whites were together in mixed churches for many decades. It was only towards the close of the eighteenth century and in the nineteenth that separation became important to both communities.[30] Blacks had become Christians in mixed churches; whites had become Baptists and Methodists at the same times and in these same mixed churches.

The very real interaction in these biracial institutions, possible because of previous shared life experiences and values, had deep and lasting effect on all parties. Black attitudes towards ecstasy, rebirth, and death deeply influenced whites. In these areas, Afro-Americans did not simply reinforce earlier white tendencies, but expanded white understandings and introduced new perceptions and values. Ecstatic spirit travels, certainly known to Englishmen, but not common, now became a common form of spiritual exercise. Africans provided role models and practical guides for this form of experience. Their joy in arousal and freedom of expression were of great significance. Rankin met with both at White's Chapel, Virginia, 1776:

I preached from Ezekiel's vision of the dry bones: And there was a great shaking. I was obliged to stop again and again, and beg of the people to compose themselves. But they could not: some on their knees, and some on their faces, were crying mightily to God all the time I was preaching. Hundreds of Negroes were among them, with the tears streaming down their faces.[31]

Whites recorded memories of crucial interactions with blacks. Anne Randolph Page, mistress of some 200 slaves, was brought to a spiritual rebirth (c. 1800) through contact with 'an old blind negro woman ... who was a dear child of God.... I owe her, under God, much of my religious joy in after-years'. Page went to the black quarter to share in black ecstasy, turning away from the white social rounds which were her duty: 'I often visited her in her cottage; and witnessed the evidences of her triumphant faith. She was a living example of Christ formed in the soul, the hope of glory'.[32]

African attitudes to death – their expectation of family reunification and life after death – also deeply influenced whites, who widely expressed a new view of the afterlife after the Great Awakenings. The proper attitude of the dying person became one of joy, while the afterlife was pictured as a heavenly home where, much in African fashion, family and clan life continued. In the 1760s, for example, slave owner Rev. James Maury wrote that his mother had 'made a most glorious end! Which God grant we may all have the happiness to make whenever we shall be called upon!' Maury expressed his hope to join her in the heavenly Jerusalem 'where alone in fullness of joys and pleasures for evermore'.[33]

White Southerners began to enter ecstatic states as funerals, as well as at revivals, and African symbols and quasi-African patterns of celebration were found in white cemeteries.[34] In a popular Methodist hymn whites sang:

I hope to praise him when I die
And shout salvation as I fly.

The shout, involving ecstatic body movement as well as vocalisation, had come into the white tradition from the black experience. It was *the* way to get 'happy' or 'high'. Blacks sang:

I wonder where's my dear mother
She's been gone so long
I think I hear her shouting
Around the Throne of God.[35]

Overall, African perceptions and values permeated the white world view, reinforcing some old aspects and introducing some very new ones. Work was slowed in pace, time and place hallowed, magic workers respected, clan ties reinforced, and heaven seen as home.

Black influence was very pervasive, and its parameters can only be suggested here. For example, as blacks did most of the building, an African aesthetic and African techniques of home building may well have deeply affected whites. (Most Africans, and most eighteenth-century Southerners, built their small, simple homes of uniform and light construction material, which was a radical departure from English and New England building methods.) As is well known, blacks often told children and adults stories and both their language and their values were transmitted. Blacks expected whites to think of family and clan as they did, and as they often preserved and passed on white family history, their values permeated white values.[36]

Through family, work and church contact, in daily living and in special celebrations, blacks and whites forged a new Anglo-African culture-pool, from which they took values of the other. In the greater racial separation of the nineteenth century, brought about in part due to upper-class fear of lower-class white and black interaction (and potential action), both groups lost contact with their pasts. The whites became ashamed of their formal interactions with blacks and felt that separation in the churches exhibited their superiority, while the blacks viewed separation as helping them to maintain an area of self-control. Notwithstanding these changes, the eighteenth century had witnessed a racial closeness and interaction that had left an African impress on Southern perceptions and values, and both Southern whites and Southern blacks were heirs to a new cultural mix, with ties to medieval Europe and Africa.

Notes

1 Frazier (1964), p. 82. For an excellent survey of the new scholarship, see Wood (1978).
2 An excellent presentation of the latest research on and evaluation of early slavery can be found in Kulikoff (1986). For black culture, see Ch. 9.
3 Levine (1977), p. 80.
4 Isaac (1982), p. 407 note 16.
5 Genovese (1969a); *ibid.* (1975).
6 See Vlach (1978); Wood (1974).
7 Herskovitz (1966); Nash (1974); Berlin (1980); see also Mintz and Price (1976).

8 Sobel (forthcoming).
9 Curtin (1969); Klein (1978).
10 Wood (1974), pp. 131–66; Jordan (1968), p. 103.
11 Lovejoy (1983), pp. 8–11.
12 Galenson (1981), pp. 131–3, 138–9, 166, 174.
13 Wood (1974), p. 160; Kulikoff (1986), Ch. 10.
14 Pinchbeck (1926), p. 40; 'Number and occupation of certain slave owners in Richmond in 1782' compiled from *Heads of Families, First Census of the United States 1790*, State Enumeration of Virginia, 1782 to 1785, Washington, DC, 1908, pp 57, 94–6.
15 Carter (1965), 17 June 1773, p. 758. See also pp. 769, 776, 781, 793, 797, 811, 946, and *ibid.* (1976).
16 Byrd (1941); *ibid.* (1958); *ibid.* (1942); Washington (1976–79); Fithian (1943); Fairfax (1903–4); Blodget (1946).
17 Williams (1978).
18 Watson (1861), p. 300.
19 Williamson (1980).
20 Thomas (1971); Hill (1982).
21 Hill (1963); Wrightson and Levine (1979).
22 Forde (1963); Booth (1975); Fernandez (1982).
23 George Washington to William Pearce, 25 Jan 1795, in Fitzpatrick (1931), vol. 34, p. 103.
24 Sobel (1979); Butler (1980).
25 Perry (1969), vol. I, 'Virginia', pp. 270–3, 299, 305, 346–8.
26 On the early conditions of southern whites, see Morgan (1975) and Main (1982).
27 Davies (1761), pp 10, 12, 28, 41.
28 See the bibliography of extant 'Eighteenth-Century Virginia Baptist Maunuscript Church Books' compiled by Gardner (1980), pp. 910–15.
29 Thomas Rankin in Asbury (1958), vol. I, 30 June and 1 July I, 1776, pp. 221–2; 7 July 1776, p. 222.
30 Mathews (1977).
31 Rankin in Asbury (1958), vol. I, 30 June, 1 July I and 7 July 1776, pp. 221–2; Walker (1972); Johnson (1969).
32 Andrews (1844), pp. 10, 17–19, 24, 86, 88.
33 James Maury in Fontaine (1973), pp 398–9. See Lewis (1983); Bruce (1978).
34 Sobel (forthcoming), Part Three.
35 Jackson (1943), p. 57; Work (1940), pp. 61–6.
36 These issues are discussed at length in Sobel (forthcoming). See McDaniel (1982).

Further reading

Of the works referenced in the notes above, the following would be most recommended: Rhys (1982); Kulikoff (1986); Levine (1982); Mintz and Price (1976); Sobel (forthcoming).

Thirteen

Slave Trading and the Mentalities of Masters and Slaves in Ante-Bellum America

Michael Tadman

At one level, this study is concerned with the practical character of the slave trade between the states of the Old South, that is, with the scale of that traffic, the extent of the forcible separations it produced, and with the circumstances which led masters to sell to the trader (or, as contemporaries called him, the 'negro speculator'). At another level, however, examination of the structure of the trade raises issues fundamental to the whole character of slavery. By examining slave holders' attitudes towards selling and slave reactions to sale and separation, the overall purpose of the paper is to suggest, for the ante-bellum period, a general theory of master and slave mentalities and interrelationships. Indeed, the family and separations seem to be such central reference points that any general model of ante-bellum slavery must either pay close attention to these issues or risk serious error. [1]

The traffic with which we shall be concerned was internal, and from the late eighteenth century (and especially from the closure of the African slave trade in 1807) carried large numbers of slaves from the older established areas to the newer, rapidly expanding plantation regions further west and south. For most of the ante-bellum period the trade's exporting base was Maryland, Virginia, Kentucky, Tennessee, and the Carolinas, while the ever-expanding importing region would include Georgia, Alabama, Florida, Arkansas, Louisiana, and Texas. In minor part, speculators relied upon a highly specialised coastal shipping between New Orleans and a cluster of centres around the Chesapeake (especially Alexandria, Baltimore, and Richmond), but 'coffles' of slaves driven overland comprised the vast bulk of the 'negro business' – the gangs (usually about thirty or forty slaves in each) trekking some hundreds of miles to the Lower South, where they would be offered at plantations and hamlets throughout the slavemonger's adopted territory.

For the abolitionists, such a traffic represented, in naked form, the whole evil tendency of the slave system and, at the same time, was seen as providing the crucial pivot of the slave economy. In what they considered to be the exhausted land of the Upper South, slave owners, unable to make mere agriculture pay, were said to have resorted to stud farming and slave breeding for the Lower South market. As a result, a vast and sordid interregional trade was said to have developed, with forcible family separations being just one of its routine and dehumanising aspects. For the pro-slavery interest, the existence of the trade, of course, posed extremely awkward problems; but the propaganda response was vigorous. The trade, they insisted, was numerically a very minor affair. With speculators, they maintained, shunned like the plague by decent Southerners, the trader made what purchases he could, either from a few unscrupulous owners (usually written off as Yankies who had come south), or at 'involuntary sales'. These latter sales were seen as occurring perhaps at the death of a master (when estates were divided), or at sheriff's and other debt sales (where the law forced a selling off of assets). But in such circumstances, it was argued, the southern community rarely failed to rally round to keep families together and, in all but the most difficult of cases, frustrated the 'oily speculator'.

The trade and the issues it raises were not only crucial to contemporaries in the ante-bellum debate on slavery, but, as we have already suggested, have major implications for the modern debate on slave and master's attitudes. Indeed, by examining the trade, this study aims to provide a basis for commenting upon the key theories of master-slave accommodation which, with very different emphases, both Fogel and Engerman and Genovese have proposed. [2] At the heart of Fogel and Engerman's *Time on the Cross* is the claim that masters sponsored and protected the slave family and in so doing gave them a stake in the system. The slaves became diligent and highly productive workers and, as a result of their family base and of positive incentives offered by masters, were willing participants in the economic triumph of the South's capitalistic slave system. In such an accommodation between masters and slaves an extensive slave trade, with widespread family separations, could have no part.

In contrast to the model proposed in *Time on the Cross*, that of Genovese rests, not on the idea of slavery as a highly efficient and capitalistic operation, but rather on its being an inefficient pre-capitalist or seigneural system. Essentially, the master's power and 'hegemonic' control were achieved through a process of compromise over rights and privileges. Masters, in exchange for the enjoyment of labour servce, offered their slaves what they saw as 'direction and protection', together with certain 'privileges' (these including compromises on rates of work and on punishments). For their part, Genovese maintains, the slaves interpreted their privileges as 'rights', and in so doing evolved the notion (running counter to slavery) that these entitlements amounted to full human rights. Such conflicts over rights and privileges, he argues, represented important class struggles; but, he continues, what was crucial was that they were pressures *within* the system and not against it. Since planters had succeeded in locating the terrain on which conflicts would be fought out, and since that territory did not threaten the slave system, planter 'hegemony' had been achieved. Masters and slaves accommodated each other through a 'web of paternalism', and the system was perpetuated.

The study will reappraise the accommodation theories of Fogel and Engerman and Genovese and, since I find very strong evidence pointing not only towards a great volume of slave trading and forcible family separations but also towards the slave owners' enthusiastic involvement in those processes, my paper will suggest that the above models are not the most useful way to view ante-bellum slavery. Instead, an interpretation which suggests the predominance of more jarring and distanced relationships between masters and slaves will be proposed. It will be argued that accommodation was important, but was much more limited than in the models of Fogel and Engerman and Genovese, and that the worlds of master and slave were far more segregated from each other than those theories suggest. Beyond that, evidence on the peculiarities of the slave trade to Louisiana's sugar region will be used to help set master-slave relationships of the ante-bellum period into a wider comparative context.

I

In considering the role which the domestic slave trade played in the Old South we must begin by establishing the extent of that traffic. Only in the context of a reliable estimate of the trade's volume will it be useful to consider wider issues such as the motives for selling to the speculator, the scale of resultant family separations, and the impact of such separations on slaves' mentalities. The purpose in looking initally at the magnitude of the trade is not to establish that there was in the ante-bellum period a vast interregional movement of slaves – that much has been established by historians and is clear from the basic statistics of huge population growth in the importing area – but rather to disaggregate the overall movement into its two component parts, slave trading on the one hand and planter migrations on the other. These latter migrations resulted not from sales but, typically, from the decision of a slave owner to leave his plantation in the Upper South and, taking his established gang of slaves, to try his luck on the newer and richer lands of the Lower South.

Quite recently Fogel and Engerman, as part of their attempt to establish the existence of a master-sponsored slave family, proposed an estimate of the trade, with the conclusion that not more than 16 per cent of all interregional slave movements were attributable to trading, the huge remainder being accounted for by planter migrations. Their estimate turned upon an analysis of sex ratios. Having examined documents concerning the coastal trade to New Orleans, they found in that traffic a male/female ratio of sixty to forty and concluded that the trade as a whole was similarly male dominated. Since, using evidence derived from the census, they quite correctly calculated that the total interregional slave movement (combining trading and migrations) was only about 51 per cent male, the conclusion that the trade could have contributed very little to the overall movement seemed to follow. An extensive sampling of speculators' business records (documents specifying the sex of some three thousand slaves, and representing all such records which have been found in research at major American archives) reveals the problem with Fogel and Engerman's assumption (see Table 1).[3] This evidence clearly indicates that, in the interregional slave trade, it was only the New Orleans branch which was sex selective.

Since the traffic to all other markets was evenly balanced between males and females, the method of Fogel and Engerman, in fact, isolates only the extent of the New Orleans trade and provides no basis for a satisfactory estimate of the trade as a whole. From more detailed calculations of importation patterns into Louisiana and from the evidence of traders who specialised in supplying that state, it is clear, moreover, that it was only the sugar section within the state which concentrated upon male importation (the proportion of male

Table 1 Slave trading records documenting the sex ratio of the domestic slave trade†

Record Type	Trader	Sex ratio information available for period	Route traded	Numbers of slaves traded			
				Male	Female	Children of un-known age	Sex not clearly specified
S	Rives, F.E.	1817–19	VA-MS	28	25		3
S	Fields, O.	1822–28	NC-SC	18	25	6	4
S	Glen, T.	1830–37	NC-AL	221	190		12
P	Glen, T. (additional)	1830–40	NC-AL	59	66		7
S	Totten, J.S.	1832–36	NC-AL	81	87		5
S	Mitchell J.A.	1834–35	VA-AL	28	21		1
S	Whitehead, F.L.	1835–36	VA-MS	39	30		4
P	Badgett, H.	1837–50	NC-GA/AL	22	35	1	
P	Long, W.	1836–49	NC-MS	57	35	5	'3
S	Pitman, J.W.	1835	VA-LS	3	7		
S	Templeman, H.N.	1846–47	VA-LS	40	57	7	3
S	Templeman & Goodwin	1849–51	VA-GA	45	48	3	2
S	Hughes & Downing	1843–44	KY-MS	7	6		

S	Walker, A. & A.T.	1851–61	NC-AL	28	61	16	2
P	Ferguson, E.W.	1855–59	NC-LS	14	21		
S	Omohundro, S. & R.F.	1857–62	VA-LS	150	178	32	
C	SC Equity	1851–63	SC-LS	234	225	11	10
C	Charleston Probate	1850–59	SC-LS	104	132	21	144
*S	White, J.R.	1846–60	MO-LS	217	244	22	
	Totals			1,395	1,493	124	200

Notes:

† This excludes the trade to Louisiana's predominantly sugar-producing parishes.

C Purchases from Equity and probate sales by documented traders.

S Information derived from traders' accounts indicating transportation from the Upper South and sale in the Lower South.

P Information derived from traders' purchasing records. (The traders concerned were active in the long-distance trade and almost certainly resold these slaves in the Lower South.)

*S This account book includes sales (57% of them being males) to Louisiana's 13 leading sugar parishes, but these latter sales are excluded from the entry in the above table.

LS Lower South. Otherwise 'Route Traded' gives standard state abbreviations as follows: VA (Virginia), MS (Mississippi), NC (North Carolina), SC (South Carolina), AL (Alabama), GA (Georgia), KY (Kentucky), MO (Missouri).

importations in that region running at about 70 per cent). Such a specialised demand produced in the Chesapeake area specialist dealers who selected 'good shipping negroes for the Orleans market'. As traders' records abundantly demonstrate, the Louisiana sugar region had, within the ante-bellum South, a unique insistence that the great bulk of its importations should be prime adult males, with the balance being, not of children, but almost exclusively of 'sturdy young single women'.

The method of Fogel and Engerman, then, while indirectly leading to interesting insights into Louisiana's sugar region (and indeed into the special demographic characteristics of sugar regions in the Americas generally), did not provide a basis for estimating the trade as a whole. Evidence from the traders themselves makes it plain, however, that while the interregional traffic was not usually sex selective it was consistently *age selective*. Traders' bills of sale, account books, letters, and advertisements demonstrate a strong and unmistakable concentration on slaves of around ten to thirty-five years (and within that a further preference for those of about fifteen to twenty-five years of age). Against this, it seems to be quite clear that planter migrations were not sex selective. Evidence for this comes not just from migrants' letters and travellers' accounts, but from samples of manifests describing coastal movements of slaves. Migrations, overall, carried a representative cross-section of the whole Upper South slave population, the young children and aged sometimes making the difficult journey in wagons while the rest usually travelled on foot.

Since it is clear that the age structure of planter migrations contrasted greatly with that of the trade, what is now needed is an age profile of the total movement of slaves. Such a profile will allow us to disaggregate that movement into its trading and migration components. Fortunately, a method which allows us to calculate the age structure of the total movement is available, this being the survival rate technique. Behind this method is the assumption that those (in our case slaves) of the same age and sex would, across the South as a whole, display the same percentage mortality (and therefore survival) rates. Thus, for example, if for the South as a whole, 90 per cent of male slaves aged ten to nineteen years in 1850 survived and were recorded in the census of 1860, the same 90 per cent survival rate would be expected across the South.[4] When we find, however, that in exporting states such as Maryland survival rates for this group (as recorded in census statistics) were as low as perhaps 40 per cent, and that in importing states such as Texas they approached 200 per cent, we can conclude that importation and exportation (in fact age-selective movements) had occurred.

From survival rate comparisons of the sort just indicated, we can in fact (for each age and sex cohort) estimate the numbers of importations and exportations occurring in a particular decade. And having found, for example, the numbers of children, of prime adults, and of aged slaves exported from the Upper South as a whole, we can then calculate (and eventually contrast) the percentage rates at which each age group was exported. To find these rates we need simply compare, for example, the numbers of prime adult males exported over the 1850s with the number of such slaves present in the exporting states at the start of that decade. The results of such calculations are very striking and show far higher percentages (as well as, of course, absolute numbers) of prime adults exported than of children, middle-aged, or older slaves. The pattern, in fact, corresponds closely to that which speculators' advertisements and business records establish for the trade, and contrasts very sharply with that of planter migrations.

Limitations of space preclude a detailed exposition of the evidence employed in the calculations here outlined, but Table 2 and Fig. 1 (for the 1820s) give some indication of the sort of procedures involved. The key element in disaggregating the trade from planter migration is the fact that migrations would have drawn at the *same percentage rate* (though not, of course, in the same absolute numbers) from *all* age groups. But, from Figure 1, we find that in the 1820s, while as many as about 14 per cent of prime adults were drawn from the exporting states, the percentage for slaves over forty-five years old in 1820 was only about three. Since planter migration would have drawn at the same percentage rate from all age groups, we can conclude that those migrations drew not more than some 47,000 slaves (or 3 per cent) from the exporting states' total 1820s population of more than 1,600,000. It follows, therefore, that, with an estimated total of some 150,000 interregional movements for the decade, not more than about 30 per cent of 1820s slave movements could have been produced by migration, with the huge remainder being the result of trading. Similar calculations are possible for the 1850s and again suggest that the trade accounted for some 60 to 70 per cent of all movements. Detailed calculations suggest, in fact, that the ratio between the trade

Table 2 Interregional slave transfers, 1820–29

	A	B	C	D	E	F	G	G
Age in 1820	0–13		14–25		26–44		45+	
Age in 1830	10–23		24–35		36–54		55+	
	Male	Female	Male	Female	Male	Female	Male	Female
1 1820 slave population of net exporting states	256,227	241,478	146,218	144,037	119,144	111,570	59,557	55,430
2 Southern slave survival Rate % for 1820s	0.911	0.952	0.921	0.924	0.728	0.735	0.550	0.602
3 Expected 1830 slave population of net exporting states	233,423	229,887	134,667	133,090	86,737	82,004	32,756	33,369
4 Actual 1830 slave population of net exporting states	198,701	195,415	116,264	116,738	80,479	76,207	31,259	31,870
5 Preliminary transfer totals	34,722	34,472	18,403	16,352	6,258	5,797	1,497	1,499
6 Final transfer totals	35,804	35,051	18,912	16,787	6,854	6,335	1,733	1,707

Sources and notes Statistics are derived from federal censuses.

Note (a)   The cumulative slave population total for the exporting states in 1820 was (combining line 1, columns A to H) 1,133,661, and the exporting states' 1830 total of slaves aged 0 to 9 was 461,444. For slaves aged 0 to 9 in 1830 the estimated exportation total was 30,994.

(b)   Final transfer totals add to the preliminary total those slaves who would have been exported in the 1820–29 period but who would have died before the census of 1830.

(c)   The estimated 1820s exportation total was (combining line 6, columns A to H) 123,184 slaves, plus 30,994 slaves aged 0 to 9 in 1830, making a *final total* of 154,178. This suggests an overall exportation *rate* of 9.48% for the decade.

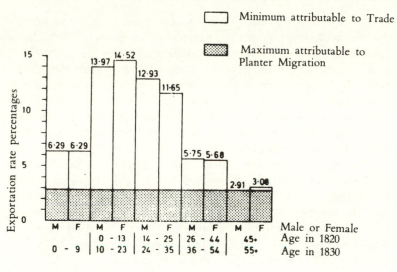

Source: Derived from federal censuses.

Figure 1   Structure of the total interregional slave movement, 1820–29

and migration was fairly constant and that in the first half of the ante-bellum period trading averaged 70,000 to 100,000 slaves per decade, rising to an average approaching 200,000 slaves per decade after 1830.

In order to test the above results, an entirely separate method of calculation was also adopted, and it revealed the same conclusion – that the trade accounted for the great bulk of all interregional slave movements. The second approach was to take a sample state, South Carolina, and to make a direct count of all traders found to be active in that state during a particular decade, the 1850s. Numbers of documented traders were then compared with estimates (derived from survival rate calculations) of total slave out-movements from the state. The head-count of traders stretched over all of South Carolina's twenty-nine counties, although in nine of those counties a key preliminary basis of evidence (local newspapers, which can be searched for traders' advertisements) was not extant. Clearly many traders were omitted in the analysis in counties where newspapers did not survive. Nevertheless, what emerged for the 1850s was that in a state exporting (by a combination of trading and migration) some

6,500 slaves per year, there were ninety-four conclusively documented trading firms operating exclusively or almost exclusively out of that state.[5] In addition, many more (sixty-three) probable trading firms were very strongly suggested, though not conclusively documented. The basic ratio of documented firms to annual slave exportations (one firm for every sixty-nine slaves) itself suggests that the trade would have accounted for a very high percentage of the total slave movement. But in some sections of the state where accidental bonuses of evidence survive, the case for a very intensively conducted slave trade, accounting for the huge majority of exportations, is overwhelming. This is especially so in the Sumter county area, an otherwise unremarkable section of the state. For that area, by the chance intervention of an abolitionist at the close of the Civil War, a huge supplement to the preliminary evidence of newspapers survives in the form of the Ziba Oakes slave trading papers. Detailed county evidence, state-wide South Carolina documentation, and data for the South as a whole, combine, therefore, to demonstrate a massively important traffic in slaves.

II

As we have seen, planters were, according to the pro-slavery tradition, supposed to sell to the trader only in circumstances of dire necessity. Speculators' records, however, suggest a dramatically different picture. From a sample of several thousand slaves documented in the bills of sale of slave traders, only about 5 per cent at most can have been purchased at probate or public sales for debt. With the huge remainder, instead of some public official conducting the transaction, the owner sold directly to the trader. A sample check suggests, moreover, that the financial status of the sellers was generally sound, for very few (if any) faced sheriffs' levies for debt in the several years before and after the transactions studied. Not only that but, as annual listings of South Carolina slaves show (the lists being made by the state authorities for tax purposes), years of high slave exportation from that sample state corresponded very closely with periods when there was not only especially high demand for slaves in the importing states, but when South Carolina itself (through its basic agriculture) would have been enjoying unusually high prosperity. Fogel and Engerman's calculations seem, in fact, to establish that the agriculture of the Upper South (as well as of the importing states) flourished in the ante-bellum period.

Intensive selling of slaves at periods of special agricultural prosperity, and selling at private transactions (rather than at public probate or debt sales), suggest for those sales an overwhelmingly speculative character – that is to say, one based not on necessity but on an urge to cash in on lucrative market circumstances.

Slave traders' records also reveal family separations on a huge scale. Fogel and Engerman employed New Orleans evidence and concluded that forcible separations were very rare indeed, not accounting for more than a few per cent of the interregional slave movement as a whole. Their method was to take as separations all instances where records indicated a mother and her offspring sold as a unit but without a father. We have already noted, however, that the New Orleans trade systematically under-represented both women and children, so that an unusually low proportion of mother and offspring units could be expected at that city. Moreover, Fogel and Engerman's method would have omitted husbands sold separately, children sold without parents, and wives sold without either offspring or spouse.

In order to arrive at a more reliable estimate of forcible separations, a broad sample of the trade as a whole (rather than just the New Orleans traffic) was taken by the present writer. This sample amounted to some 8,600 slaves and was arrived at simply by taking all available traders' records which described (with indications of ages) trading to areas other than southern Louisiana. The procedure then adopted was to record the units in which masters sold to traders (so that slave holders' rather than traders' actions were focused upon). Overall what emerged was that at least (and very probably more than) 43 per cent of all slaves traded experienced, as a direct result of sale to the trader, either separation from a spouse or, as a child, separation from both parents. More specifically, 7.1 per cent of all slaves sold to the trader were accounted for by mothers sold in mother and offspring units (and, since the sex ratio of the trade was balanced, a further 7.1 per cent should be added for husbands sold without wife and offspring). In addition, 9.3 per cent of all slaves were accounted for by children sold in mother and offspring units. Beyond this, 7.8 per cent of slaves traded were children under twelve years old and sold without either parent, and 12.1 per cent were children aged twelve to fourteen and sold without either parent. Detailed evidence suggests that the overall 43 per cent rate of forcible separation is indeed an underestimate, no account being taken for example of wives sold separately from children and husband.

The implications of these separation patterns will be considered later, but for the moment we should note that the sellers involved were very unlikely to have been a group of unrepresentative and particularly unscrupulous slave owners. Firstly, the sheer volume of the trade argues against this. But, more specifically, it is clear that southern states never, on moral grounds, introduced prohibitions against the trade. Those limited prohibitions which did occur sprang from such motives as repudiating debts to traders at times of occasional economic panics. From a detailed sample of traders' careers, it is very clear, moreover, that 'negro speculation' was never, or almost never, a hindrance to social advancement. Indeed, most reasonably successful traders were important and respected members of their community, being involved in various business ventures, and likely to enter politics and to serve in local charities and other associations. Perhaps even more telling is the fact that while, in the very extensive correspondence collections which are available across the South, traders complained of a great range of inconveniences in their business (especially trader competition in buying markets, and the problems of selling for cash or short credit in the Lower South), their letters recorded barely a hint of resistance to dealing or associating with them on the grounds of their being speculators in slaves.

III

While as we have seen, the New Orleans traffic was an atypical and unusually specialist branch of the South's interregional slave trade, its very atypicality leads to evidence which is significant for the wider discussion of slavery in the Americas as a whole. In particular, the Louisiana material helps to explain why North America displayed strongly positive rates of slave natural increase (around 25 per cent per decade in the nineteenth century), while the slaves of the West Indies and South America generally showed natural *decrease* or at best very low natural increase. The answer, as the Louisiana evidence suggests, is the sugar crop. Such a conclusion has, in a fairly tentative way, been drawn previously by Barry Higman, but Louisiana data helps both to assert this conclusion more boldly and to explain the interlinking of the factors concerned.[6]

As census-based calculations show, the crude slave increase rate for Louisiana in the 1850s was, despite being swollen by at least some 8,000 interregional importations in that decade, only 18.3 per cent (in contrast with the southern slave average of 23.4 per cent for that decade). When importations are subtracted, the real natural increase is shown as not more than (and was in fact probably far lower than) 7.6 per cent – a rate almost as low as that usually found among West Indian and South American slaves. In explaining the low natural increase of South America and the West Indian islands, a variety of factors (whose interrelationships are not usually made clear) is normally suggested – these including high sex ratios, climate, disease environment, harsh treatment, high percentages African, and the persistence of African child-rearing traditions. The Louisiana material, however, points to the key trigger factor – the very strong preference of sugar areas (because of the especially demanding work involved) for a more or less permanent male domination in the labour force. In the period of the African slave trade, all areas imported some 60 per cent males (that proportion being available from Africa). But the crucial difference within the African traffic was that the sugar-dominated areas of the West Indies and South America, not wanting their work force to return to a balanced sex ratio, imported male-dominated African cargoes far more intensively than did North America.

The male preference in sugar areas appeared strikingly in my evidence on the interregional trade to ante-bellum Louisiana, and that bias set up a series of adverse demographic circumstances. It meant, firstly, that relatively few females were available for child-bearing and, Louisiana evidence suggests, it also meant unusually high adult mortality rates as well as depressed fertility rates. Significantly, however, natural increase rates for ante-bellum Louisiana did not fall to the disastrous levels of the West Indies and South America – the principal reason being, it seems, that the males imported by the inter-regional trade were acclimatised Afro-Americans. In the sugar areas beyond North America, however, the factor of newly imported Africans, confronted with a new and therefore hostile disease environment, set up a devastating combination. Nevertheless, with Louisiana as with the West Indies and South America, it seems to have been the sugar crop and its deliberate preference for males which launched the adverse demographic syndrome. Such patterns would mean, in areas outside of North America, high percentages of young adult African males – and these circumstances would do much to explain the higher incidence of revolt in those areas than in North America.

IV

My main concern, however, has been with North America and, ultimately, the mentalities of her masters and slaves. What has emerged is, firstly, a pattern of speculation and deliberate separation of slave families which seems to make it difficult to sustain the view, advanced by Fogel and Engerman, that masters sponsored the slave family. Beyond that, the whole *Time on the Cross* model of a slave economy based on positive incentives, diligent workers, and the willing co-operation of slaves, would seem to be brought into question. Moreover, it seems hard, in the light of evidence on the trade, to argue as Genovese did that masters and slaves accommodated each other by a delicate set of compromises over rights and privileges. Since, as Genovese wrote, masters who separated husband from wife would have been hated by their slaves, and since, as he maintained, a withdrawal of rights and privileges would have 'threatened crisis for the whole system', a hegemonic model based on an organic system of compromises does not seem to be the best conceptual framework for the ante-bellum South. Furthermore, while speculative slave selling on a huge scale could perhaps be reconciled with a version of pre-capitalist and seigneural planter values, this profit-for-profit's sake approach to the sale of slaves suggests the possibility of a very different model – one of rather callous capitalism.

It would not be sensible, however, to lump all planter or all slave attitudes together as being essentially the same. What seems likely to have obtained, in fact, is a range of planter attitudes – and it might be useful to suggest within slave holder racism three rough general types. Firstly, we might suggest a genuinely benevolent group which conscientiously protected slave familes. A second type might represent those who, while generally pursuing a business-first, uncaring attitude to slaves, selected certain favoured individuals for special indulgence. Beyond that, we might suggest a third type, one pursuing undiluted business-first racism (and within that might appear a subgroup, probably a minority, which habitually engaged in gratuitious acts of violence and ill treatment towards slaves). The evidence of the trade suggests that we do not need merely to list such types, but that we can assume within the spectrum of planter racism, a strong skewing towards the second and third of our notional categories.

Slave attitudes and reactions would have been very much

influenced by such a range of slave-owner types. But we must set slave attitudes within the context of recent major studies (especially work by Gutman) which have very strongly indicated the basic strength of the North American slave family.[7] Gutman's discussion of such questions as slave-naming practices, exogamous marriage patterns, length of marriage, and the rate of black marriage registration in the decades following slavery, has presented very weighty evidence in support of a vigorous slave family – a family with strong awareness of and attachment to kin (as well as to 'fictive' non-kin connections), and with the marked dominance of two-parent households. Systematic 'slave breeding' seems to have been little more than an abolitionist propaganda myth – certainly specialist 'breeding farms' do not appear in traders' correspondence, and such hypothetical enterprises would surely have had to wait an unacceptably long period of years for their 'crop' to reach maturity. What the interregional traffic in slaves seems to have meant in immediate terms was, in the Upper South, a high chance of the separation of first marriages and of loss of children by sale. Nevertheless, the trade did not prevent the flourishing of a strongly family-based slave society.

But the trade and separations had wider implications. Given the great vigour of the slave's family sense, forcible separations would have been deeply resented. Indeed, it seems likely that they would have given slaves a vital yard-stick by which to judge, not only individual masters, but the whole of the system which affronted their basic family loyalties. Slaves, to be sure, would have made accommodations – over work loads, rest periods, and the like. At the same time, however, the evidence of family separations suggests that accommodations would have been severely restricted in scope: they seem likely to have been limited day-to-day adjustments to power, rather than being the basis of a 'Protestant work ethic' or a broad system of planter hegemony.

Slaves are likely to have been influenced partly by their family culture and partly by the attitudes of their masters. Thus, there would have been slaves (with genuinely benevolent masters, or who received special individual indulgences) who might have been bought-off or be otherwise docile (although, as Frederick Douglass suggested, 'good' treatment could sometimes lead masters into the problem of rising expectations among their slaves).[8] But the balance of masters' attitudes and the slave's strength of family suggest, for the substantial majority of slaves, a distanced and profoundly distrustful attitude towards masters. The worlds of masters and slaves would, it seems, while overlapping at points, have been largely separate and segregated. Segregations seems likely to have dated not from emancipation or 'Jim Crow' laws but from slavery itself. A model of segregation combined with limited accommodation to power seems more useful for the ante-bellum South than the all-embracing accommodation models recently advanced by some historians. During the seventeenth and eighteenth centuries, with a higher African-born presence, slave-master adjustments would have been somewhat different from those of the ante-bellum period – but the African presence does not suggest a less segregated pattern. Again, the experience of the ante-bellum South would have contrasted with that of the West Indies and South America where (because of the interconnections of crop and demography) a high African presence would have been a central feature – that presence tending to produce, on a wider scale than in North America, direct revolt by slaves.

Notes

1 In this article limitations of space do not permit a full elaboration of evidence and method. Detailed evidence on the extent of the trade does, however, appear in Tadman (1979). On this and other issues, see also Tadman (1977), and ibid. (forthcoming).

2 Fogel and Engerman (1974); Genovese (1975); and also Genovese and Genovese (1983).

3 The following slave traders' papers and accounts (many of which constitute rich sources of information on a whole range of aspects of the trade) were used: the papers of F. E. Rives, O. Fields, J. A. Mitchell, F. L. Whitehead, T. Glen (and also on Glen, the Jarret-Puryear Papers), all in the Duke University Library; the papers of J. S. Totten, H. Badgett, W. Long, and E. W. Ferguson (all the North Carolina's State Archives); J. W. Pittman Papers (Library of Congress); H. N. Templeman Account Book (New York Public Library); Templeman and Goodwin Account book and A. and A. T., Walker Account Book (Southern Historical Collection); S. and R. F. Omohundro Slaves Sales Book (Virginia University Library); and the J. R. White Account Book, Chinn Collection (Missouri Historical Society). Also used are the Sales Books (1851–67) of James Tupper, Master in Equity for Charleston District, and the Book of Inventories, Appraisals, and Sales (1850–59) for Charleston District (South Carolina Archives); and for Hughes and Downing see J. W. Coleman 'Lexington Slave Dealers and their Southern Trade,' *Filsom Club Historical Quarterly*, **22**, (1938), pp. 1–23.

4 The only real exception seems to be in the sugar area of Louisiana where, as we shall see, mortality rates seem to have been higher. This 'disappearance' of slaves in Louisiana will, however, only have a minor effect on our calculations – that effect being, not to exaggerate the volume of the trade, but rather to give our estimate of the relative contribution of trading a downward bias.

5 With almost all of the ninety-four documented firms, evidence derived from newspaper advertisements was supplemented by other sources (manuscript court records, census enumerations, local histories, and other material). Where evidence was drawn exclusively from newspapers, the style of the advertisements concerned was so similar to that of known traders (long-running advertisements, numbers of slaves wanted, ages, insistence that cash would be paid), and so dissimilar to that for other buyers (small numbers, mixed ages, payment on credit), that traders can confidently be assumed.

6 See Higman (1976); and *ibid*. (1984).

7 See especially Gutman (1976).

8 See Douglass (1965), pp. 263–4.

Further reading

The works already cited in the footnotes by Fogel and Engerman, Genovese, and Gutman are of central importance. In addition, the following are suggested; Bancroft (1931); Levine (1977); David *et al*. (1976); Sutch (1975); Stephenson (1938); Stowe (1852); *ibid*. (1853); Andrews (1836); Weld (1839); Rawick (1972).

Fourteen

Runaway Slaves in Nineteenth-Century Barbados

Gad Heuman

I

Runaway slaves in nineteenth-century Barbados were a significant aspect of the slave society. Little research has thus far been done on runaways in Barbados, in part because it is surprising that slaves managed to run away at all. Barbadian slaves did not have the possibilities of *grand marronage* which Richard Price, Silvia de Groot, and others had documented for Jamaica and Surinam.[1] By the nineteenth century, there was no scope for the establishment of communities of runaways. Barbados was a relatively small and settled colony; the forests and caves which may have helped earlier generations of slaves to escape no longer existed. In addition, the proportionately high ratio of whites to blacks which characterised Barbados must have made running away a distinctly difficult enterprise.

Yet the slave advertisements in the Barbadian press indicate that running away was hardly uncommon. It is impossible to quantify precisely the numbers of such slaves; but scarcely an issue of a Barbadian newspaper in the first two decades of the nineteenth century is without an advertisement for a runaway slave or a report of a slave being discovered or lodged in gaol.

Whatever their numbers, Barbadian runaways did not generally pose a threat to the slave system. Yet running away was a form of resistance to their enslavement. At the very least, it was a denial of labour to a particular master. At the other extreme, running away was an attempt to escape the system altogether. We therefore need to know about runaways – who they were, where they went, and who harboured them. But the evidence on running away is not just important in describing individuals; it is also suggestive about the nature of slavery in Barbados during this period. This paper will seek to address both points: the runaways themselves and some of the wider issues which they raise.

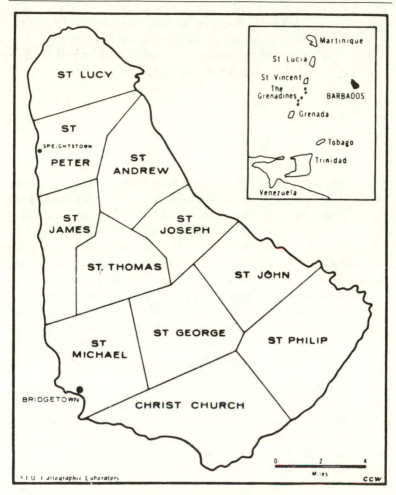

BARBADOS: PARISH BOUNDARIES
Kindly supplied by Jerome S. Handler

II

The statistical evidence on runaways was collected from advertisements in the Barbadian press at roughly five-year intervals from 1805
to 1830. As certain runs of newspapers were unavailable in the
Barbados Archives, the years included in the survey were 1805, 1810,
1815, 1819, 1824 and 1830. Two newspapers, *The Barbados Mercury and
Bridgetown Gazette* and *The Barbadian*, were the sources of the

advertisements. Where it was possible, the press was also examined for other years during this period for general information on the runaways. The statistical material was coded and run through a computer, using the program SPSS.[2]

There are obvious hazards in using data of this kind. The information is often sketchy. It is usually possible to ascertain the name, the sex, and the date first advertised of any slave. Colour, country of birth, occupation, and age are to varying degrees less available. For the years after 1817, it was possible to examine the Slave Registers for additional data, especially for the slaves' occupation, colour, and age.[3] But this only added significant material for 1819. The most revealing information in the advertisements was often the description of the slaves rather than their age or sex; in many cases, however, there were no such data at all.

Other problems also arose with the material. In some cases, the country of birth was cited, especially when the slave was African. When this information was not cited, it was assumed that the slave was Barbadian. The evidence of origin in the Slave Registers reinforced this supposition. A more insoluble problem concerns the length of absence of any slave. All that is generally known is the elapsed time of the advertisements, although in some cases, the owner indicated the period the slave had already been away before the advertisement appeared in the press. The time that advertised slaves were away is therefore seriously understated, although the data do provide an indication of this important variable. As in the case of the Jamaican material, slaves who were caught had rarely been sought in advertisements, thus making it impossible to make use of this information to ascertain length of absence.[4] It is also likely that owners would have been more eager to get back their most valuable slaves; as a result, the sample includes more skilled and elite slaves than in the general population of runaways.

It could be argued that the descriptive material in the advertisements is itself not very reliable. In many cases, owners were guessing where their runaway slaves might be. Information must also have come from other slaves, some of whom may have sought to mislead their masters. Yet, as Michael Mullin has suggested, this data was unbiased; it was not intended for use by propagandists, let alone historians. With all its faults, the evidence from slave advertisements may therefore be 'more appropriate for the study of a people who could not or were not inclined to write things down'.[5]

III

The sample consisted of 368 slaves, a large proportion of whom were male (see Table 1).[6] Since the sex ratio of the Barbadian slave population had become balanced by the early nineteenth century, it is clear that males were disproportionately represented among the cohort of runaways. Similarly, creoles (who were slaves born on the island) made up the overwhelming majority of runaways. For those slaves for whom there are data on origins, over 90 per cent were creole while about 9 per cent were African. These figures are not very different from the proportions of creoles and Africans in the slave population generally in 1817; if anything, the proportion of African runaways is slightly larger than in the general population (see Table 1).

Table 1   Runaways in the slave population

	(%) Runaways	(%) Total slave population
Sex		
Males	63.5	45.6
Females	36.5	54.4
Nation		
African	9.2	7.1
Creole	90.8	92.9
Colour		
Black	46.8	85.1
Coloured	53.2	14.9
Population	360	77,493

Sources: B.W. Higman, *Slave Populations of the British Caribbean, 1807–1834* (Baltimore, 1984), pp. 413, 116; sample survey.

Most of the runaways were relatively young, if young is defined to include those under thirty years of age. Nearly three–quarters of all runaways were in this age range. When the age ranges were broken down by sex, it was found that male and female runaways were represented roughly in proportion to their respective percentages in the overall sample of runaways.

Not surprisingly, the percentage of coloured runaways was high:[7] 53 per cent of slaves for whom there is such evidence were of mixed colour while 47 per cent were black (see Table 1). Since the percentage of brown slaves in the Barbadian slave population was about 15 per cent the large proportion of coloured runaways is immediately evident.[8]

The data for Jamaica provide an interesting contrast with some of these figures. While the male/female ratios in the Jamaican case are roughly similar to those of Barbados, the origins of the runaway slaves in the two colonies differ widely. Pat Bishop calculated that nearly 70 per cent of runaways in Jamaica had been born in Africa. Allowing for the longer time span of her study and the greater proportion of Africans in the Jamaican slave population, the evidence nonetheless suggests a very different origins for runaways in Jamaica and Barbados.[9]

Owners were often very clear about the type of slaves who escaped. They were generally creoles or behaved like creoles. For instance, Chloe was an African woman who had gone out to sell some glassware one day but had not been heard of since. Her owner, E. S. Bascom, could think of no reason for her disappearance; moreover, he noted that 'by her appearance and speech, she may be taken for a Barbadian'. Many slaves sought to pass as free people; this meant that they could usually act the part. Words like 'plausible' and 'artful' appear quite frequently in the advertisements to describe such slaves. Thomas 'is a very artful fellow, and may undertake to pass himself as a free man'.[10] The owner of the slave, Hamlet, put it another way: Hamlet 'has a [good] deal to say for himself, [and] may easily pass for a free man'. These were generally highly assimilated and often skilled slaves who could merge into the black and brown free community.

Skilled slaves were far more likely to escape. An analysis of 92 occupations listed in the advertisements reveals that the overwhelming number were skilled or semi-skilled. Just over 20 per cent were carpenters, 12 per cent sold goods of one kind or another, and nearly 9 per cent were tailors or domestic slaves. Other occupations represented in significant proportions included shoemakers, masons, and sailors; there were also smaller proportions of a wide range of other skilled workers. On the other hand, field slaves formed less than 5 per cent of this occupational cohort. The slave elite – and particularly the artisan elite – were therefore heavily represented in the occupations of the runaways, far more than their proportion of the total slave population.

A breakdown of the sex of the runaways for whom there are data on occupations is quite revealing. The only categories cited for female occupations were hucksters, house servants, and field slaves. Approximately three-quarters of those runaways who sold goods were women while just over 60 per cent of house servants were females. Only one-quarter of the runaway field slaves were females. In every other occupational category – most of which were skilled – no women were listed at all. The dominance of male runaways in the skilled occupations and in the slave elite reinforces what is known about the respective position of men and women in Caribbean slave society.

The colour of these slaves is also interesting. All of the field slaves were black as were three-quarters of the domestics. Women whose occupations are known were more likely to be black than brown. By virtue of their colour and their occupations, women generally would have had a more difficult time merging into the free community. The exception to this was runaway hucksters, nearly 70 per cent of whom were coloured.

As expected, most skilled runaways were coloureds: there were usually two skilled coloureds to each one skilled black. This was the case for carpenters, cooks, masons and tailors. Porters and fishermen violated this rule, as both categories included only blacks. Nearly all the runaway slaves for whom occupations were known were creoles; almost 95 per cent were in this category.

But where did the runaways go? In many cases, the owners did not know, but in a large number of instances, they were able to be quite specific about their slaves' possible destinations. One of the obvious places was a town, especially Bridgetown or Speightstown. For skilled slaves, towns probably offered greater possibilities of employment. The relatively large free black and brown communities there must have made it easier for a runaway to pass as a free person. Of those runaways whose destinations are known, more than a quarter of them were said to be in a town.

What is perhaps surprising is that a similar proportion – over 25 per cent of the runaways – found refuge in the country, presumably on other plantations. Roughly 6 per cent of runaways were either abroad or on a ship and a similar percentage were attempting to pass as free, most probably in a town. Owners knew nothing about the destination of another quarter of their slaves, and the remaining 8 per cent were thought to be employed either in a town or in the country.

These categories clearly overlap, and many slaves were in more than one grouping. The figures suggest that running away to the country was a more significant destination than might have been expected.

It is also interesting to examine the destinations of slaves by sex. Table 2 demonstrates that more female runaways went to the country than to the town, while males favoured the towns. This correlates with earlier data about the occupations and colour of female and male runaways. Since the women were more likely to be in less skilled occupations than the men, female runaways seem to have escaped more frequently to the country where they may have had kin to harbour them. On the other hand, skilled males more often attempted to blend into the free urban community, looking for employment and trying to pass as free. Male runaways also sought to get abroad: 90 per cent of this cohort were male.

Table 2   Destination of runaways by sex

		Town	Country	Pass as free	Abroad
M	No.	68	55	17	10
	%	71.6	60.4	77.3	90.9
F	No.	27	36	5	1
	%	28.4	39.6	22.7	9.1

Source: Sample survey.

There are tantalising suggestions about slaves who fled abroad and who may have formed an earlier generation of 'boat-people'. In 1805, a slave was picked up in a boat by a Mr Todd near St Vincent. Since the runaway claimed to have a Barbadian master, Todd, who was from St. Vincent, was prepared to have the slave returned on proof of ownership. Fourteen years later, a seaman slave named James Cuttery absconded from a mail boat. He stole a smaller boat, a bucket, and a sail and probably also headed for St Vincent. Cuttery had a good reason for getting to St Vincent; he had formerly lived there. As the island was to the windward of Barbados, it is quite plausible that other slaves sought to escape in the same way.[11]

St. Vincent was not the only foreign destination of Barbadian runaways. Nancy Efey was the mother of two mulatto children and perhaps therefore had a better chance of obtaining 'spurious papers'. Her owner reported that Nancy intended to go to Demerara, where she had a sister. Another owner thought that her slave, Jane Frances, would leave Barbados, but did not make any specific suggestions about where she might go. Jane 'endeavours to pass as a free woman, and, in all probability, will wish to quit the Island. All masters and owners of vessels are hereby cautioned not to take her off the Country, and other persons from harbouring or employing her'.[12]

This was a frequent warning, but it is unclear what effect it had. Jacob was a well-known slave who worked on board English ships, and whose professional name was Samson. 'He went down the river on the 15th inst. on board the ship FAIRY, Capt. Francis, and has not since been heard of'.[13] Another slave, identified in the Slave Registers as John Maycock, was a 15-year-old butler. He seems to have 'imposed himself on the master of either the ship Constantine or Tiger, as a free man ... [and] quitted the island'.[14] Ships' captains may have found it in their interest to have runaways on board. Runaways were potential extra hands, they could be sold at another port, or they could possibly pay for their passage. The constant warnings about the complicity of captains not only suggest that this was one of the possible escape routes for runaways but also that it was of considerable concern to Barbadian slave holders.

Whether they fled abroad or remained in Barbados, runaway slaves seem to have been quite consistent in the month or the season they chose to escape (see Figure 1). Based on the month the owners first advertised for their runaways, the data reveal that slaves most frequently left in July and August. The least popular month for running away was February. One possible explanation for these various months, at least for plantation slaves, is related to the plantation cycle. Slaves may have escaped after the crop had been harvested in the early summer, partly because supervision was more lax or because the dead season meant fewer extra perks for slaves. Barry Higman's research adds weight to this view: he found that food supplies from the plantations as well as from the slaves' provision grounds were most stretched in this season. Since Barbadian slaves knew this time of year as the 'hungry-time' or 'hard-time', seasonal nutritional stress could have been an additional factor in increasing the number of runaways in July and August.[15] It is also

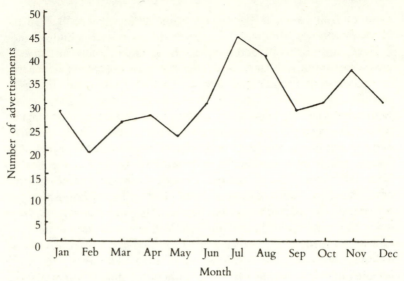

Source: Sample survey.

Figure 1   Runaways by month first advertised

important to note that owners may have been less concerned by slaves running away in the slow season. This view is supported by the unpopularity of February as a time to escape; at that point, sugar was being harvested and the planters would have needed all their labour.

There are other data to support this interpretation. It is possible to examine the date each slave was first advertised and how long the advertisements continued. In this way, it can be shown in which months slaves were absent for the longest and the shortest periods of time. The analysis reveals that slaves were away for the greatest average time in December, January, and February and for the least number of days in August. July is in the middle range of this cohort. This evidence would suggest that planters may have been quite desperate to get back their labour for crop-time and therefore advertised heavily for their slaves during these winter months. Similarly, it adds weight to the belief that owners generally were less concerned about slaves' running away after the crop was over. Another possibility for the relative popularity of staying away during the winter months was the Christmas festivities and the importance of slave families and friends being together then. It may also be that slaves may have sought to avoid returning to the most difficult work of all: harvesting the crop.

Data on the slaves' length of absence are revealing in other areas as well, especially if the time elapsed is broken down into the following categories: short (under two weeks), medium (two weeks to three months), and long (over three months). In this case, a slightly higher proportion of female runaways is among the short stayers than their proportion in the overall runaway sample. Male runaways were more heavily represented in the medium and long categories. These figures reinforce the possibility that women may have escaped more often for relatively short periods to visit family or friends. On the other hand, males were more likely to have escaped for longer periods – seeking more frequently, as we have seen, to merge into the free community or to escape abroad. The data may also reflect the differential importance owners placed on male and female runaways. Males were usually more valuable economically, and this may have been reflected in the number of advertisements placed for them.

Other categories for the elapsed time slaves were gone are perhaps more predictable. The average figure for creoles' length of absence was twice as high as for Africans and that for coloured three times the figure for blacks. Slaves aged between 18 and 29 years of age were away considerably longer than those in the younger and older age ranges. According to the data, slaves over 40 were gone the least amount of time. For those slaves whose occupations are known, field slaves were away for among the shortest periods of time, while domestics and shoemakers were gone for twice the average of this occupational cohort. Carpenters, fishermen, hucksters, and tailors were all near the average length of absence. Again, it is clear that runaways who were creole, coloured, and skilled had a far greater chance of escaping for a longer duration than those who were African, black, and unskilled.

The evidence also suggests that the overwhelming majority of slaves were gone for a relatively short time. Nearly 65 per cent of runaways were in this category. It would be fair to assume that many of these slaves had left their owners temporarily and intended to return. But what of the 35 per cent of slave runaways who were gone for a longer period, and within that grouping, the 8 per cent who had escaped for at least three months?

It may be instructive to examine some cases of slaves who stayed away for a very long time, even within the confines of Barbados.

One of the most striking examples involved a slave named Johnny Beckles, who was caught in 1805 on the Pool Plantation in St John. Beckles was about 45 years old, and the man who discovered him reported that 'from the best information I can collect, [Beckles] has been living in the Pool Negro-yard for many years before the storm of 1780'. This would mean that Beckles had run away at least 25 years previously. Another long-term runaway was a shoemaker named Sam, who was about twenty years old. Sam had been harboured by his father 'for nearly 16 years when by accident he was discovered to be a slave; and it was fairly proved that he was stolen by his parents when the mother was leased on Haymond's Plantation, and he a child'. For all those years, Sam had successfully passed as free, but was now possibly harboured with his mother.[16]

An even more curious case involved an African man named Buffy, who was discovered at Lancaster Plantation in St James in 1806. According to Buffy, his owner was a Frenchman in Jamaica who had died about six years previously. At that point and somewhat mysteriously, Buffy 'came over as a cook on board a vessel, and ... has remained on the island ever since'. The advertiser pointed out that Buffy spoke broken English 'but plain enough to be understood by any person' and 'has his country marks on both cheeks'.[17] Buffy was hardly an assimilated slave, although he did have a profession. Yet he had been able to live for six years in Barbados before being discovered as a slave.

Even an unacculturated African slave was able to escape for nearly two months. Betsy 'can speak little or no English, having been purchased from a Guinea ship about 10 months ago'. The first advertisement for her appeared on 5 October 1805 and she was not caught until 23 November of that year. This is one of the few cases where an advertised slave was caught and for whom there was an additional advertisement. Betsy's experience suggests that slaves appearing in the advertisements were probably away a minimum of two months and perhaps longer.[18]

One of the interesting questions to ask is whether the pattern of running away altered in any way during the period 1805 to 1830. It is immediately clear that the highest number of advertisements, 105, appeared in 1815, with 101 advertisements in 1805 and 91 in 1810 (see Table 3). There were far fewer advertisements in the years after 1815. Although it is not possible to account for the significant drop in the number of advertisements after 1815, one of the consequences of the 1816 slave rebellion may have been an alteration in the system of dealing with runaways. The law may have changed, or the apprehension of slaves may have become more rigorous. It seems unlikely that the actual number of runaways would have dropped significantly in the period after the rebellion.

Table 3   Number of runaways advertised and their mean number of days gone by year

	1805	1810	1815	1819	1824	1830
No. runaways advertised	101	91	105	48	6	12
Mean length of stay in days	32.3	10	52	41	18	?

Source: Sample survey.

The year 1815 did not just experience the largest number of advertisements; it also witnessed the highest average length of stay for runaways, apart from 1830 which was distorted statistically (see Table 3). When absence is examined as previously by short, medium, and long stays, 1815 is the year with the largest number of slaves who were absent for the longest period of time. The destination of runaways in 1815 is also suggestive: far more than the statistical average went to the country than to the towns. Nearly 43 per cent of all the slaves escaping to the country in the sample went there in 1815, contrasted with only 31 per cent of slaves going to the towns. The 1816 Rebellion was not an urban phenomenon: it broke out in St Philip. The evidence about the number of runaways in 1815, their length of stay, and their destinations points to the conclusion that runaways were not simply merging into the free community or temporarily visiting kin. Although runaways did not normally pose a threat to the system, they apparently could do so. It would be unwise to correlate runaways with rebellion; however, the increase in the number of runaways in 1815 may have been symptomatic of the heightened tension in Barbados which ultimately resulted in the 1816 Rebellion.[19]

Owners were very aware of the dangers posed by runaways. The year after Bussa's Rebellion in 1816, the master of a female slave named Massey sought to warn planters about runaways generally and his escaped slave in particular. Massey probably had a forged pass and was working as a laundress. Her owner believed that 'gentleman proprietors and managers are not aware of the evil in suffering absent slaves about their property, as they certainly will imbibe pernicious maxims, and afterwards afford a ready asylum to such of their slaves as may abscond'.[20] One problem, then, was the potential example of successful runaways. But there were also more serious cases to worry about.

Appea was a tall, fifty-year-old man with a

> surly countenance, has several scars about his head occasioned by fighting, and a piece off one of his ears, bit out by the same cause; he has been absent upwards of 12 months, and has eluded every vigilant attempt to take him. He is perhaps one of the most notorious villains the Country ever possessed; and a dangerous person to be at large amongst Plantation Negroes.

Yet this dangerous runaway – whose advertisement appeared in the middle of 1815 – was able to survive by 'drawing the figure of negroes on paper, by which means he gets a subsistence, going from one Estate to another; although he seldom stays long on any'.[21]

A final example reveals the potential danger of trying to arrest runaways as well as an important aspect of the system of apprehending escaped slaves. In October, 1815, the driver of Mount Wilton Plantation, Primus, was sent to search for a runaway and given a pass for ten days. 'Primus not returning home since, though invited to do so through his connections, it became necessary to seek him; he has a Wife at Mr Searles' in St Joseph'. The owner of Primus, Reynold Ellcock, hired Frank, the ranger of Pickering Plantation, and two other men in January 1816 to find the runaways.

> As they were returning at midnight, on Saturday the 20th instant, without finding the Runaways, they were suddenly attacked in the public road, not far from the buildings at Mount Wilton, and Frank, who seemed to be the sole object of their vengeance, was barbarously murdered by 5 or 6 men

who had concealed themselves in a corn-field near the road. The subscriber offers a reward of £25 to any person or persons who will give evidence to convict the perpetrators of this horrid murder, it being natural to suppose Prince [the first runaway] and Primus had gotten notice of this search, and had waylaid the men sent after them.[22]

This murder followed a particularly difficult year in Barbados. Michael Craton has documented the economic problems as well as the political ferment in the island in 1815 over the act for slave registration.[23] These developments may have given Primus as well as Appea more determination to flee in the first instance and subsequently to resist arrest.

One other interesting point is worth noting about this case. Primus had been sent out to catch a runaway and then Frank had been sent to get him. Indeed, the system depended on drivers and other elite slaves helping to apprehend escaped slaves. But slaves often used this system to their own advantage: when running away themselves and when challenged, they claimed to be searching for escaped slaves.

Like many slaves, Primus had run away to kin; in his case, it was to his wife. More than twice as many slaves in the sample were supposedly harboured by family as by non-family members. While a significant proportion of runaways were harboured either by a wife or a husband, it is interesting that a greater percentage of this cohort were thought to be with their parents. Siblings played a slightly lesser role than husbands and wives, but they too were not insignificant.

If these data are examined by length of absence, parents emerge as the kin who harboured runaways for the longest average time. Parents are above the mean time for the cohort of all familes as harbourers (twenty-eight days) as are husbands, while wives are just below this figure. Siblings, grandparents and children are well below the mean figure for families generally.

Families were an obvious destination for runaways. But the evidence goes further than this: it points to the strength of family ties and to that of the extended family. Betty Beck was a mulatto slave who was 'supposed to be harboured in the Plantation of Richard Cobham, Esq. called Stepney, where she was born, and many of her family belong'. Jack Charles was also well connected: he had numerous family in St Philip, St George and St Michael. His owner knew that Jack had aready spent time with his wife in St Philip, but there was a mother and an uncle to worry about as well. Families not only hid their escaped kin; they sometimes put them to work. Bob was a carpenter who had 'been seen at work with his father, by the name of Johnny Gittens, living in Milk Market'. Bob's sister also lived in the same district.[24]

The data are also suggestive in other ways about the family relationships of escaped slaves. Nearly a third of all the slaves who were harboured by wives had more than one of them; in several cases, owners mentioned three wives for their runaways. It is also interesting that the harbouring family members were not necessarily all slaves; many slaves had free kin. Clarissa, who was about twenty years old, had a free black mother 'living under the green trees in the Roebuck; and her father a black man belonging to James Holligan, Esq. called Mingo – by either of whom it is supposed she may be harboured'. It was obviously a considerable help to have free kin: Sanco 'passes as a free man, having family of that description in town'. Mimbah was doing even better. She had been a retailer of dry goods and had a house where she lived with her free black husband.[25] These harbourers suggest a complex pattern of relationships. They provide evidence of the existence of the slave family and should redirect efforts to examine the intricate and connected world of slave and free people.

Many slaves were not harboured by kin, but by friends, by employers, or by the soldiers of the West India Regiment. Judged by the length of their absence, those runaways harboured by non-family may have been able to stay away longer than those hidden by families. In part, this was because of the relative success of the runaways harboured by whites.

Although there were not many slaves in this cohort, planters were concerned about the implications of whites harbouring runaways. Sarah Jane was though to be harboured by her mother 'or by some evil-disposed white person or other in behalf of her mother'. April 'had been harboured at [Codrington] College and at a white man's house' in St John, although on a previous escape, he had been hidden by slaves. More important was the type of advertisement for Jacob: 'a further £10 to any person who will give information of any free subject who has employed him'.[26] The implication here is that whites may have often hired runaways; alternatively, that escaped slaves may have sought particular whites as employers. These slaves were not threatening the slave system generally but were making choices about their owners. White collusion with runaway slaves was not uncommon elsewhere as well; discussing runaways in the United States, Mullin concluded that a large number of runaway slaves were successful 'because for a variety of reasons, many whites who "harboured" them were willing to challenge the slave code at its weakest point'.[27]

It was not only whites who employed runaways; slaves did so as well. Ceafor was a mason who was 'supposed to be harboured by black masons employed upon the King's Works'. Another escaped slave named James was a fisherman who had lost his right leg and used crutches; nonetheless, he was thought 'to be employed and harboured by some of the fishermen about Fontabelle, particularly by a man belonging to Isaac Green'.[28] Slaves working for other slaves are indicative of a more elaborate structure of employment and harbouring than has previously been recognised.

Slaves were also harboured in and around the Castle, the home of the West India Regiment. Runaways could more easily pass as free among the black soldiers and among the free community which served them. There were some amusing cases in this group. For instance, Marissa 'had been repeatedly seen at St Ann's [the Castle], and was once taken from there, and rescued by some soldiers, before she could be delivered up to her owner'. This was despite her being 'remarkably stout'. Fortune had escaped once before as well and 'by virtue of a certificate given by some evil-disposed person of his freedom, he enlisted in the black corps under the name of Thomas Panton, a native of Jamaica'. The Castle also offered a refuge for two Africans who had several countrymen there but who spoke little English.[29] For a variety of reasons, then, white West Indians may have been right to worry about the effects of free black soldiers on a slave society.[30]

IV

It is clear from the evidence that the majority of advertised runaways were male, creole, coloured, and skilled slaves. Runaways escaped to the country as well as to the towns, with males apparently preferring the towns where they were more likely to pass as free men, gain employment, or try to get abroad. Women, on the other hand, opted more often for the country where they sought refuge among kin. Runaways more frequently chose to leave in the dead season, after the crop had been harvested. The majority seem to have stayed away a relatively short time, although a significant percentage of runaways were gone for over three months. There were also some prominent examples of slaves who managed to hide for several years, even within Barbados. More slaves in the sample left in 1815 than any another year and those slaves stayed away the longest period of time. This suggests a possible link to the 1816 slave rebellion and to the political ferment in Barbados in 1815. Slaves were harboured by both family and non-family; interestingly enough, whites as well as slaves were among the harbourers who hid and sometimes employed runaways. These are some of the conclusions of the study, but there are a number of other points worth emphasising.

On the one hand, it was sometimes in the masters' interest to allow slaves to run away. As we have seen, planters may well have regarded the July/August period as a more convenient time for slaves to be absent. Owners undoubtedly wanted to get rid of some of their runaways, and some runaways who were caught were apparently never claimed. Joe and William were two such runaways; they were arrested, put in gaol, and first advertised in January, 1830. Almost a year later, they were still unclaimed and unsold.[31]

Other masters had specific reasons to get rid of their slaves. The owner of Nelly reported that she had escaped along with £104 worth of dry goods. He was prepared to 'dispose of her for £100, and her child, and give the goods into the bargain to the purchaser'. Another case involved Betty Phyllis: she 'was well known . . . to be the object who set on fire the bed and curtains of her former owner, Mrs Griffith'. The owner of Ben reported he would probably try to pass as a free man and get employed, but she had clearly had enough and would 'be glad to dispose of the said Man'.[32]

On the other hand, there were many masters who were quite determined to get their slaves back. The owner of two runaways who were brothers offered the extraordinary reward of £50 for them. He also made it clear that 'if they will both or either of them return to their business of their own accord, I will freely pardon them, and inflict no kind of punishment upon them whatsoever, nor ask any questions where they may have been harboured'. John H. P. King was another anxious owner. His slave, Richard, had run away and was probably harboured by his father or mother. Richard's father had 'lately expressed a great wish that [Richard] be also sold to his present owners, the Messrs Cumberbatch'. However, King was not about to sell, 'it being the subscribers unalterable determination not to dispose of him'. King placed sixteen advertisements in the press for Richard without apparent success.[33]

Richard's case suggests that some slaves ran away to put pressure on their owners to sell them. In some instances, masters promised that their runaways would be able to choose new owners on their return. Phill had run away, and was now offered for sale, but 'should he voluntarily return, the privilege of choosing an owner will be granted to him'. Similarly for Hamlet, 'if he will return of his own accord in eight days from this date, he shall have a paper to look for another owner'. Or in the case of Charlotte, should she 'return home accompanied by a ready money purchaser, she will be pardoned, and sold reasonably'.[34]

Running away, then, could serve a variety of purposes. Some slaves managed to escape altogether; others used it to change their owners while most probably sought to make life more bearable for a while. In the process, runaways revealed the strength of family and personal ties in Barbadian slave society as well as the collusion of free people in their escape. While runaway slaves were clearly resisting aspects of the slave society, they were also testimony to 'the role of the powerless in affecting, and even controlling important parts of the lives of the masters'.[35]

Acknowledgment

I am grateful to Iain Liddell of the Computer Unit at the University of Warwick for guiding me through the labyrinth of SPSS and to Seymour Drescher, Stanley L. Engerman, Barry Higman, and James Walvin for their helpful comments on this essay. It is a revised version of a paper originally given at the 16th Annual Conference of Caribbean Historians, Cave Hill, Barbados in April 1984 and subsequently the History Workshop Conference on Slavery in Oxford in 1985. Delegates to these conferences also made useful suggestions. The research for this paper was funded by the Nuffield Foundation. It has been published in *Slavery and Abolition* (December, 1985), pp. 95–111 and in Gad heuman (ed.), *Out of the House of Boudage: Runaways, Resistance and Marronage in Africa and the New World* (London, 1986), pp. 95–111.

Notes

1 Price (1973), and Groot (1963). See also Thompson (1976), and Gaspar (1979).

2 For a useful introduction, see Norusis (1982).

3 T71/520–33; T71/540–6.

4 Bishop (1970), p. 151.

5 Mullin (1972), p. x.

6 The statistical material in the paper is derived from the sample survey and from an SPSS analysis of this data.

7 'Coloured' is used here to mean slaves of mixed colour. Synonyms include browns and mulattoes.

8 Higman (1984), p. 116.

9 Bishop, *op. cit.*, p. 22.

10 *The Barbados Mercury and Bridgetown Gazette* (hereafter *BM*): 4 March, 24 June 1817; 19 August 1815.

11 *BM*: 8 June 1805; 6 November 1819; see also Craton (1982), p. 147.

12 *BM*: 6 April 1819; 14 October 1817.

13 *BM*: 20 August 1805.

14 T71/520, f. 456; T71/524, f. 271; BM, 24 April 1819.

15 Higman, *op. cit.*, p. 215.

16 *BM*: 11 June 1805; 24 October 1818.

17 *BM*: 19 June 1806.

18 *BM*: 5 October, 23 November 1805.

19 For a further discussion of this argument, see Beckles (1985), p. 71.

20 *BM*: 4 October 1817.

21 *BM*: 15 July 1815.

22 *BM*: 27 January 1816.

23 Craton, *op. cit.*, pp. 259–60.

24 *BM:* 30 December, 8 August 1815; 19 October 1805.

25 *BM:* 23 February 1819, 3 June 1815; 17 December 1805.

26 *BM:* 10 November 1810; 21 January 1815; 10 November 1810.

27 Mullin, *op. cit.*, p. 106.

28 *BM:* 18 June 1805; 24 July 1816.

29 *BM:* 27 April, 16 November, 9 November 1805.

30 For further information on these regiments, see Buckley (1979).

31 *The Barbadian:* 19 January, 18 December 1830.

32 *BM:* 9 October 1810; 28 November 1815; 24 November 1810.

33 *BM:* 22 December 1810; 6 August 1805.

34 *BM:* 29 November 1817; 1 September 1810; 11 February 1809.

35 Mintz and Price (1976), p. 16.

Further reading

Blassingame (1979); Greene (1944); Schwartz (1970).

Fifteen

Haiti: Race, Slavery and Independence (1804-1825)

David Nicholls

'Recognition of a Black Empire founded upon insurrection and upon the massacre of the white population', the French prime minister told the British ambassador in 1825, 'would have a most pernicious moral effect'[1] Haiti posed, for the colonial and slave-owning powers, a potential threat. It was seen as a symbol of emancipation and was a sign of hope for the black slaves of the Caribbean and of the southern states of the USA. Yet despite Villèle's warning, the French government recognised the independence of Haiti in that year, manifestly believing that the economic and political benefits for France outweighed the pernicious moral effects.

The black and mulatto armies under Jean-Jacques Dessalines had expelled the French and proclaimed the independence of Haiti in November 1803 – and, more formally, on 1 January 1804 in the city of Gonaïves. The new state comprised the former French colony of Saint Domingue, situated at the western end of the island if Hispaniola, and also laid claim to the Spanish colony of Santo Domingo, on the eastern two-thirds of the island. Dessalines named the new state 'Haïti', which was the pre-Columbian Indian name for the island. For over twenty years Haiti's independence had remained unrecognised by the international community.

Largely as a result of a series of slave revolts which began in the northern department of Saint Domingue in 1791, slavery had been abolished in the colony in 1793 and in the following year throughout the French dominions. It was, however, reintroduced into Saint Domingue by the British in the areas they occupied,[2] and by the French when they regained control of the wayward colony in 1802. Slavery was finally abolished only with the victory of Dessalines and the end of the colonial regime. Independence thus came to be seen by Haitians as a necessary condition of freedom and was, moreover, for them as for many foreign observers – friendly and hostile – a symbol of racial equality and a challenge to slavery in the new world. In this paper I wish to consider the symbolic role played by Haiti in the early nineteenth century.

The colonial situation

It was evidently the case, in eighteenth-century Saint Domingue, that slavery, race and colonial status were linked. The *raison d'être* of the colony was to supply cheap tropical goods to the metropolitan country and to provide a market for French manufactured products. It was generally believed that sugar could be grown cheaply only on large plantations manned by slave labour. The system of slavery was in turn justified by theories of the racial inferiority of black people. Yet the relationship between race and slavery was more complicated. By the time of the French revolution of 1789 a considerable proportion of the colonial population was of mixed race, mostly being offspring of white fathers and black mothers. Many of these *gens de couleur* (or *mulâtres*) had been freed from slavery and constituted – together with some free blacks – a distinct caste, known as *affranchis*. This group theoretically enjoyed equal rights with the whites, under the *Code Noir* of 1685, but were in fact discriminated against in a number of ways and deeply resented the role of second class citizen which they were forced to play. It should be noted, however, that there were a number of free blacks and that a small proportion of slaves were mulatto. So distinctions of colour largely, but not completely, overlapped with distinctions of caste.

In 1791 the colony of Saint Domingue was composed of almost half a million slaves, about 40,000 whites and 30,000 *affranchis*; though it is possible that the latter were more numerous than this.[3] In any case the *affranchis* represented an important sector of the population, owning much of the land and many of the slaves. They were not themselves keen on emancipation and during the disturbed years from 1789 to 1803 frequently joined the whites in defence of property. Yet it was their ultimate alliance with the blacks in 1802 which brought slavery and the colonial system to an end.

Independence and race: Haitian attitudes

National independence was seen quite explicitly by the Haitian leaders as being based upon a conception of race. Both mulattoes and blacks regarded themselves as members of the African race, who had been discriminated against by the whites. The racial basis of the Haitian state was enshrined in the first constitution of 1805 which stated that all Haitians of whatever shade were to be known as '*noirs*'; it also decreed that no white ('*aucun blanc*') could own property in the country. Pétion later introduced into the 1816 constitution of his republic a clause allowing people of African and Indian extraction to receive full Haitian nationality after one year's residence.

The early leaders of Haiti were openly committed to the abolition of slavery and to the maintenance of full independence. It is difficult for us, in a period when so many ex-colonial countries have gained independence, to understand the full significance of what the Haitian generals were doing. The only precedent was the action of the American colonies, but there it was an elite of European origin who had led the country into independence. In Haiti this had been done by former black slaves and despised mulattoes, thereby constituting an assault on slavery, racial discrimination and colonialism. On defeating the French armies, Dessalines announced that he intended to liberate the neighbouring Spanish colony of Santo Domingo and regretted that he did not have the means to invade Martinique and Guadeloupe, urging the blacks of these French colonies to take action for themselves. He found it necessary, however, to reassure other European powers, particularly Britain, that he had no intention of intervening in their colonies. His aim was to secure British and United States support against the French.

French efforts to restore the slave colony

With the death of Dessalines in October 1806, the country split into a northern state (which later became a kingdom) under the black Henry Christophe and a mulatto-dominated republic in the west and south, presided over by Alexandre Pétion. On the issue of slavery they were agreed. On no account could they consent to its restoration. There is evidence, however, to suggest that some of the republican leaders may have considered at one time the possibility of restoring Haiti to some kind of French suzerainty.

The fall of Napoleon and the restoration of the monarchy in France led to new efforts being made in Paris by the dispossessed planters to persuade the French government to reconquer the country. Intelligence from various sources in Haiti convinced the government that such a step would be unwise and the Minister of Marine, Malouet, sent Dauxion Lavaysse, Dravermann and Franco de Medina on a mission to negotiate a settlement with the two Haitian governments. Lavaysse went to Port-au-Prince where he was received by Pétion. Medina entered the northern kingdom by

way of Spanish Santo Domingo but was arrested and brought to Cap
Haïtien. After extensive questioning of the prisoner a solemn *Te
Deum* was sung in the cathedral in thanksgiving for the unmasking of
the French proposals, which included the partial reintroduction of
slavery. At this celebration the secret instructions from Malouet to
the three agents, which had been confiscated from Medina, were
read out.

The plan proposed treating Haitians differentially, according
largely to the colour of skin:

a. Pétion, Borgella and a few others would be given equality
with whites. Others admitted as honorary whites by being
given *lettres des blancs* either for 'the fairness of their complexion, their fortune, their education, or their public
services'.

b. The rest of the mulattoes were to be placed 'somewhat
below the white caste'. 'It is of the first importance to
preserve for the whites some superiority over the coloured
class of the first rank.'

c. 'Shades intermediate between the mulatto and the negro'
would enjoy less rights.

d. The free blacks would be even less privileged.

e. 'With respect to the most numerous class, that of the
blacks attached to the cultivation and manufacture of sugar,
indigo, etc., it is necessary that it should return to or
continue in the situation in which it stood before 1789' with
new regulations to ensure discipline 'without being too
severe'.

f. A final category of trouble-makers would be 'transported
to the island of Ratau'. When asked where this island was
Medina explained that it meant that they were to be killed.
'It is an invention of the Minister Malouet, not to wound
the philanthropic feelings of his majesty.'[4]

Vastey described how Medina was placed, standing on a bench,
during this bizarre event. No doubt this is the origin of Beaubrun
Ardouin's (surely apocryphal) description of a 'requiem' for Medina
celebrated in his presence. Ardouin stated that during the ceremony
Baron de Vastey preached a sermon in which he denounced the
activities of Medina in such violent language that the officers in the

congregation drew their swords and threatened the prisoner with death.[5]

With the failure of this mission, rumours of a military intervention were revived. The reactions of Christophe and Pétion were swift. The latter told his people:

Your will is be free and independent. You will be so, or exhibit to the world the dreadful example of burying ourselves beneath the ruins of our country rather than return to a state of slavery, however modified. When all Europe has combined, at the voice of philanthropy, to annihilate the last trace of that most shameful traffic, the traffic in men; and when the most polished nations prepared and meditate a general plan of emancipation for those who yet groan beneath oppression; we see with regret that governments, which pique themselves on being the most religious, cherish principles which both justice and humanity condemn. Haytians! Your security is in your arms!

Christophe asserted the Haitian resolve 'to fight to extermination rather than submit again to the yoke of France and slavery'.[6] Extensive plans were layed for guerrilla warfare in the event of an invasion.

The French government continued to maintain contact with the republic and in 1816 sent a mission headed by Fontanges and Esmangart to pursue the matter. 'From the first moment Pétion made it clear,' reported Esmangart, 'that he would reject any proposition which would not result in the recognition of Haitian independence'.[7] A much revised proposal was made by the French government rejecting any idea of reintroducing slavery and recognising the rights of all Haitians as French citizens, but this was unacceptable to Pétion. By 1821 Esmangart had come to the conclusion that France must recognise Haitian independence and give up any attempt to re-establish slavery or colonialism. Nevertheless, all was not lost:

We can negotiate a treaty with Haiti which will be more or less advantageous to France according to the skill of the negotiator.... The treaty of commerce... would leave matters in the condition in which they were placed by the revolution and would enable us to carry on openly what we now do clandestinely.[8]

References began to appear in French diplomatic papers to '*un nouveau genre de colonisation...la colonie commerciale*' (a new species of colonisation... the commercial colony). In 1817 Leborgne de Boigne wrote his *Nouveau système de colonisation pour Saint-Domingue.* Esmangart advocated a treaty which would recognise political independence but which would bind Haiti financially and commercially to the former metropolis. Haitians were not, however, unware of this neo-colonial plan.[9]

The colonial system unveiled

Outstanding among Haitian writers of this period was Pompée Valentin Vastey, created Baron de Vastey in the Kingdom of Haiti. Though a mulatoo, he had identified himself early on with Toussaint Louverture and with the black tendency in Haiti. He stressed the economic basis of the colonial system and maintained that slavery with all its attendant barbarities was due to the 'insatiable avarice' of the European colonists.[10] With the revolution, however, the colonial system was destroyed and political independence was proclaimed. Vastey insisted that there were certain economic conditions necessary for the maintenance of a true political independence and foresaw the danger of French neo-colonial ambitions. Already, as we have seen, such men as Esmangart and other ex-colonists had advocated the economic domination of Haiti without the administrative costs of colonial government. Vastey wrote:

> *Independence*, say the ex-colonists, is the *hobby* of this people; by means of a *nominal* independence, they might be led to any thing. Well, let us grant them what they ask, and we shall immediately succeed in leading them wherever we wish![11]

He pointed to the economic conditions of an effective independence:

> We do not wish for a *merely nominal* and *fictitious* Independence...we equally design to have our trade free from all restrictions; that is to say, we will not grant an *exclusive* commerce to any nation whatever.[12]

Furthermore, changes must, he insisted, be made in the plantation economy. Much of the infrastructure had been damaged or destroyed in the revolutionary years. Irrigation systems, plantation houses and sugar mills lay in ruins. Vastey argued that there must be a move away from exclusive concern with export crops and the development of self-sufficiency in foodstuffs. 'We were bound to adopt a new agricultural system, fitted to our wants, and worthy of a free people', he wrote,

> A nation must be able to supply herself with every thing she principally wants. If she depends for subsistence on foreign markets, she has no more her independence in her own hands.[13]

Pétion's republic had already taken effective steps to this end by breaking up some of the large estates and selling or giving plots of varying sizes to army personnel, civil servants and other citizens.[14]

Foreign affairs

The policy pursued by the two Haitian states was similar in certain respects. Both endeavoured to play off one great power against another in order to retain a degree of independence. Both were at pains to keep on good relations with Britain, and Christophe sought support from the leaders of the anti-slavery movement. He engaged in an extensive correspondence with Wilberforce and Clarkson, who furnished him with intelligence on French plans and who sent school-teachers to the kingdom.[15] Christophe was so keen to retain international support that he actually refused to take any steps to interfere with the Spanish slave trade and denied giving any encouragement to slaves in the British colonies, stating that their situation was quite different from that against which the slaves of Saint Domingue had revolted. Much of what Vastey and other northern publicists said about the British must be seen in this context, rather than as mere flattery. Their emphasis upon the fact that Haiti did not constitute any danger to the colonial system in other parts of the Caribbean was part of the attempt to reassure the British government and also Haitian sympathisers in England and to retain their support. 'England is the principal power in Europe that took a lively interest in our fate,' de Vastey declared,

> It is England, who first of all proposed the abolition of the slave trade, and endeavoured to ameliorate the condition of

slaves. It is England, who, by an order in council, considered us neutral and independent, and sent directly and legally her ships to Hayti. We should then be, of all beings, the most ungrateful and unjust, were we ever deficient in gratitude to the people and government of England. Far from being dangerous to that equitable and loyal power, it will always find us ready to espouse its interests, which are identified with our own.[16]

Pétion was somewhat less cautious in these matters and, as is well known, gave material assistance to Simón Bolívar in the liberation of Spanish colonies on the mainland on the condition that slavery would be abolished in the newly independent states. He was criticised by northern spokesmen for supporting Bolívar and for including a constitutional article which allowed all Africans, Indians and their descendants to assume full Haitian nationality after a residence of only twelve months. This provision, it was claimed, constituted an appeal to the black and coloured population of other European colonies in the region, and thus 'tends directly to disturb the peace and internal government of these foreign colonies or countries'.[17]

Vastey's principal quarrel with Pétion's republic was, however, its alleged willingness to entertain French overtures and consider a re-establishment of the colonial system and even some form of slavery. By receiving Frenchmen like Dauxion Lavaysse, Pétion encouraged the Bourbon government to think in terms of once more bringing Haiti under French sovereignty. Pétion would not, in fact, agree to anything less than a French recognition of the full independence of Haiti, though he was willing to negotiate terms which included compensation for the dispossessed plantation owners.

As noted above, Dessalines had insisted, even prior to the final victory, that white foreigners would be forbidden from owning property in independent Haiti. Though the republic retained this prohibition the northern state abolished it. Neither in the constitution of 1807 nor in the royal constitution of 1811 did the prohibition of foreign ownership occur. This was no mere oversight. Spokesmen of the kingdom explicitly condemned the republic for maintaining this prohibition. Certainly it was reasonable to forbid French nationals from owning property, for Haiti was still at war with the former metropolis. To prevent citizens of other countries from owning property was, however, unnecessary, unjust and unwise.[18]

Attitudes to Africa

The attitude of Haitians to Africa, the continent of their origin, was highly ambivalent. On the one hand they declared almost unanimously that Haitian independence was a signal of joy and hope for the 'immense and unfortunate regions of Africa'.[19] It marked the beginning of a new era in which Africa would progress according to the European model. Baron de Vastey, together with a number of other Haitian writers, argued that civilisation, as known in his day, had originated in North Africa, claiming that this alone was enough to prove that black people are in no way inherently inferior to whites. Nevertheless they did accept the idea that civilisation in the nineteenth century was most fully developed in Europe this being due to particular historical and cultural factors, rather than to any racial inferiority of Africans. De Vastey also observed that the most recent anthropological evidence suggested that the tribes of central Africa were by no means as primitive and savage as European prejudice had assumed.

Africa was, for De Vastey, 'the cradle of the sciences and the arts', and the people of Egypt, Ethiopia and Carthage were advanced in culture in a time when the Gauls were sunk in primitive ignorance. Did there not exist in the Africa of his own day an infinity of empires, kingdoms and states, he demanded of Baron de Malouet, who had declared Africa to be incapable of independence.[20] The explorer Mungo Park, who had penetrated many hundreds of miles into Africa, attested to the many excellent qualities of the people of the interior.

Yet despite these positive ideas about Africa, past and present, de Vastey believed that Africa was generally uncivilised and that it was the vocation of 'noble and generous England' to be the channel by which illumination and culture would be conveyed to the African people. He praised British colonial policy, particularly in the creation of Sierra Leone in West Africa as a home for liberated slaves. Africa, he declared, 'can be civilised only by a conquest, of which the object is civilisation, and not in imitation of the conduct of the Spaniards and Portuguese in the two Indies'.[21]

Early Haitian writers, then, saw Haitian independence as a sign of hope especially for the black or African race throughout the world and some of them had an even broader vision of the Haitian revolution as heralding a 'third world' movement of liberation. F. D. Chanlatte, a republican writer, saw events in Haiti as presaging the end of the colonial system and 'men of all colours throughout the universe' being freed. Baron de Vastey in turn pointed to Haitian independence as the first fruit of a colonial revolution in which 'five hundred million men, black, yellow and brown, spread over the surface of the globe, are reclaiming the rights and privileges which they have received from the author of nature'.[22]

Voodoo, marronage and revolution

The role played by the Voodoo religion in the process of liberation is much debated, as is the contribution of the maroons. Voodoo – an amalgamation of various African religions, which incorporates elements of Christianity – certainly provided a means by which the slaves of different plantations were able to meet and thus to communicate. Perhaps more importantly it preserved the African identity of the slaves. It has played a generally conservative role in Haitian history, but at certain times it may have supplied inspiration for radical action. The legend, probably having some basis in fact, is that the slave revolt in the north was begun with a Voodoo ceremony presided over by an *houngan* (voodoo priest) called Boukmann. Toussaint, Dessalines, Christophe and most of the other black and mulatto leaders, being *creoles* (i.e., born in Saint Domingue), were fiercely opposed to the practice of the religion, which was largely under the control of *bossals* (slaves born in Africa). This hostility has, with a few notable exceptions, continued to the present day among the black and mulatoo elites.

What part was played in the revolution by the *marrons* (maroons or runaway slaves) is difficult to say. One school of historians insists that they were essentially conservative – being interested simply in maintaining their own settlements. They even were known to return later runaway slaves to their owners. On the other hand it is asserted that the *marrons* were a source of continual inspiration to the slaves, preserving among them the desire for freedom, and that the fact of *marronage* was a running sore in the colonial regime.[23]

Foreign appraisals of Haitian independence

As the opening quotation shows, the French government regarded the loss of its most lucrative colony not only as an economic blow but as a dangerous precedent. In the early years of Haitian independence the British feared an invasion of British colonies, particularly Jamaica. This apprehension soon receded, but there remained the danger of Haiti as a sign of hope for the blacks of the colonies. Henry Brougham's comments in the *Edinburgh Review* of 1805 reflect the impact which events in Haiti had made:

> negroes organizing immense armies; laying plans of
> campaign and sieges, which, if not scientific, have at least
> been to a certain degree successful against the finest
> European troops; arranging forms of government, and even
> proceeding some length in entering the most difficult of
> human enterprizes; entering into commercial relations with
> foreigners, and conceiving the idea of contracting alliances;
> acquiring something like a maritime force, and at any rate,
> navigating vessels in the tropical seas, with as much skill and
> foresight as that complicated operation requires (6, p. 346).

This was a matter for concern and Brougham argued that it behoved the British to improve the conditions of slaves in their Caribbean colonies. 'What are all the fears of banishment to Siberia, or of French conscription', he demanded,

> compared with the risks to which every white inhabitant of
> Jamaica is exposed, so long as Dessalines is emperor of
> Hayti, and has a troop of allies in the slaves of every British
> plantation? (*ibid.*, p. 342).

The abolitionists, Wilberforce, Clarkson, James Stephen, Zarchary Macaulay and others took a considerable interest in Haitian developments and used information from their agent W.W. Harvey to show how emancipation leads to progress and to prosperity.[24] Of the Haitians, Harvey wrote;

> Though of the same race, and possessing the same general
> traits of character as the negroes of the other West Indian
> islands, they are already distinguished from them by habits of
> industry and activity, such as slaves are seldom known to
> exhibit.[25]

Similarly in France Henri Grégoire, formerly Bishop of Blois, wrote in 1826, 'The Haitian republic, by the mere fact of its existence, will perhaps be a great influence on the destiny of Africans in the new world'.[26]

The British government was cautious in its relations with the new black state. British agents had visited Haiti to negotiate with Dessalines in November 1803 and merchants soon established themselves in the principal ports of the country. In December 1808 an Order in Council authorised trade with the northern state and with the southern republic. While eager to take advantage of commercial openings, the British refused to give diplomatic recognition to Haiti. It was only after French recognition of Haitian independence in 1825 that the British sent a consul in the person of Charles Mackenzie. Even so the British refused to allow Haitian consuls to be sent to their West Indian colonies. Similarly merchants in the United States were keen to trade with Haiti, but senators – mostly from the slave-owning South – prevented diplomatic recognition of the country until 1862. Thomas Hart Benton, of Missouri, objected to diplomatic relations with Haiti, on the ground that it would exhibit the fruits of a successful negro insurrection. The USA, he continued,

> will not permit black ambassadors and consuls to ... give their fellow blacks in the United states proof in hand of the honors that await them for a like successful effort on their part.[27]

Not only in Europe and the USA was Haiti seen as a threat; the governing elites in the newly independent republics of South and Central America were worried that their black population might be encouraged to demand equal rights. Despite the aid given by Dessalines and Pétion to the independence movement headed by Miranda and Bolívar, Haiti was not invited to the Panama Conference of 1825. President Jean-Pierre Boyer complained that this insult to Haiti was due to colour prejudice.[28]

Conclusion

On Pétion's death in 1818, Boyer had succeeded to the presidency of the republic; with Christophe's suicide two years later he was able to unify the western part of the island; in 1822 Haitian troops moved into the former Spanish colony of Santo Domingo and the whole island became one state. By this time the French had given up any possibility of restoring the colonial status of Haiti and after protracted negotiations and some sabre rattling by France, Boyer agreed to pay a huge sum in compensation to the dispossessed planters. France then conceded to the inhabitants of the former French colony 'the full and complete independence of their government'.[29]

The succeeding years represent a sad story of economic decline, financial corruption on the part of competing elites and a growing dependence on foreign powers, culminating in the US invasion of 1915. There is, however, more to the story than this. An extraordinary succession of Haitian writers throughout the nineteenth century defended the black race against the prejudice of European and American publicists and contributed to the growth of a sophisticated cultural tradition far outshining anything to be found in the colonial Caribbean.[30] Also a sturdy and dignified peasantry grew up in the countryside. Haiti was poor, but life was sufficiently agreeable to attract many hundreds of Jamaican immigrants to the land where black people first threw off the chains of slavery.

Notes

1 Granville to Canning 13 January 1825, Public Record Office, London, FO 27/329.
2 Geggus (1982).
3 Estimates differ considerably, see Nicholls (1979), p. 259 note 43, on the relation between caste, colour and class, see *ibid.* (1985), pp. 21f.
4 De Vastey (1823), p. xxxv.
5 Ardouin (1958), 8, pp. 26f. Cole (1967) generally follows Ardouin's account of the incident (p. 220).
6 De Vastey, *op. cit.*, pp. lxxxiv and lxxxviii.
7 'Note sur St Domingue', Archives du Ministère des Affaires Etrangères, Paris (AAE), correspondence Politique: Haïti 2.
8 Esmangart to Ministre Pasquier, 2 January 1821, AAE, CP: Haïti 2,
9 'Mémoire sur Haïti', 9 February 1820, AAE, CP: Haïti 2. For an excellent discussion of this theme, see Joachim (1971).
10 De Vastey (1818), p. 53.
11 *ibid.* (1823), p. 236.
12 *ibid.* (1823), p. 245.
13 *ibid.* (1818). p. 54.
14 On early land policy, see Manigat (1962); Nicholls (1974); Lacerte (1975).

15 The correspondence with Clarkson is readily available in Griggs and Prator (1952). Some letters to Wilberforce can be found in Wilberforce and Wilberforce (1838).
16 De Vastey (1818), p. 26.
17 *ibid.* (1823), p. 209.
18 *ibid.* (1823), p. 207.
19 Rosiers (1819), p. 5.
20 De Vastey (1816), pp. 31f; *ibid.* (1814a), pp. 19f.; *ibid.* (1814b), p. 20.
21 *ibid.* (1814a), pp. 18–19; *ibid.* (1818), p. 74 note.
22 Chanlatte (1817), p. 4; De Vastey (1816), p. 14.
23 On the role of the *marrons*, see Fouchard (1972); Manigat (1971); Debien (1974), pp. 411f.; Debbasch (1961); *ibid.* (1962).
24 Harvey worked in northern Haiti as a teacher in the last months of Christophe's reign and wrote *Sketches of Hayti from the Expulsion of the French to the Death of Christophe*, (London, 1827). For a fuller discussion of the attitude of abolitionists to Haiti, see Geggus (1985).
25 Harvey, *op. cit.*, p. 266.
26 Grégoire (1826), p. 44.
27 Quoted in Montague (1940), p. 53.
28 Boyer to Lafayette, quoted in Ardouin (1958), 9, p. 75 notes.
29 *Le Moniteur* (Paris), 12 August 1825.
30 These writers are discussed in Nicholls (1979).

Further reading

In addition to Nicholls (1979); Geggus (1982); Cole (1967); and Griggs and Prato (1952) cited above, see James (1963); Korngold (1945). For the later period see Holly and Harris (1970); Dean (1979).

Sixteen

The Social-Psychological Analysis of Manumission

L. Mee-Yan Cheung-Judge

Introduction

Manumission was a common feature in many slave societies. It was the act of freeing individual slaves from the bondage of slavery, and in Latin it actually means 'release, liberate from one's hand'. Schwartz (1974, pp. 604–5) defines it as 'a juridicial action in which property rights were surrendered and in which the former slave assumed a new legal personality and new legal responsibility'. The phenomenon of manumission has been extensively examined and studied by scholars in various disciplines (see *Further reading*). Topics such as the nature and origin of manumission, types of manumission, the demographic characteristics of the manumitted, the status of the freed persons, and many others have been well documented. Such, however, is not the case for the social-psychological study of manumission, particularly the area of the identity structure of the manumitted.

Even though manumission was a common phenomenon in slavery societies, the process and character of manumission varied immensely, dependent upon what complex of separate or interwoven factors were at work in a given community, for example, the prevailing socio-political and economic climate within the society where manumission occurred; the reasons or motives behind manumission (e.g., humanitarian, religious, economic, military, political); the degree of involvement of the state (restricting or encouraging); the racial differentiation between masters and slaves, slaves and freed persons, freed persons and freed persons; the types of manumission (e.g., unconditional, conditional with obligations attached, self-purchase of either partial or full freedom, legal or 'popular'); and the presence of pressure groups from various religious and humanitarian societies. Such factors, singly or in combination, not only dictated the consequences of manumission for individuals and groups, but also created a wide spectrum of freed persons (completely freed, partially freed with contractual obligations to ex-master; partially self-purchased, tenants, peons, etc.). Therefore, it is difficult and would be inaccurate to generalise the condition and consequences of manumission. Each situation has to be studied and analysed before any conclusive comparisons can be made.

Assumptions

The social-psychological analysis of manumission starts with the tremendous status inconsistency which existed in the lives of the manumitted slaves as a result of the existence of any or all of the above factors. Although objectively and technically freed by their masters, in fact many aspects of the lives of the freed persons either remained the same or grew worse. For example, even though all Roman ex-slaves received Roman citizenship, their legal status was inferior to that of members of the master class and they were always regulated by the government by paying tribute and taxation, not to mention being subject to the presence of continuous prejudice because of the stigma of their previous slave status (Hopkins, 1978). In Spanish America where racial and ethnic differentiation between master class and freedmen was greater than in the Roman world, the fate imposed on the freed slaves was even more brutal. From the seventeenth to the nineteenth century manumission occurred in most parts of the New World and freed persons, though significantly better off than slaves, still suffered tremendous restrictions socially, religiously, and educationally. As a form of social control, many of them were forbidden to use coffins for their dead, were not allowed to be buried in the cathedral, and were not allowed to worship in the same church as the master class. Freedmen of known African origin were barred from the educational facilities. Many of them were hired out to Spanish masters, so that their whereabouts might be known and taxes could be collected easily from them. Those who had broken out to work elsewhere had to contend with a great deal of social prejudice which served as a serious obstacle to any hope of socio-economic advancement (Bowser, 1972). During a similar period such status inconsistency was even more glaring in Curaçao where no freed slave could receive his/her civil rights until two years after manumission, and any offence against a former master could result in the freed person reverting to slavehood (Hoetink, 1972). Such was the case in Surinam also. Because of the fear of numerical superiority, the colonial authorities limited the number of manumissions and enforced great social, legal, religious, educational, and economic restrictions on them. Similarly, in the Republic of Venezuela, government played a crucial role in regulating the lives of those manumitted. Rather than allowing them to do as they pleased, work and live where they desired, the government restricted them to the same kind of job, being contracted preferably to the same master as their mother. Even though many of the peons had the freedom to sell their labour to the highest bidder, they still had to register with the local judge and carry a booklet certifying their status (Lombardi, 1969).

This situation of tremendous status inconsistency among the manumitted was succintly summarised by Berlin (1974) in his work on the slavery system in the American South. According to him, the gap between slavery and freed status was never quite what some abolitionists made it out to be. Once freed, the blacks generally remained at the bottom of the social order, despised by whites, burdened with increasingly oppressive racial prescriptions and subject to verbal and physical abuse. Although legally no longer dominated by a master, in the eyes of many whites, their place in society had not been significantly altered. They were 'slaves without masters' and they were not free. The freed slaves often found themselves balanced precariously between abject slavery, which they rejected, and full freedom, which was denied them. This glaring discrepancy between expectation and reality in their legal, social, political, educational, and religious rights was often bitterly resented by the freed persons and this resentment is believed to have had a substantial impact on their self-perception, their identity structure, interpersonal relations, and their social and communal life. Were they slaves or were they free? From this fundamental question spring a range of other ones, for example, could they participate fully in educational, religious, and social life as they chose to? Could they prosecute those who obstructed their passage to freedom? Which community would they choose to live in, if such choices were permitted? Who would they choose to be their intimate friends? What career structure was open to them? The basic issue which I am concerned with in this paper is how did manumitted slaves answer such questions and how did they react to this situation of inconsistent rankings and life style on the stratification differentials? On the personal level, did they incorporate the negative effects of their new membership in their self-definition and therefore suffer negative self-feeling? On the social level, which group (master class, freed persons, slaves) did they identify themselves with and therefore enact such identity in social interaction? On the collective level, did they move towards a stronger communal link with people of the same fate or did they discard such collective identity and move towards the master class? Moreover in the face of such injustice, did they collectively seek changes, changes that would restore congruency between their legal, political, economic, religious, educational, and social status? This paper assumes that the effects such status inconsistency had on the manumitted led to different coping mechanisms. On the basis of the corresponding behavioural manifestations as recorded in various historical material I hope to be able to find out how the manumitted coped with status inconsistency.

The paper is of an exploratory nature, attempting to analyse theoretically the social-psychological consequences of manumission on individuals and groups through the use of an identity model which I first used in studying the resurgence of ethnic phenomenon (Cheung, 1979). The model aims to analyse how any social factor affects the individual's identity structure personally, socially, and collectively and what type of behavioural manifestations there are at each level. I believe that the search for answers to some of the afore-mentioned questions can be significantly facilitated by the application of the identity model. Finally, I hope that this theoretical analysis will stimulate historians to study further the social-psychological aspects of manumission using in-depth historical cases.

The identity model

The model shown in Figure 1 has three interrelated levels of analysis: the personal, the social, and the collective. Each level has two distinct dimensions to it, the subjective and objective.

On the personal level, the focus is on how status in life (for example, ethnic/racial background, gender, free or slave status, class and others) bears on the psychological and psychosexual stages of development, that is, upon the formation of ego, superego, self-concept, self-esteem, self-definition and self-feeling. Research questions in this area would include, for example, what type of effects a *group's* deprived status in society would have on the *individual's* self-concept when he/she takes that status personally, or internalises the group dynamic/label.

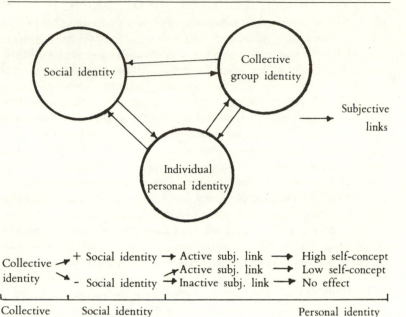

Figure 1   The identity model

The social level of analysis, as expounded by social psychology, focuses special attention on ascribed or prescribed status and the use of such particular frames of reference in social interaction. The concern is with the social categorisation of people based on their ascribed and/or prescribed status, and the differential behaviour which ensues from this. It also refers to the use of that frame of reference by others in the perception and treatment of an individual.

The collective or group dimension, as mainly expounded by both sociologists and anthropologists, focuses on the basis by which groups are identified, how the identity is preserved or changes over time, and what occurs in the intergroup contact situation.

The distinction between the three levels of identity is closely related to the two separate dimensions noted earlier, the subjective (attitude-cognitive) and the objective (socio-demographic). At the individual or personal level, the subjective dimension refers to an active awareness or consciousness of one's status as a source of identity, while the objective or the socio-demographic characteristics refers to any outward or objective basis of categorising people. In other words, the objective dimension (for example gender, racial/ethnic linkage, physical characteristics, skin colour, food habits and others) refers to the indisputable characteristics of the individual which place him/her in some specific category. These objective criteria are important constituent elements in the collective identity of any group, though they do not necessarily play a large role in the identity system of the individual. For example, for some slaves (especially those who had intimate and close relationships with the master), the awareness of being a slave was no more significant than, say, also being 'male', 'young,' and 'head of the household slaves'. In a situation like this, the objective knowledge of one's slavery status need be only a minor component of one's self-identity and would not have led to voluntary participation in that collective group. One can be aware of the unique status of oneself and the group one belongs to and yet choose to undervalue or not to be self-conscious of such status.

In other instances, the subjective identification would have assumed considerable importance *vis-à-vis* other personal characteristics to the extent that particular ascribed and prescribed status became the mode of identity. Unlike the earlier example, there could be slaves to whom this status was the most significant aspect of self-definition.

The linkage between the three components is crucial in our analysis of how manumission affected the various levels of the freed person's identity structure and its subsequent psychological and behavioural manifestations socially and politically. In those instances in which individuals chose not be conscious of their status personally, and therefore of their group attachment in their self-identity, then the link between personal, social, and collective identity was broken. Under such circumstances, even if treated as slaves in a social situation, individuals would not feel the impact of the collective identity on their personal identity. However, if they were actively aware of how the slavery status was brutally imposed not only on their self-definition, but also on how they were being treated and related to in social situations, then the link between the personal, social and collective could be highly active. I shall deal with this extensively in the following section.

Application and analysis

In the various cases briefly described at the start of this paper, it was shown that a glaring inconsistency pertained in most of the lives of the manumitted and that the differences between various societies was only a matter of degree. Hence the following application of the identity model to manumission will start with the social situation of status inconsistency, and will speculate that there will be different psychological, and behavioural manifestations in the manumitted's social, communal and political life, depending on (1) whether there was subjective awareness of such inconsistency in either collective identity and/or personal identity, (2) whether the individuals valued their freed status, and (3) whether there were links between the collective/social and personal identity, and how strong these links were. I shall examine each of these three factors in more detail.

(1)   Subjective awareness

The level of subjective awareness of status inconsistency in either the personal and/or collective identity was a crucial factor in determining the type of consequences such situation had on the individual. Without knowledge, one cannot act. If the individual was not aware of either the status differentiation between slaves and freed persons or the severity of the discrepancy between reality and expectation of the freed status, then the effects of status inconsistency on the individual's identity structure would be minimal. There were many factors which might have contributed to a low level of awareness. Some individuals lived in a very insulated environment where their relationships with the former master were still intimate, or where objective knowledge of the full legal rights of the manumitted were not well publicised or even blocked, or where the individuals employed selective psychological mechanisms which aimed to keep painful information out of their consciousness. Whatever the causes were, the subjective awareness of the objective differences between being slaves and being freed and/or the deplorable condition of their lives did not register in the individuals' identity structure, and hence would not lead to any forms of psychological responses nor the corresponding behavioural manifestations of such conditions of life.

On the contrary, if there was a high level of subjective awareness among the freed persons concerning what manumission was supposed to bring and what was denied to them, then one would have expected status inconsistency to generate various types of response. However, whether such responses were manifested behaviourally was determined by two other factors: how much the individual valued the freed status, and whether there were links between the personal and social/collective identity of the individual. In other words, subjective awareness (of the differences between being freed and being slaves and/or what they were entitled to and what was denied them), though a significant factor in determining the individual's response to status inconsistency, was not sufficient to dictate the degree, extensiveness, and manifestation of the response.

(2)   Value placed on the freed status
Objectively, manumission was supposed to offer the end of bondage and to put ex-slaves in control of their destinies. It is therefore hard to imagine that there would be any freed slaves who did not value this new status. However, there is ample evidence that there were a number of ex-slaves who placed a low value on the new-found freed status due to some of the following factors: age of the slaves when manumitted, the prevailing economic situation outside the plantations or former situation, the degree of hostility in the outside world, the number of family members left with the former master, the degrees of emotional attachment to the former master, and the employment of the classic denial defence mechanism.

On the personal level, if individuals were actively aware of the brutal injustice suffered even in their new-found freedom and also placed high value on such status, then they would have suffered psychologically, especially in self-esteem. The incorporation of negative group membership in one's personal identity would usually lead to the loss of self-confidence and esteem. On the social level, those who valued the new status but had their rights and entitlements denied them may have either tried to hide their new membership in any form of social interaction, or tried to pass as free born, or avoid any form of social interaction altogether. On the collective level, individuals might have either have turned to building stronger communal links with other freed persons in order to strengthen their own sense of value or have rejected membership with a collective group which the society despised. On the other hand, if a person did not value something (even though that something was denied them), then on the personal level one would not expect him or her to suffer negative effects in his/her self-feeling. Similarly, on a social level, individuals would not be anxious in using such status in social interaction as they would not care which categories people put them in, nor would they receive a serious blow if they were treated negatively because of their new membership. On the collective level, we would expect those who did not value their new freed status to have been less active in forming cohesive communal life with other freed persons and to have been less active politically in collective bargaining to improve their lot. However, how those individuals who were actively aware and placed high value on their freed status responded to status inconsistency would have been further determined by whether there were any links between the three levels of identity structure and how strong the links were.

(3)   Links between the three levels of identity
If there were strong links between the three levels of identity, individuals who might have suffered from loss of self-esteem due to the high value they placed in the freed status would have been pro-tected/insulated from the full impact of the derogatory effects of the subjugated membership by having other points of reference. More-over, the cohesive communal relationship (especially with the enactment of its internal value) would have counteracted the negative effects externally. Hence those individuals who had active links between the three levels of identity and who identified them-selves as freed persons in their personal identity would have (a) chosen to enact such identity in social situations in spite of difficult circumstances, (b) have asserted themselves in social interaction without yielding to the derogatory treatment imposed on them, and (c) would have chosen deliberately not to associate themselves with the master class. Further, when there were strong links with people in a similar position, we would expect these freed persons to have maintained a high political collective profile in fighting for the restoration of their rights. Any evidence of organised political groups would be a clear indication.

Based on the above discussion, I propose the following hypotheses which sum up the previous analysis of the effects of status inconsis-tency on the identity structure of the manumitted.

In a society where manumission occurred but with a high level of status inconsistency imposed on the lives of the manumitted:
(1) The more the individual freed slave valued his/her freed status, was aware of status inconsistency, and incorporated the subjugation

situation into his/her status, the more he/she suffered psychologically, especially in the area of self-esteem.

(2) The less the individual freed slave valued his/her freed status, was aware of such inconsistency, and incorporated the subjugation situation, the less he/she suffered psychologically, especially in the area of self-esteem.

(3) The more aware the individual freed slave was of such inconsistency, and the stronger the link between personal and collective identity, the more active he/she would be in the political struggle of restoring equity, and the more he/she would form cohesive social and communal life with other freed slaves.

(4) The less aware the individual freed slave was of such inconsistency, and the weaker the link between personal and collective identity, the less active he/she would be in the political struggle of restoring equity, and the less he/she would form cohesive social and communal life with other freedmen.

Conclusion

As has been stated, the social-psychological analysis of manumission starts with the tremendous status inconsistency which existed in the lives of the manumitted slaves. Hence, if there was minimal status inconsistency in the society where the manumitted resided – that is, equity was accorded to the freed person – then the manumitted slaves who took their freed status into their self-definition would have enjoyed a higher self-esteem and a more positive self-definition in their identity structure. However, if there was great status inconsistency in the society where the manumitted resided, then those manumitted slaves who took their free status seriously in their self-definition would have suffered a lower self-esteem and lower self-confidence. However, if individuals in this latter group had strong links with others who were in a similar position, I believe that they would have been insulated from the full impact of the subjugated membership. If this was the case, then I believe that the combination of active awareness of inequality accorded to their new status, and the rejection of such negative effects in their personal identity system, together with strong links with groups of people sharing the same fate, would tend to make individuals in this group more active politically in fighting for real freedom.

The issue of the social communal cohesion with other manumitted individuals is of considerable interest. As has been mentioned, cohesive communal life often has an insulating effect on the individuals' self-esteem, but there are further questions that must be asked. For example, did a high level of consciousness of being free necessarily lead to higher cohesive communal life with people of the same kind? Or did it lead to a higher level of integration with the master class? At the opposite end from the possibility of social cohesion of the manumitted, there are instances when freed slaves did not acknowledge the status differentiation in their self-definition, especially if they were still bound to the former situation of subjugation. In that situation, the freed status would not be significant to their personal identity system. In fact they may not have seem themselves as being any different from slaves. One wonders whether individuals in this group would have been affected by their free status with respect to their self-definition and identity structure and whether without a high level of active awareness of their status they would relate to other freed slaves in forming their communal, social life. I speculate that this group would have been politically less active than the former group, and would have had a less active group cohesion with the other freed slaves.

Similar situations probably occurred in the cases of individuals with strong links between their personal and collective identity. If they had a high collective consciousness of their status, and/or status inconsistency, and such inconsistency was often enacted in social situations, then the group with strong links between personal, social and collective identity would exhibit a stronger social and communal life with other freedmen, a lower level of integration with the master class (even in those cases where they were allowed so to do), and politically be more active in fighting for equality (given that the power balance was not a completely closed one). In contrast, if such individuals were not aware of their freed status, did not have active group consciousness with other freed persons, avoided perceiving themselves as such in social situations, and did not associate themselves with others, then we would expect them not only to be inactive politically but also to manifest accommodation tendencies.

However, in the above analysis, we must also bear in mind that there were a number of important modifying factors that need to be taken into consideration: the level of status inconsistency in the society where manumission occurred; the degree of power closure between the two groups; the demographic spread of the freed population (whether there was enough of them to form some sort of communal life); the degree of stratification within the society (whether the manumitted ever interacted with the master class, or after being freed, they still remained on plantations or in similar bondage contexts); and not least, the physical distinction between the master class and the freed persons. In the application of the model, each of these modifying factors would need to be systematically introduced to explain the outcome of how active *vs* inactive identification with the free status personally, socially, and collectively would affect the individual, not only psychologically in his/her identity structure, but also in the enactment of such identity in either or both social and political life.[1]

Notes

1 Texts drawn upon for this paper include Berlin (1974); Bowser (1972); Cheung (1979); Coen and Greene (1972); Hoetink (1972); Hopkins (1978); Lombardi (1969); and Schwartz (1974).

Further reading

Booker (1966); Buckland (1970); Craton (1978); Curtin (1977); Davis (1966); Finely (1972); *ibid.* (1985); Foner and Genovese (1969); Genovese (1965); Kilson and De Barenne (1971); Klein (1971); Kloosterboer (1972); Patterson (1967); *ibid.* (1977a); *ibid.* (1977b); Ransom and Sutch (1977); Rice (1977); Ruben and Tuden (1977); Turton (1980); Watson (1980a); and *ibid.* (1980b).

Seventeen

'Many Clear Words to Say': Afro-American, Oral and Feminist History

Susan Grayzel

This talk was intended to be a work in progress; it was
written as a workshop piece with no intention of publication.
It therefore lacks a wide research base, and those interested
in the history of Afro-American women, their experience of
slavery and accounts of their lives through oral history,
should consult the bibliography at the end of this piece.
Moreoever, as the historiography of this topic continues to
expand at a rapid rate, this work, like the bibliography, may
well be outdated. It merely attempts to bring to the
attention of a wider audience the existence of one significant
oral history project on the lives of Afro-American women.
In addition, this piece is a shortened version of the talk
presented at the conference.

In 1976 an oral history project on the lives of American Black women
born between 1870 and 1920 was begun under the auspices of the
Arthur and Elizabeth Schlesinger Library on the History of Women
in America at Radcliffe College. The intention of the project was to
provide accounts of the lives of women of this generation, removed
by one or two generations from the actual experience of slavery,
before they completely disappeared from recorded history. In the
mid-1970s, women's history, Afro-American and oral history were
relatively new additions to academia. I was pleased to participate in
this endeavour at a later stage (1983 onwards) by working as an
intern with the Black Women Oral History Project and by
continuing as a volunteer for a period of some two years. Although
my involvement with the project was not extensive, it significantly
changed my perspective on history and my ideas about what can be
learned from listening to women. My intention here is to share some
of the experiences of the women in this oral history, to let us listen to
their words and voices. Then we can begin to pose some difficult

questions: what do these records teach us about the enduring influence of slavery? What can we learn about the lives of women? Why is oral history relevant, even crucial, in forcing us to listen to the stories left out of history?

The importance of oral history lies in its great potential to give history back to those who live it. As a vital tool in studying the history of minorities and ignored groups, it virtually redefined Afro-American history in the popular mind after the success of Alex Haley's *Roots*.[1] Its contributions have enhanced our understanding of women and of the doubly neglected Afro-American woman. Though I have no definitive statements to make, I have a few ideas about the ultimate benefits which the evidence of an oral history project focusing on Afro-American women can provide for students of slavery.

Firstly, it is important to examine how perceptions and accounts of the slave experience affected later generations. Secondly, it seems central to an understanding of the historical strength of black women to examine the fortitude of these memories and the impact of strong foremothers. Finally, it is incumbent upon us to learn from these records that decision-making power over their lives did not become a reality for Southern Afro-Americans, in particular, for decades after the legal end of slavery.

The women whose voices and experiences I wish to share were interviewed in the late 1970s and early 1980s. The ideas which led to the creation of the Black Women Oral History Project were not novel outside mainstream, white, Western academic endeavours, and indeed oral history hearkens back to African traditions. In 1977, Ann Schockley wrote in the *Negro History Bulletin* that 'it is a recognised fact that... the history of Afro-Americans is basically an oral history'. She argued further that 'one of the essential needs for collecting black oral history lies in the long neglect and racist attitudes of some historical societies, libraries, colleges and universities in believing that the collecting of... materials belonging or relating to blacks was unimportant'.[2] The Schlesinger library was already well aware of this archival discrimination against black records and women's records when it decided to establish the Black Women Oral History Project. Eventually collecting the stories of seventy-two women, the project focused on those who, to give the stated aim, 'had made significant contributions to American society in the early and middle decades of the twentieth century'.[3]

These women represented a cross-section of American women of African descent. Not only were the interviewees emblematic of the diversity and dynamism of Afro-American women, but many of the interviewers were also of African ancestry. The included the project's coordinator, Ruth Edmonds Hill, who interviewed her own mother. In this sense, the interviews themselves reflected a passing on of knowledge from one generation of Afro-American women to another.

All of this relates to a central theme in my work with the project which has to do with feminism and the connections between women across generations as well as across social, economic and racial barriers. There is an enormous amount of information in the Black Women Oral History Project about women, Afro-Americans, communities, family and education. From that wealth of information, I have chosen to focus on the influence of older women on the interviewees' lives. This did not require any special effort on my part or particular research skills as the transgenerational support and inspiration gained from women was something which the records themselves pointed to and affirmed. It should be said, however, that in taking this focus, I in no way wish to ignore the other influences on these women's lives or to negate the importance of fathers, brothers, husbands or grandfathers. Each woman lived a unique experience. Yet, as does a poem by Margaret Walker Alexander – one of the interviewees – I wish to pay tribute to the legacy left by women. In her poem 'Lineage' from her award-winning 1942 collection *For My People*, she writes;

> My grandmothers are full of memories
> Smelling of soap and onions and wet clay
> with veins rolling roughly over quick hands
> they have many clear words to say
> My grandmothers were strong
> Why am I not as they?[4]

Initially I approached this paper by trying to understand where and how group loyalties develop and by asking questions concerning race, class and/or gender solidarity. I since learned that these questions are to some extent irrelevant at least in so far as they relate to the women in the Black Women Oral History Project. If one idea encapsulates the lives and struggles of these women, it is 'race uplift', the idea that individual actions must work for the benefit of all Afro-American people.[5] Behind this overarching sense of needing self-pride and respect as part of an affirming racial identity, lie three crucial elements of their lives: family, education and religion. All spoke eloquently about these forces.

Within this family history, they speak of the presence of strong women – grandmothers, mothers, sisters, community leaders and educators – who helped to shape lives in times of immense difficulty. Though the influence of these foremothers in no way eclipsed that of supportive fathers and male community leaders, the women interviewed paid particular homage to them. In addition, these women, in many cases, described their experiences in terms of their family, rather than solely as an individual account. They discussed their family's collective oppression not merely their own. For example, Addie William, an interviewee born in 1874 and the oldest child of parents who had been slaves, moves quite naturally from 'I' to 'we' in describing her life as a sharecropper's daughter:

> I had to work in the field but I had to milk two cows,
> scrub the children, etc.... before I went to the field to work
> every day of my life. We worked from sunup until sundown
> and in planting tobacco time, when there was much rain,
> we'd plant tobacco all day long in the rain.[6]

At her mother's insistence, the family moved from the country to Danville, a larger town, in order that she might receive an education. After one year's training, she taught school in rural areas for fity-four years and insisted that all her children go to universities – 'Lord only knows I had to work hard'.[7]

Hard work dominated many of these women's lives. One woman was raised by her grandmother, a former slave. Her life was affected by the impact slavery left on her grandmother, a woman who resisted her owner and emphasised self-determination in her later struggles to secure education for herself, her granddaughter and the larger Afro-American community.[8]

This highly-valued education was not so easily obtained by women, and the following anecdote illustrates the lack of control over self-destiny experienced by these women due to racial discrimination. The 'trouble' a young, black woman could encounter in early twentieth-century America is vividly portrayed by these words from Minnie L.

Fisher. Born in 1896, Minnie Fisher is the oldest native born citizen of Mound Bayou, Mississippi, an all-black township founded in 1887. In speaking of the settling of her community, she describes what it was like to create a refuge for former slaves:

> When they came land had to be cleared, huts ... to be built, wild animals had to be destroyed. There was no comfort for them here but they were determined to ... build a place for their children where they could worship God and be educated.[9]

While struggling to receive an education, she had – unlike white women of her generation – to defend her right *not* to work.

> One morning when I was on my way to the post office ... one of the ladies walked to the gate and said 'Who are you?' I said 'I'm Minnie L. Fisher'. 'Where do you work?' I say 'I'm not working yet. I'm still in college.' 'You are in college?' I say 'Yes, I am'. 'Well, what are you doing in Cleveland?' I said 'My sister is working ... and I stay awhile with her every year and then I go back to school.' So she found out that I was telling her the truth. But my sister said 'Well don't go up to that post office no more in the morning by her house ... because I don't want no trouble'.[10]

The type of work it was assumed that Ms Fisher was available to perform was domestic labour, a standard type of employment for Afro-American women. Yet the majority of women interviewed in the Black Women Oral History Project were educators of some sort, a tribute indeed to the emphasis placed on service to the community.

One of the courageous women who led the struggle for black education was Mary McLeod Bethune, daughter of former slaves. She had a profound impact on several interviewees, among them Lucy Miller Mitchell. As both a student and teacher at the school Mrs Behune established for Afro-American girls, she tells us how the motivation for education was not merely the desire to be educated in abstract, but the desire to challenge a system of institutionalised discrimination and informal terror. She begins her anecdote about Mrs Bethune by recalling the words Mary Behune taught her to live by:

One of her constant expressions was, 'You are being trained to serve, go out into your community and be an example of what education and training can mean to an individual'. We heard this over and over again. 'Help your fellow man.' ... And so in-grained was this concern and feeling of individual responsibility for the less fortunate of my people, that all of my adult life has been spent in work with the under-privileged of my race. Maybe that is why you haven't heard so much about me, because it's been the unspectacular things....

Mrs Bethune was a woman of extraordinary courage, and I recall an incident that occurred when I went back to teach after graduating from college. There were two candidates for mayor of the town: one who had promised to erect a new high school in the black community, and another candidate who was of the Ku Klux Klan. Mrs Bethune and many other prominent citizens, both black and white, backed the candidate promising the high school to the black community. On the eve of the election, I had taken a group of students on one of these entertainment missions to one of the hotels to give a concert...This was in 1922. And I received a telephone call from Mrs Bethune saying, 'Lucy, bring the students home immediately.'.... Mrs. Bethune didn't tell me why I had to cut short the program, and I leaned out of the window to ask another person... 'Why the hold-up?' They said, 'Don't you know, the Klu Klux Klan is marching tonight?' ... [We] arrived on campus, Mrs Bethune said, 'Get the students into the dormitory, get them into bed, do not share what is happening right now.' ... 'We have been informed that the KKK is marching on our campus, and that they intend to burn some buildings.' She said that the black men in the community had been advised and they are on this campus ... if there is any move by a Klansman to set fire, there will be violence. She said, 'But God is not going to let that happen.' She said, 'I am going to protect this campus.'

Well, we had barely time to man our stations .... Mrs Bethune ... stood out in the quadrangle with her arms folded, as the message came down that the Klan was coming. It was a bright moonlight night, and you could see

the Spanish moss hanging from the trees. It just made a
perfect arch for the marchers, but it was an eerie scene.
Evidently, the presence and courage which Mrs Bethune
exemplified, as those men marched in their white robes,
coming down that street, must have intimidated them,
because all that they did was to march in one entrance
around the quadrangle and out the other entrance of the
campus. They never broke ranks. But the courageous part
was that by six o'clock the next morning, the black
community was mobilised to go to the polls and vote for
that candidate. They went in one huge group. There were
five hundred blacks eligible to vote in that community; they
were there, led by Mrs Bethune to the polling booth.
Wasn't that something? They voted their man in and they
got their high school.

Probably not one woman interviewed escaped the joint
discrimination endemic in a world of sexual and racial inequality, but
neither would one admit defeat. Communities of women came
together to combat their problems through the Black Women's Club
movement, through voluntary organisations such as the Young
Women's Christian Association – a predominantly middle-class
women's organisation – and through Church groups within the
powerful and independent black Churches, amongst others.[12] This
does not mean that the women separated their own struggle from the
struggle for their people as a whole. There was, however, the
recognition that Afro-American women had a uniquely difficult role
in American society. They were more likely to work outside the
home at the lowest paid wages than either white women or black
men, and often they did not relinquish the roles of family
management they had played in the slave family.[13]

Due to the limits of this forum, I have only been able to share a
tiny part of the Black Women Oral History Project, but clearly there
is much to be learned from these women's perspective on life. Their
stories can truly alter our expectations concerning the motives for
historic acts as one more salient example will show. Rosa Parks, a
woman so soft spoken that her voice was barely caught on tape, is
responsible for initiating one of the most significant events of the civil
rights movement. In December of 1955, she refused to give up her
seat in the 'white' section of a Montgomery, Alabama bus. This one

act of civil disobedience triggered a successful bus boycott led by the then-emerging civil rights leader, Martin Luther King, Jr.

Rosa Parks was raised by her grandmother, and while sharing little of her grandmother's experience, she speaks of growing up in the rural South and of her mother and grandmother's efforts to secure her an education.

> I didn't have too much leisure. Well, first of all, when I was going to Miss White's school ... My mother obtained what was called a scholarship, where I could clean two classrooms after school and sweep the floor and dust the desks and tidy it up for the evening ... At that time, I lived quite a long way from the school, so I was walking home from school....
>
> I never had a whole lot of leisure time just to play. There were always duties and things to do. When we were in Pine Level, however, I used to go fishing with my grandmother a great deal....
>
> I learned to sew and one of the things I liked to do was piece quilts. We took little squares and we sewed them together to make a quilt....
>
> My mother had hoped, I think, that I would be a teacher, but life as a teacher in a rural community seemed so very hard that it didn't much appeal to me at that time that much. I was concerned with trying to get an education and be prepared to have a career.[14]

In 1955 Rosa Parks was working as a seamstress in Montgomery. Her account of what stands out to many as the impetus of the civil rights movement can begin, as I observed earlier, to challenge our assumptions about community and racial solidarity. Her interview also illustrates the interaction between the interviewer's expectations and the participant's view of the situation.

> Question: On the first of December 1955, you refused to give up your seat to a white passenger on a Montgomery bus ... everyone else dutifully acquiesced to the white bus driver's demand that they move. Only you stayed in your seat. Why?
>
> I think it was because I was so involved with the attempt

to bring about freedom from this kind of thing ... I felt
that there was nothing else I could do to show that I was
not pleased with ... People have said I was a great
Democrat, people say things like that, but I was not
conscious of being ... I felt just resigned to give what I
could to protest against the way I was being treated.

First of all, I wanted to say that at this point on the bus
ride, I didn't consider myself breaking any segregation
laws... There were just certain drivers that would insist on
you going to the back of the bus after you give him the fare
... And neither did all of them ask you to stand up if there
was white people standing. So it seemed like each driver
was at his own discretion.

Question: What was the reaction of other black people on
the bus when this [her refusal] happened?

They didn't any of them say anything to me ... during
the time I was there all remained the same exactly where
they were.

Question: Nobody tried to interfere?

No.

Question: Did you resent that in any way?

No.

Question: Did you expect some support?

No, I didn't. It didn't even enter my mind. Because I
knew the attitude of the people. It was pretty rough to go
against the system.... There was one man who was on the
bus, he lived next door to where we lived, and he could
have, if he'd wanted to, gotten off the bus to let my
husband know that I was arrested.[15]

Yet there was solidarity enough to launch a boycott of buses until it
was possible to sit wherever one chose regardless of race. As this
excerpt demonstrates, until we have more oral history, our understanding of the motives and impetus for 'significant' acts within our
historical knowledge may well be skewed by our own expectations
and by what the dominant historiography has given us.

In closing, I would like to discuss the benefits of these connections
between oral history and the history of Afro–American women. In

doing so, I would like first to quote from another interviewee Olivia Pearl Stokes. In reflecting on her life and her community, she offers a less optimistic view of future progress for black women and men:

> We have moved from community good to individual fulfilment in terms of the acquisition of material goods. The blacks have gotten caught up in this, they are rugged individualists and no longer the community people, remembering that their heritage was out of Africa, or their heritage was out of the struggle to survive during the days of slavery.[16]

Hers are provocative words and they, as well as oral history itself, challenge us regarding both our questions about and our analysis of contemporary history. This method of historical inquiry teaches us to listen to what the participants in 'ordinary' history feel, rather than relying on our own assumptions. We have the technology to record these lives and to listen. We should then rethink the experience of slavery, not only from the point of view of those who inherited its legacy or from a desire to insert women's experiences into the framework, but more fundamentally to reorder what we question and why.

We might begin by looking at how the experience of work affects the relationship between pride and alienation; at how and why solidarity sometimes fails across and within boundaries of race and gender; at how women do not have just one community or solidarity base from which they draw support but several; at how this multiplicity of support works; at the possibility for women to become part of a political community, and finally at how different loyalties and roles come into conflict – for example, being Afro-American and an educator/wife/daughter/mother/activist, or combination thereof.

Whether or not one agrees with Olivia Stokes' words, her message remains disturbing. If the history of these women evinces one thing, it is how change can be implemented through working towards a collective end, by having a strong sense of community. If, as Olivia Stokes feels, this community spirit and sense of collective endeavour have to some extent been lost in the present generation, it is for us as students of history to find out where it remained strong and why it may have disintegrated. Nonetheless, the testimony of these women remains an ongoing source of strength, their lives an ongoing source of inspiration. There is much that we can all learn on a personal as well as an historical level from their example.

Acknowledgments

Thanks to Léonie Archer who persuaded me to present this paper and bore with my long-delayed revision process, to Sarah Lloyd for helping me with an early draft, to Nicky McIntyre and Andrea Fellows for their support, to Guy Boanas and Lyndal Roper for their technical assistance and especially to Lyndal for her editorial help, to Terri Bullen and all the participants in the Oxford Workshop session. Finally, I would like to express my deep appreciation to Patricia Miller and the Schlesinger Library on the History of Women in America for permission to quote from the interviews and to Lucy Miller Mitchell for permission to quote from her interview and to all the interviewees in the Black Women Oral History Project for their inspiring words and lives. Above all, I would like to thank Ruth Edmonds Hill whose assistance has been invaluable.

Notes

1 Published 1976, New York. This enormously popular book recounts the genealogy of this writer and was later made into a successful television mini-series.
2 Shockley (1978), p. 789.
3 Quoted in 'Origins and history' in *Women of Courage: A Catalog of an Exhibition of Photographs based on the Black Women Oral History Project* (Cambridge, MA, 1984), p. 3.
4 Margaret Walker, 'Lineage', in *For My People* (New York, 1968).
5 See Perkins (1984).
6 Schlesinger Library, Radcliffe College, Black Women Oral History Project, Interview with Adelie Williams, p. 5.
7 *ibid.*, p. 15.
8 Information from the archives of the Schlesinger Library, Black Women History Project.
9 *ibid.*, Interview with Minnie L. Fisher, p. 1.
10 *ibid.*, pp. 5–6.
11 *ibid.*, Interview with Lucy Miller Mitchell, pp. 13–14. Used by special permission of Lucy Miller Mitchell.
12 See Hill (1984) which describes the Black Women's Club Movement.
13 See Blassingame (1982), p. 78.
14 Schlesinger Library, Radcliffe College, Black Women Oral History Project, Interview with Rosa Parks, pp. 3–4.
15 *ibid.*, pp. 10–11.
16 Quoted in Perkins, *op. cit.*, p. 20.

Eighteen

Defining Slavery - its Special Features and Social Role

Robin Blackburn

The Concise Oxford English Dictionary gives the following primary entry for 'slave': 'Person who is the legal property of another or others and is bound to absolute obedience.' The same source defines slavery as 'condition of the slave ... exhausting labour, drudgery'.[1] The reference to legal property, and the equation of slavery with hard labour reflect the specific modern sense of the slave condition, a sense fixed to a considerable extent by New World slavery in the wake of European conquest and colonisation, but with some echoes from the ancient world, where slaves were also legal property and forced labourers.

The second part of the OED definition refers to a condition of subordination – of the person 'bound to absolute obedience' – for which equivalents may be found in many cultures and epochs, but which is still specified in rather general, abrupt and enigmatic terms. A French dictionary, Littrés *Dictionnaire*, offers a similar formula: 'The slave is a person, male or female, subject to the absolute dominion of the master in virtue of purchase, inheritance or war'.[2] In an essay on 'War and servitude in Segou' the anthropologist Jean Bazin explores the significance of the word *jon*, usually translated as 'captive' or 'slave', amongst the people of this West African state in the eighteenth and nineteenth centuries. Bazin observes that the primary sense of the word *jon* is indeed the 'purely factual situation of captive' though he adds: 'if capture effectively produces the *jon*, it only serves to reproduce his dependence to the extent that this strictly individual event is transformed into a social taint which is transmitted to the descendants although weakening from one generation to the next.' Bazin writes that the condition of the *jon* can be intensified and fixed chiefly by exchange or sale: 'If in the production of total servitude, capture is the first stage the second is sale, or in many cases a series of purchases or sales, through which the individual is definitively separated from his society of origin'.[3] Being a slave (*jonya*) is contrasted with *horonya*, which refers not to freedom in its 'legal-bourgeois sense' but to free membership of the given community: 'what is denied in *jonya* is the concrete individual, particularly defined, man of this land, of that name, of that kin and his freedom (*horonya*) understood as real autonomy, as mastery of the conditions of his existence (which he may at least have in his role as head of the household)'.

The people of Segou were within the field of force of the Atlantic slave trade yet their concept of *jonya* had at its core a sense of identity existing, even if in less sharp form, prior to, and apart from, the terrible pressures of that trade. Slavery, by annulling all prior rights and identity, has been the mechanism by which an individual is violently and permanently transferred from one community to another, without ever acquiring membership of the community of destination. While slaves have often been forced labourers their special status as shadow members of society, stripped of the rights of belonging, have also enabled them to be used as soldiers, concubines, or administrators.

In what follows I will attempt to establish whether there has been a core of features common to the slave status, beyond the great diversity of uses to which slaves have been put. It will be helpful as a preliminary to explore the variety of forms and meanings of enslavement, distinguishing it from other species of social oppression; indeed it will be suggested that the relations of slavery contrast with those based on marriage and kinship, with which they have so often been compared, and that this helps to explain the distinctive role which slavery plays in history.

There is evidence of enslavement from the dawn of recorded history and the institution of slavery, in one form or another, has accompanied most of the great world civilisations. From a wide-ranging comparative survey Orlando Patterson concludes: 'Probably there is no group of people whose ancestors were not at one time slaves or slave holders'.[4] Or, on his evidence, both. The only social relations which span a wider variety of cultures and epochs than slavery are those springing directly from family and kinship. In one of their earliest but most fascinating sketches of the stages of human development Marx and Engels argued that primitive slavery was itself a product of family relations in the early phase of tribal ownership:

The division of labour is at this stage still very elementary and is confined to a further extension of the natural division of labour existing in the family. The social structure is, therefore, limited to an extension of the family; patriarchal chieftains, below them the members of the tribe, finally slaves. The slavery latent in the family only develops gradually with the increase in population, the growth of wants, and with the extension of external relations, both of war and of barter.[5]

Thus Marx and Engels postulated both a primary potential for enslavement, arising out of the nature of kin relations, and a development or extension of this servitude consequent upon socio-economic development, war and barter. In certain respects the status, if not condition, of the slave has often paralleled that of wives, concubines, children and other minors, all of whom have been forbidden to hold property in their own name, participate in political decision-making, give legal testimony and so forth. Such significant parallels can make it seem that slavery has grown out of the seeds of primitive patriarchy. There may be an element of truth in this but it should not obscure the discontinuity and distinction between the status of dependent kin and that of the slave. Women and children, if not enslaved, helped to constitute the family and the lineage – even more essentially they brought together different kin groups and lineages, a function and role with its own moment of autonomy. While the specific social being of the slave can be changed at will by the slave holder, including release from the slave condition through manumission, these other statuses have a destiny which cannot be altered at will by anyone. There was an accidental quality to the very existence of the slave: the condition and prospects of the junior wife, or youngest son, might be wretched but they reflected a more or less well-defined pact between the social and natural order, and between one human group and another.

In the text already quoted, *The German Ideology*, Marx and Engels argue that the matrix of production and reproduction constitutes the social structure and rests upon a determinate division of labour:

The production of life, both of one's own in labour and of fresh life in procreation, now appears as a double relationship: on the one hand as a natural, on the other as a social relationship.[6]

When Engels came to elaborate on these ideas in *The Origin of the Family, Private Property and the State* he sketched a theory both of the origins of male domination and of the historical emergence and significance of slavery. The notion of an aboriginal matriarchy which Engels took over from Morgan now seems empirically dubious. Maurice Godelier has suggested that male dominance has been widespread, probably universal, in human history, while still leaving room for considerable variation in the position of women.[7] If Engels' theses on matriarchy are set aside there is still something essential in the approach of Marx and Engels to these questions, especially the attempt to think through the relationship between production and reproduction, the natural and the social. More specifically, there is the thesis that the development of slavery and property helped to strengthen the hand of men and to foster differentiation and economic development.

The distribution of roles in the realm of reproduction is obviously not a question of arbitrary social attribution but rests on the distinct biological capacities of men and women. The fact that women exercise a natural monopoly over pregnancy, and hold a strong natural advantage in lactation, must have lent its own bias to the division of labour between the sexes in pre-history; since in pre-modern demographic conditions women would be bearing two or three times as many children as in today's advanced countries but living only half as long. Child-bearing and the nursing of infants would occupy a great part, probably the greater part, of women's adult life. Men could be more mobile and were more expendable. From the standpoint of the reproduction of the human group there was a survival value in allotting to men the larger part in the more hazardous occupations requiring the use of force – hunting and warfare. If this was so then the division of labour between the sexes would tend towards male supremacy since it would give male warriors and hunters the leverage implied by control of organised force. This leverage could be exercised in relations with other groups, as well as in internal social organisation and symbolic representation.[8]

If slavery has been the means for the forcible transfer of persons from one group to another marriage has been a means for the negotiated or contractual transfer of women between groups. In Lévi-Strauss's classic study, *Les Structures élémentaires de la parenté*, the reciprocal bond basic to marriage was not set up between men and women but between male dominated lineages by means of women, who were only the occasion for it. Though variously privileged and powerful, individual men were still constrained by the natural and social facts of reproduction and kinship. Short of enslavement women could still be subject to a harsh regime of labour and punishment, in addition to the burdens of child-bearing and child-care; but if the wider tasks of reproduction were to be sustained then the extremities of slave exploitation and oppression had to be avoided. Women's status as wives and mothers could never be wholly degraded without degrading their husbands and sons. Glory might be achieved in war rather than childbirth but there was surely a harsher dichotomy within each of these spheres – between the conqueror and the captive, between the legitimate and the bastard. Death, or slavery, the 'living death', could easily be the fate of those condemned by arms or illegitimacy. Women given in marriage between one group of men and another continued to represent a link with their society of origin. The slave's origins were entirely effaced and there was no continuing link. The status of the slave was an inherently dishonourable one; though this dishonour could be partially alleviated precisely by becoming either the mother of a recognised child, or a soldier.

Marx and Engels were right to postulate a latent slavery in the division of labour practised by the primitive kin group in the sense both that the family tended to generate a category of potential slave holders and in the sense that kin relations could expose to slavery all those who fell outside its categories. But they also believed that the domination of women by men, or of children by parents, itself had a slave-like character or represented the germ of slavery: in *The Origin of the Family* Engels points out that the term itself actually derived from *famulus*, meaning a household slave, and *familia*, meaning 'the slaves belonging to a particular master'. As Engels observed, this suggested something very different from the family in 'the ideal of our modern Philistine, which is a compound of sentimentality and domestic discord'. But Engels' etymology yields ambiguous results since it could as well be that it was slavery which generated the Roman notion of family, rather than the other way about.

The equation of the family and slavery pinpoints the usually, though not exclusively, male sex of the slave holder and it can draw attention to certain common features of all forms of oppression or domination, or between the specific situation of women and slaves in societies where the former have few rights and little autonomy. But on the other hand it misses important dimensions of the slave relation, many of which stem precisely from slavery's *negation* of family and kinship. The slave is subject to the absolute dominion of the slave holder in large part because he or she lacks rights or restrictions pertaining to a member of the kin group or family. The slave lacked such belonging. The slave 'belonged' to one man or a group as a piece of property not as a member with an identity and ancestry of his or her own. In the pre-individualist world of the primitive kin group each family member partakes of the group's identity but the slave was excluded from it. The slave's identity did not see the light of day; it was the shadow cast by the owner. The slave brought no name but was given a name just as domestic animals might be. Distinctive dress, body markings or hairstyle were imposed on slaves to set them apart. The slave was, in principle, a pure instrument, even if, as the Romans put it, a talking instrument – an *instrumentum vocale* in contrast to livestock, *instrumentum semi-vocale*, and the work tool, *instrumentum mutum*. Unlike distinctions of gender or generation the slave status was a purely social construct.

Marx and Engels refer to slavery developing in the wake of war and barter. Heraclitus, in one of the earliest known theories of enslavement, argued that it was the concomitant of the inevitable conflict between human groups. Capture in warfare, or as a result of raiding expeditions or kidnapping, has certainly been one of the most common sources of the enslavement of free persons.[9] There is likewise very early evidence for the barter or sale of slaves. The captive whose life was spared could no longer claim rights or identity derived from his or her society of origin but owed life itself to the slave holder. The foundling or the orphan could be delivered into slavery by an analogous logic. Slaves could be selected and formed by extrusion – by the condemnation of insiders as well as by acquisition of outsiders. Social membership could be lost by those who had once possessed it. Chronic endebtedness could be transformed into slavery. Famine or natural disaster might force the victims to sell or pawn themselves or their children as an alternative to starvation or homelessness. One derivation of the most common Latin term for slave, *servus*, traces it to the term for a person whose life has been spared (*servatus*) by the captor. A common theme of slave-holder ideology maintained that in allowing their life to be spared slaves bound themselves to their masters. Similarly penal enslavement was a punishment given to those who had committed a capital offence; it was a commutation of the death sentence.

Those captured in war were, by definition, enemies but not necessarily fully alien. They were close enough to be fought and might one day become necessary allies. Retaining their captives as slaves would be a permanent provocation and risk. Moreover the slave captive could escape or be recaptured. Neighbours made difficult slaves: this is, perhaps, one of the reasons why the warriors of Segou preferred to sell their captives. Even if a whole neighbouring people were conquered then outright enslavement would be a most arduous option. It has been extremely rare for a people to be enslaved in its own native land. The conquered could usually dispose of sufficient communal resources and collective solidarity to enable them successfully to resist complete slavery, though individuals might be enslaved and the conquered community as a whole might succumb to some less extreme dependence.

That the slave was essentially a stranger and a foreigner has been argued by Henri Lévy-Bruhl in his *Théorie de l'esclavage* and by M. I. Finley in his contribution to the *Encyclopedia of the Social Sciences*.[10] Athenian and Roman citizenship was held to incorporate a guarantee against enslavement, though grave crimes could incur penal servitude. Thus Solon's laws protected Athenian citizens from enslavement for debt. The slave was an outsider, a barbarian, someone with no claim on civic rights or indeed on anyone who might diminish the rights of the slaveholder. Most were purchased from slave traders and many originated from the border regions or beyond. But, of course, there were second generation slaves or slaves from civilised regions. To complicate further the equation of foreigner and slave there were also resident foreigners, such as the Athenian metics, and freedmen of foriegn extraction, who were not enslaved though not citizens. Slaves were outsiders wherever they were born and however long they had lived 'inside'. Plato's theory of natural slavery, according to which some people were fitted only for menial or banausic employment, could supplement and strengthen the metaphor of strangeness based on a mainly ethnic justification of slavery. But later Greek and Roman slave holders did not always insist on a fully consistent theory of natural slavery; of course, some very able Greeks were enslaved to Romans while Roman slave holders became quite ethnically heterogeneous themselves. Late Roman writers conceded that some actual slaves might not deserve to be so. They then comforted themselves with the notion that slavery could not degrade those who were not 'really' slaves. While, as G. E. M. Ste. Croix insists, this was a self-serving and hypocritical doctrine, it may also have been linked both to a certain receptivity towards manumission and to the increasing difficulty of drawing clear lines between insider and outsider, natural slaves and citizens.

The ancient Hebrews also had a dichotomous system for specifying those who could be enslaved, with the added reinforcement of a stronger ethno-religious identity. And, as with Solon, the designation of the enslaveable was coupled with the Jews' own privileged exemption. God instructed Moses that the children of Israel should not take one another as slaves:

> as for thy bondmen, and thy bondmaids, which thou shalt have; of the nations that are round about you, of them, shall ye buy bondmen and bondmaids. Moreover of the children of the strangers that do sojourn among you, of them shall ye buy, and of their families that are with you, which they have begotten in your land: and they shall be your possession. And ye shall make them an inheritance for your children after you, to hold for a possession; of them shall ye take your bondmen forever: but over your brethren the children of Israel ye shall not rule, one over another, with rigour (*Leviticus* 25: 42–6).

The Lord's advice could scarcely have been clearer. Not only Jews but Christians and Moslems were to heed it. Yet the bare fact of being a stranger or an unbeliever was not sufficient to produce the slave. Not all strangers or unbelievers were enslaved. There was also the awkward fact that slaves could, and did, become believers. This may have been encouraged since many of the slaves were Canaanites, a neighbouring people – conversion and assimilation would have placed a barrier between the slave and return to the land of his or her ancestors. After a few generations how did the assimilated children of strangers remain strangers? The alien status of the slave was fixed by a tale of hereditary guilt. Following the story about Noah's Ark in *Genesis* comes the following passage:

> And Noah began to be an husbandman, and planted a vineyard: and he drank of the wine, and was drunken; and

he was uncovered within his tent. And Ham, the father of
Canaan, saw the nakedness of his father, and told his two
brethren without. And Shem and Japeth took a garment,
and laid it upon both their shoulders, and went backward,
and covered the nakedness of their father; and their faces
were backward and they saw not the nakedness of their
father. And Noah awoke from his wine, and knew what his
youngest son had done unto him. And he said, Cursed be
Canaan; A servant of servants shall he be unto his brethren
(*Genesis*, 9, 20–6).

Again, not only Jews but Christians and Moslems came to believe
that Ham's sexual offence, whatever it was, condemned Canaan's
issue to servitude – as the next chapter of *Genesis* points out, amongst
Canaan's descendants were the inhabitants of Sodom and Gomorrah.
The puzzling aspects to this story – the precise nature of the offence
and the fact that the curse falls not on Ham but on one of his children
– did nothing to reduce its mythic potency as a justification of why
some should be slaves and other not. Given the arbitrariness of enslavement and the ubiquity of sexual anxiety, quite the contrary.
Moreover stigmatising the slave as sexually unclean, which the
Canaanite myth certainly did (e.g., *Leviticus* claimed that Canaanites
had the habit of congress with animals), offered important guarantees
to legitimate members of the patriarch's family. Slave holders have
had a universal proclivity for sexually abusing female slaves. Myths
of the Canaanite variety might discourage this and would certainly
make it very difficult for the slave holder to manumit natural
children by 'Canaanite' mothers, with the consequent danger that he
might bequeath property to them, diminishing the patrimony.
Legitimate wives and children had good reason to support what has
been termed a 'legitimist' myth, in contrast to the paternalist
inclinations of the master who had nothing to lose from a multiplica-
tion of legitimate offspring. At all events the ancient Hebrews
continued to hold 'Canaanite' slaves for centuries, though not in large
numbers.[11] It is interesting to note that a sexual offence against
patriarchy also furnished the one instance in Solon's laws permitting
the enslavement of a citizen – a father could sell into slavery a
daughter who had had illicit sexual relatons. However, this was not
converted into a more general theory of slave origins as happened to
the story of Noah's curse. The institution of monogamy, as in Greece

or Rome, would also give support to legitimist preoccupations.

When it came to forging myths the Greeks and Hebrews were evidently in a class of their own. Yet these justifications for, and explanations of, enslavement contain ingredients found in other slave-holder ideologies. The theme of the stranger is reinforced by a conviction of strangeness that survives – is even intensified by – familiarity. Crucially the stigma of slavery also confers recognition on those non-slaveholding free persons on whose support slave holders depended.

Summarising his impressive comparative survey Patterson has proposed the following sociological definition: 'slavery is the permanent, violent domination of natally alienated and generally dishonoured persons'.[13] The slave status was *permanent*, even though it might be ended by manumission, in the sense that it was not inherently transitional or temporary like that of a prisoner being held for ransom or condemned to labour for a term of years. Greek or Roman slaves could be referred to as 'boys' (*pais* or *puer*) but unlike minors they could never, as slaves, reach adulthood. The status of the slave was defined by, and saturated with, violence to a greater extent that any other social relations. Slaves were acquired by violence, maintained in their servitude by violence and constantly at risk of physical abuse: since the very life of the slave had been spared so it could be expended in the service of the slave holder.

Perhaps the most important element in Patterson's definition is his description of the slave as *natally alienated*, in the sense that they had no birthright of their own. In all societies up to and including those of the modern world birth confers essential rights concerning citizenship, nationality and property. In many pre-capitalist societies kinship has played the central role in ordering social relations and structuring economic and political power. To be officially kinless, like the slave, was thus the most fundamental species of deprivation of social rights. And even in those societies where co-residence was more important than kinship, probably the case in much of the ancient world, it was still birth which furnished primary access to civic belonging.

Paradoxically this condition of natal alienation could be inherited: in any functioning slave system many slaves, perhaps the majority, would be slaves by birth. There was a social logic to this in so far as the child of a person without positive social attributes inherited none.

Moreover the kin ties that would develop in the slave community itself would not be recognised by the slave-holding regime. If the slave holder found it convenient to break up a slave family by sale nothing stood in his way; the threat, by itself, served as a guarantee of slave subordination. Though there have been many patterns of slave inheritance – Patterson identifies seven types – that of ancient Rome had the advantage of being easy to determine and was most common in the large-scale slave systems. Ancient Rome was a patrilineal society but nevertheless slavery was inherited through the mother, irrespective of the status of the father. The children of a slave mother belonged to the owner of the mother at the time she gave birth.[14]

There could be some tendency for an alleviation of the slave's condition in the second or third generation. Attachment to one family or place could lead to some subordinate incorporation, to the acquisition of a specific social identity. The slave holder might even tolerate such a mitigation of pure slavery. Likewise the offer of manumission on condition of years of loyal service could encourage slave industry and reduce the costs of invigilation. Where there was a vigorous slave trade the passage of some slaves to a condition of sponsored freedom or serf-like dependence would not necessarily weaken the slave system. But there remained a fundamental question for any slave-holding social formation. Could they continually reproduce the slave condition, regardless of whether new slaves were acquired by means of a slave trade or through natural reproduction? To some extent the term 'slave trade' is a misnomer since the eventual status of the person purchased would have to be established by the enslaving society. Of course it helped that the person purchased knew that they had been the objects of a degrading transaction. Having expended the purchase price the purchaser also would have felt more secure and justified in his possession. But it was still necessary for the enslaving social formation to sustain the social relations of slavery for itself. Slaves might be resigned or fatalistic – or even grateful that they had not suffered a worse fate – but the prudent slave holder would not place all his faith in involuntary servitude. Both the slave holder and the slave-holding society would make provision for runaways or insubordination. Those who owned a sizeable number of slaves would employ armed slave drivers and overseers – though the latter, as in Rome, might often themselves be slaves. The outsider status of the slaves would normally mean that the hand of every insider would be against them. Reinforcing such hoped-for solidarity would be the realm of symbolic representations, denying sympathy to the slave. Ideologies which justified slavery played a crucial role in securing the support of those citizens who owned no slaves. Civil privileges, ethnic conceit and religious taboos could all, as we have seen, be tied up with the justification of servitude, though the mixture might not always work, especially where links had nevertheless developed between the free and the enslaved.

Slaves who challenged servile subordination would be the targets of exemplary punishments, in the first instance from their own masters, failing that from public agencies. In ancient Rome it was the rule that if a slave murdered the master then all slave members of the household would be put to death. Ste. Croix writes of the controversy sparked by the application of this rule under the Principate:

> 'You will not restrain that scum except by terror,' said the Roman lawyer, Gaius Cassius, to the nervous senators during the debate on whether there should be the traditional mass execution of all the 400 urban slaves of Pedanius Secundus, the Praefectus Urbi, who had been murdered by one of his slaves in AD 61. The execution was duly carried out in spite of a vigorous protest by the common people of Rome, who demonstrated violently for the relaxation of the savage ancient rule – which, by the way, was still the law in the legislation of the Christian Emperor Justinian five centuries later.[15]

Modern notions of slavery tend to equate it with property in persons and coercive labour regimes. The anti-slavery Conventions which outlawed human bondage in the modern world identified it with chattel slavery and forced labour, other than penal labour. Because slavery has been, as it were, overidentified with the trade in human chattels and the exploitation of slave labour it is quite understandable why social theorists have wished to achieve a more profound and comprehensive understanding by exploring other dimensions and determinants of the slave condition than these. But it would be wrong to discount the notion that slaves have always been, in some relevant sense, *the property of slave holders*, whether individuals or a corporation, that this has exposed them to the risk of being bought and sold, and that a very large number of slaves have ended up as forced labourers.

Ste. Croix writes:

> Slavery is defined in the 1926 Convention as 'the status or condition of a person over whom any or all of the powers attaching to the right of onwership are exercised'. I accept this definition of 'chattel slavery' (as it is often called) for the ancient as well as the modern world, the more willingly since what stresses is not so much the fact that the slave is the *legal property* of another as that '*the powers attaching* to the *right of ownership* are *exercised over him*'; for the essential elements in the slave's condition are that *his labour and other activities are totally controlled* by his master, and that he is virtually without rights, at least without enforceable legal rights. In Roman law, enslavement was regarded as closely resembling death'.[16]

The definition cited by Ste. Croix does go too far in one respect since it refers to *any* as well as *all* powers attaching to ownership. In fact employers in a capitalist society do exercise some of the powers of owners over the labouring capacity of their employees; spouses can have some ownership rights over one another's wealth or income; and sports' clubs or finance houses can ask a hefty transfer fee for purchase of the service of those contracted to them.[17] It is the comprehensive extent of the property rights claimed by the slave owner which distinguish slavery. In principle the slave holder owns/controls all the time powers of the slave, in reproduction as well as production and notwithstanding the parcel of personal possessions, in ancient Rome the *peculium*, permitted to the slave. The slave's *peculium* might be quite considerable and, in the case of slaves, discharging high responsibilities, often included the possession of slaves, known as *vicarii*. But as the latter term implies this was a form of proxy ownership, or possession on behalf of the owner with a right of usufruct. Where the slave was able to accumulate money, such as the earnings of a slave artisan or prostitute, then it is true that this provided leverage over the slave holder who could not hope to make an inventory of it as he could with most other possessions. But slave holders still did very well out of such slaves; sometimes they might allow them to buy their freedom as a way of maximising their take.

In Islamic states slaves were recruited as soldiers but still remained the ruler's property. The fact that they bore arms meant some mitigation in their condition but the ruler would count on military discipline and social isolation as guarantees of loyalty. Years of service would often bring manumission. Similarly the slave imperial administrator, in ancient Rome or Byzantium or ancient China, would remain the property of the ruler. Such slaves sometimes exhibited a tendency to levitate beyond their servile condition, wielding power and not simply influence, amassing wealth and slaves, which they could put to purposes of their own, notably manumission. But so long as they remained slaves they could be stripped of all their offices and possessions – a not infrequent occurrence on the death of a ruler. As a double guarantee of kinlessness the imperial slave administrators were often eunuchs. The slave concubine could also escape from a purely servile state if she bore children who extended the lineage of her master. Beyond a certain point it was no longer true of these slaves that they could be simply bought and sold. But to that extent their slave condition had been qualified and they were in transit to some less absolute form of bondage.

In some social formations the weak development of exchange relations would have made it difficult or impossible for the slave holder to find a purchaser for the slave. But where there was private ownership and a market in slaves then the true slave was saleable. While the slave traffic was probably amongst the earliest branches of commerce there can be no doubt that the considerable development of exchange relations associated with the rise of Greek and Roman civilisation allowed for a clearer and stronger definition of economic property, in land, in moveable objects and in persons conceived of as objects or instruments. Indeed Patterson suggests that the strong sense of property conveyed by Roman law derived to a significant extent from its preoccupation with the ownership of slaves, a form of ownership corresponding to the comprehensive powers of the slave holder.[17]

Of course even the strongest powers attributed by the law of property to owners do not allow them to do literally anything they like with their possessions: such laws codify the general interests of property holders, and will discourage them from jeopardising the holdings of their fellow proprietors by wanton neglect or misuse. In the case of slavery this raised vital security questions. Just as a proprietor may be restrained from burning his house without due precautions so a slave holder might be restrained from arbitrarily killing his slave. Systems of law relating to slavery would consider the slave a person as well as a piece of property, albeit a person of a baser sort. The slave could always be beaten, if necessary tortured. Slaves would not enjoy free movement without specific authorisation. In Greek and Roman antiquity to kill another person's slave was a crime equivalent to manslaughter, usually leading to a fine of perhaps twice the slave's value. In Rome a certain category of slaves, the gladiators, were expected to kill one another for sport, at private gatherings as well as in the Circus. For a slave holder to kill his own slave for no good reason was much frowned upon. But no slave holder could be punished for it. The slave's life was held at the good pleasure of the slave holder. Likewise the slave holder was enjoined to treat his slaves well but there was no effective sanction behind this prescription, save public opinion.

In so far as the slave holder required the support of law to uphold his absolute dominion it could be argued that this dominion was not, in fact, absolute. The term 'property' precisely registers this paradox. In the case of slavery the slave holder did sometimes suffer a notional price for the protection he gained from the state or the law, where these existed. Thus in the Roman Empire the slave could, in theory, appeal against misuse by appearing at an imperial shrine as a supplicant. In Book IX of Plato's *Republic* the defence of slave holders is identified as a crucial function of the polity. Legal notions of property both normalised the violent domination of the slave and defined the terms on which the polity would support the slave holder.

To summarise, the slave status and condition has been a purely social construction – that of a social isolate, an outsider, a person without kin, a person subject to the complete and arbitrary authority of the master, a person who could be whipped or tortured or sexually abused, a piece of property, and, by virtue of the foregoing, an instrument. The very enumeration of such qualities must remind us that slavery was not a suprahistorical essence but had to be produced and perpetuated, enlisting the support of the free population and adapting the slave to the particular use required.

Notes

1 *The Concise Oxford Dictionary* (Oxford, 1931), pp. 1132–3.
2 Quoted Dockes (1982), p. 4.
3 Bazin (1974), p. 109. The conditions under which captivity is transformed into servitude are explored by several of the contributors to the
useful collection of essays edited by Meillassoux (1975), in which Bazin's
original way also appears. See also Meillassoux (1986).
4 Patterson (1982), p. vii.
5 Marx and Engels, *The German Ideology*, p. 33.
6 *ibid.*, p. 41.
7 Godelier (1981). The sketch which follows of the consequences of the
sexual division of labour is taken from Godelier, see especially p. 12. In
this text, Godelier responds to the qualified defence of Engels advanced
by Leacock (1972).
8 Engels (1969), p. 496.
9 Patterson, *op. cit.*, pp. 105–31.
10 Lévy-Bruhl (1960); Finley (1968).
11 Ste. Croix (1981), pp. 416–25. The natural slavery doctrine held that the
slave actually needed and benefited by subjection to the rule of the
master. It was little invoked in the Hellenistic period and empire. Ste.
Croix points out that the formally manumitted slave of a Roman was to
become not just a free person but a citizen. In Athens the manumitted
slave became a 'metic' but in a number of Greek states could subsequently acquire citizen status (pp. 174–5). Ethno-religious conceptions
of slavery, of the sort discussed below, precluded such transitions. On the
other hand it should be said that Romans, such as Cicero, could condemn
whole peoples, such as the Syrians and the Jews, as 'born to slavery'
(quoted Ste. Croix, *op. cit.*, p. 417).
12 For the remarkable itinerary of these ideas see the fascinating essay by
Evans (1980). While Evans rightly draws attention to the complex of
'legitimism' placing restraints on the paternalist inclinations of the
patriarchal slaveholder it should be said that despite its obsessive detail on
so many questions *Leviticus* contains no strong or specific warning against
sexual relations with slave girls. Eating prawns, seeing the nakedness of
the uncle's wife, or having sex with a wife during menstruation were
evidently far more grave offences. The Canaanite taboo ruled out offspring of slave mothers as legitimate inheritors but was probably less
effective at protecting slave women from the sexual attentions of their
masters. So far as the story of Noah and Ham is concerned the link
between vineyards, wine and servitude could be a significant inversion
since viticulture did indeed permit an intensive exploitation of servile
labour. Rabbinical commentators on this passage argued that since Noah
had no more children after this incident perhaps Ham's offence had been

to castrate his father; since Noah was over five hundred years old at the time his subsequent childlessness does not require such a dramatic explantation.

13 Patterson, *op. cit.*, p. 13. In this sentence the adverb 'generally' is, in context, meant to strengthen not weaken the association between slavery and dishonour. I remain somewhat sceptical of the very great importance Patterson attributes to dishonour as an attribute of slavery. He bravely takes very influential slaves, such as those who helped administer empires, to test the limits of his theory showing that nevertheless they enjoyed no independent honour of their own and were often the target of cruel stereotypes, as were the eunuchs (pp. 299–333). But the inevitably ambivalent attitude towards powerful slaves may make them bad texts. The faithful and hard-working slave servant or craftsman or nurse might be accorded a modicum of respect, possibly more than that given to some lowly or disreputable free persons. At all events such a comparison would be the hardest test of Patterson's thesis. Patterson is quite right to stress the way violence constituted slavery but does not consider that the known fact that slaves were under duress could mitigate their 'dishonour' as could the notion that they were not 'natural slaves'.

14 *ibid.*, pp. 132–47.

15 Ste. Croix, *op. cit.*, p. 409. The response of the 'common people', many of them probably descendants of slaves themselves, is as remarkable as the punishment meted out. In an earlier passage Ste. Croix draws attention to the slave holder's expectation of civil solidarity: 'In the background, always, was the fact that fellow-citizens could be relied upon, in Xenophon's phrase, to act as unpaid bodyguards of one another against their slaves' (p. 147).

16 *ibid.*, p. 135. See also p. 141.

17 Patterson cites some of the examples given above of partial property rights exercised over persons to argue against the idea that slaves were defined by being the property of their masters. Perhaps it is the low value assigned by Patterson to the slave's status as a piece of property which leads him to overstress, in compensation, the more purely ideological notion of 'dishonour'. That notions of the slave as property have not been confined to social formations with a strong market economy is clear from the illuminating discussion by James Watson, 'Slavery as an institution' in Watson (1980), pp. 1–16. However, I believe Patterson is right to insist that being a piece of property is not the sole defining feature of the slave's status; it must also be conceded that the powers that parents exercise over children do often have a proprietorial stamp – extending sometimes to the power to sell, or kill, them to alleviate economic distress, or for some other reason.

By refining the notion of absolute property or *dominium* the Romans certainly perfected the concept of enslavement; an innovation in the sphere of the 'organic' ideology of slave holding that should alert us to the possibility that it was associated with an innovation in the deployment of slaves. See Anderson (1974), pp. 66–7.

Bibliography

Adams, W. Y. (1977), *Nubia: Corridor to Africa*, London.

Alier, J. M. (1977), *Haciendas, Plantations and Collective Farms: Agrarian Class Societies – Cuba and Peru*, London.

Althusser, L. (1971), *Lenin and Philosophy and Other Essays*, trans. B. Brewster, London.

Anderson, P. (1974), *Passages from Antiquity to Feudalism* (sequel: *Lineages of the Absolutists State*), London.

Andrews, C. W. (1844), *Memoir of Mrs Ann R. Page*, Philadelphia.

Andrews, E. A. (1836; r.p. 1969), *Slavery and the Domestic Slave Trade in the United States, in a Series of Letters Addressed to the Executive Committee of the American Union for the Relief and Improvement of the Colored Race*, London (r.p. Detroit).

Aptheker, B. (1982), *Woman's Legacy: Essays on Race, Sex and Class in American History*, Amherst, MA.

Ardouin, A. B. (1958), *Études sur l'histoire d'Haiti suivies de la vie du général J.-M. Borgelle*, Port-au-Prince (first ed. Paris 1856).

Arnott, P. D. (1970), *An Introduction to the Roman World*, London.

Ashbury, F. (1958), *The Journal and Letters of Francis Ashbury* (ed.) E.T. Clark, 3 vols., London.

Ashe, R. P. (1889), *Two Kings of Uganda*, London.

Ayalon, D. (1979), *The Mamluk Military Society*, London.

Baer, G. (1967), 'Slavery in nineteenth-century Egypt', *Journal of African History*, vol. 8, no. 3, pp. 417–41.

Baerlein, H. (1914), *Mexico, The Land of Unrest*, London.

Bancroft, F. (1931: r.p. 1959), *Slave Trading in the Old South*, Baltimore (r.p. New York).

Barratt Brown, M. (1984), *Models in Political Economy*, Harmondsworth.

Batran, A. A. (1985), 'The "Ulama" of Fas, Mulay Isma'il, and the issue of the Haratin of Fas', in J.R. Willis (ed.), *Slaves and Slavery in Muslim Africa, vol. 2: The Servile Estate*, pp. 1–15, London.

Bauer, A. (1979), 'Rural workers in Spanish America: problems of peonage and oppression', *Hispanic American Historical Review*, vol. 54, pp. 34–63.

Bazin, J. (1974), 'War and servitude in Segou', *Economy and Society*, vol. 2, no. 2, pp. 107–14. Also in Meillassoux (1975), pp. 135–82.

Beachey, R. W. (1976), *The Slave Trade of Eastern Africa*, London.

Beckles, H. (1985), 'Emancipation by war or law? Wilberforce and the 1816 Barbados slave rebellion', in D. Richardson (ed.), *Abolition and Its Aftermath: The Historical Context 1790–1916*, pp. 80–104, London.

Bellingeri, M. (1976), 'L'economia del latifondo in Messico. L'hacienda San Antonio Tochatlaco del 1880 al 1920', *Annali della Fondazione Luigi Einaudi* vol. 10, pp. 287–428.

Benjamin, T. L. (1981a), *Passages to Leviathan: Chiapas and the Mexican State, 1891–1947*, unpublished PhD thesis, Michigan State University.

—— (1981b) 'El trabajo en las monterías de Chiapas y Tabasco, 1870–1946', *Historia Mexicana*, vol. 30, pp. 506–29.

Berlin, I. (1974), *Slaves Without Masters*, New York.

—— (1980), 'Time, space and the evolution of Afro-American society on British mainland North America', *American Historical Review*, vol. 85, pp. 44–78.

Bernabo-Brea, M. (1981), *Menandro e il teatro greco nelle terracotte liparesi*, Genoa.

Bettini, M. (1982), 'Verso un antropologia dell'intreccio. Le strutture semplici della trama nelle commedie di Plauto', *Materiali e discussioni per l'annalisi dei testi classici*, vol. 7, pp. 39–101.

Bieber, M. (1961), *The History of the Greek and Roman Theater*, Princeton and London.

Birley, E. (1953), *Roman Britain and the Roman Army*, collected papers, Kendal.

Bishop, P. A. (1970), *Runaway Slaves in Jamaica, 1740–1807*, unpublished MA thesis, University of West Indies.

Blanchard, P. (1979), 'The recruitment of workers in the Peruvian sierra at the turn of the century: the *enganche* system', *Inter-American Economic Affairs*, vol. 33, pp. 63–83.

Blassingame, J. W. (1975), 'Using the testimony of ex-slaves: approaches and problems', *Journal of Southern History*, vol. 41, pp. 473–492.

—— (1979), *The Slave Community: Plantation Life in the Ante-bellum South*, revised edition, New York.

—— (1982), *Long Memory: The Black Experience in America*, New York.

Blodget, M. (1946), 'Cawsons Virginia in 1795–1796', (ed.) M. Tinling, *William and Mary Quarterly*, series three, vol. 3, pp. 281–91.

Booker, W. T. (1966), 'Early problems of freedom', in H. Brotz (ed.), *Negro Social and Political Thought 1850–1920*, pp. 382–396, New York.

Booth, N. S. (1975), 'Time and change in African traditional thought', *Journal of Religion in Africa*, vol. 7, pp. 81–91.

Bowser, F. (1972), 'Colonial Spanish America', in D. W. Cohen and J. P. Greene (eds), *Neither Slave Nor Free*, pp. 19–58, London.

Bredin, G. (1961), 'The life-story of Yuzbashi 'Abdallah Adlan', *Sudan Notes and Records*, vol. 42, pp. 37–52.

Brenner, R. (1977), 'The origins of capitalist development: a critique of neo-Smithian Marxism', *New Left Review*, no. 104, pp. 25–92.

Bruce, D. D., Jr (1978), 'Death and testimony in the Old South', *Southern Humanities Review*, vol. 12, pp. 123–32.

Bruce, J. (1780), *Travels to Discover the Source of the Nile in the Years 1768, 1769, 1770, 1771, 1772 and 1773* (eds.) G. G. J. and J. Robinson,

Edinburgh.
—— (1804), *ibid*, second revised edition, (ed.) A. Murray, Edinburgh.
Brunt, P. A. (1958), Review of W.L. Westerman, *The Slave Systems of Greek and Roman Antiquity* (1955), in *Journal of Roman Studies*, vol. 48, pp. 164–70.
—— (1980), 'Free labour and public works at Rome', *Journal of Roman Studies*, vol. 70, pp. 81–98.
Buckland, W. W. (1970 orig. 1908), *The Roman Law of Slavery*, Cambridge.
—— (1975), *A Textbook of Roman Law*, Cambridge.
Buckley, R. N. (1979), *Slaves in Red Coats. The British West India Regiments, 1795–1815*, New Haven and London.
Burnham P. (1980), 'Raiders and traders in Adamawa: slavery as a regional system', in J. L. Watson (ed.), *Asian and African Systems of Slavery*, pp. 43–72, Oxford.
Bury, J. B. (1958), *History of the Later Roman Empire*, 2 vols, New York.
Butler, A. (1980), *The Africanisation of American Christianity*, New York.
Byrd, W. (1941), *The Secret Diary of William Byrd of Westover, 1709–1712*, (ed.) Louis B. Wright and M. Tinling, Richmond.
——(1942), *Another Secret Diary of William Byrd of Westover, 1739–1741; with Letters and Literary Exercises, 1696–1726*, (ed.) M. Tinling, Richmond.
——(1958), *The London Diary, 1717–1721 and Other Writings*, (ed.) L. B. Wright and M. Tinling, New York.
Cabanes, P. (1974), 'Les inscriptions du théâtre de Bouthrôtos', *Actes du Colloque 1972 l'Esclave* – Annales Littéraires de l'Université de Bescançon, vol II, pp. 105–209.
Cantacuzène G. (1928), 'Un papyrus relatif à la défense du bas-Danube', *Aegyptus*, vol. 9, pp. 63ff.
Cardellini, I. (1981), *Die biblischen 'Sklaven' – Gesetze im Lichte des keilschrift – lichen Sklavenrechts*, Bonn.
Cardwell, G. A. (1973), 'Mark Twain, James R. Osgood and those "suppressed" passages', *New England Quarterly*, vol. 46, pp. 163–88.
Carter, L. (1965), *The Diary of Colonel Landon Carter of Sabine Hall, 1752–1778*, (ed.) Jack P. Greene, Charlottesville.
——(1976), 'Fragment from the Carter Papers', College of William and Mary, reprinted in M. Mullin, *American Negro Slavery: A Documentary History*, pp. 108–9, Colombia.
Cartledge, P. (1979), *Sparta and Lakonia. A Regional History c. 1300–362 BC*, London and Boston.
——(1985), 'Rebels and Sambos in classical Greece; a comparative view', in P. Cartledge and F. D. Harvey (eds), *CRUX. Essays in Greek History presented to G. E. M. de Ste. Croix on his 75th Birthday*, pp. 14–46, London.

——(1986), *Agesilaos and the Crisis of Sparta*, London.

Cassuto, U. (1967), *A Commentary on the Book of Exodus*, trans. I. Abrahams, Jerusalem.

Chanlatte, F. D. (1817), *Appel aux Haytiens, ou riposte à l'attaque impreuve de al cour royale de Bordeaux et de M. Martignac, avocat*, Port–au–Prince.

Cheung Mee-Yan L. (1979) *Modernization and Ethnicity: The Divergence Model*, unpublished PhD thesis, University of Maryland.

Chirot, D. (1974–75), 'The growth of the market and servile labour systems in agriculture', *Journal of Social History*, vol. 8, pp. 67–80.

Cohen, D. and Greene J. (1972), (eds) *Neither Slave Nor Free*, London.

Cohen, G. A. (1978), *Karl Marx's Theory of History: A Defence*, Oxford.

Cole, H. (1967), *Christophe, King of Haiti*, London.

Collier, R. (1968), *The River that God forgot: The Amazon Rubber Boom*, New York.

Cooper, F. (1977), *Plantation Slavery on the East African Coast*, New Haven.

——(1979), 'The problem of slavery in African studies', *Journal of African History*, vol. 20, pp. 103–25.

——(1981), 'Islam and cultural hegemony: the ideology of slaves on the East African coast', in P. E. Lovejoy (ed.), *The Ideology of Slavery in Africa*, pp. 271–307, Beverly Hills and London.

Cowan, J. M. (1976), (ed.) *A Dictionary of Modern Written Arabic*, 3rd ed., Ithaca.

Craton, M. (1978), *Searching for the Invisible Man: Slaves and Plantation Life in Jamaica*, Cambridge, MA.

——(1982), *Testing the Chains: Resistance to Slavery in the British West Indies*, Ithaca.

Crone, P. (1980), *Slaves on Horses. The Evolution of the Islamic Polity*, Cambridge.

Cross, H.eE., (1978), 'Living standards in rural nineteenth–century Mexico: Zacatecas 1820–80', *Journal of Latin American Studies*, vol. 10, pp. 1–19.

Curtin, P. D. (1969), *The Atlantic Slave Trade: A Census*, Madison.

——(1977), 'Slavery and empire', in V. Rubin and A. Tuden (eds), *Comparative Perspectives on Slavery in the New World. Annals of the New York Academy of Sciences*, vol. 292, pp. 3–11.

Daniels, P. (1972), *The Shadow of Slavery: Peonage in the South 1901–1969*, Urbana.

——(1979), 'The metamorphosis of slavery', *Journal of American History*, vol. 66, no. 1, pp. 88–99.

David, P. A., *et al.* (1976), *Reckoning with Slavery: A Critical Study in the Quantitative History of American Negro Slavery*, New York.

Davies, S. (1761), *Letters from the Rev. Samuel Davies Shewing the State of Religion in Virginia, Particularly among the Negroes*, London.

Davis, A. (1981), *Women, Race and Class*, New York.

Davis, D. B. (1966), *The Problem of Slavery in Western Culture*, Ithaca, NY.

——(1985), *Slavery and Human Progress*, Oxford.

Davis, J. K. (1977–78), 'Athenian citizenship: the descent group and the alternatives', *Classical Journal*, vol. 73, pp. 105–21.

Daube, D. (1961), 'Direct and indirect causation in biblical law', *Vetus Testamentum*, vol. II, pp. 249–69.

Dean, D. M. (1979), *Defender of the Race: James Theodore Holy, Black Nationalist Bishop*, Boston.

Debbasch, Y. (1961), 'Le marronage: i, le marron', *l'Année Sociologique*, pp. 1–112.

——(1962), 'Le marronage: ii, la société coloniale contre le marronage', *l'Année Sociologique*, pp. 117–95.

Debien, G. (1974), *Les esclaves aux Antilles françaises*, Basse-Terre and Fort-de-France.

De Vastey (Baron de Vastey) (1814a), *Le système coloniale dévoilé*, Cap Henry.

——(1814b), *Notes à M. le Baron de V.P. Malouet*, Cap Henry.

——(1816), *Reflexions sur une lettre de Mazéres, ex-colon français, sur les noirs et les blancs*, Cap Henry.

——(1818), *Political Remarks on Some French Works and Newspapers Concerning Hayti*, London.

——(1823), *An Essay on the Causes of the Revolution and Civil Wars of Hayti*, Exeter.

Dockes, P. (1982), *Medieval Slavery and Liberation*, trans. A. Goldsmith, London.

Domar, E. J. (1970), 'The causes of slavery or serfdom: a hypothesis', *Journal of Economic History*, vol. 30, pp. 18–32.

Donham, D. and James W. (eds) (1986), *The Southern Marches of Imperial Ethiopia: Essays in History and Social Anthropology*, Cambridge.

Douglass, F. (1965; originally pub. 1855), *My Bondage and Freedom*, New York.

Ducat, J. (1974), 'Le mépris des Hilotes', *Annales (ESC)*, vol. 29, pp. 1451–64.

——(1978), 'Aspects de l'hilitisme', *Ancient Society*, vol. 9, pp. 5–46.

Ducrey, P. (1968), *Le traitement des prisonniers de guerre dans la Grèce antique*, Paris.

Egan, M. (1977), *Mark Twain's Huckleberry Finn: Race, Class and Society*, London.

Elkins, S. (1959), *Slavery: A Problem in American Institutional and Intellectual Life*, Chicago.

Ellison, M. (1974), *The Black Experience: American Blacks since 1865*, London.

Engels, F. (1969), 'The origin of the family, the state and private property', in K. Marx and F. Engels, *Selected Works in One Volume*, pp. 468–593, London.

Enloe, C. H. (1980), *Ethnic Soldiers. State Security in a Divided Society*, Harmondsworth.

Ennew, J. (1981), *Debt Bondage. A Survey*, London.

Evans, E. C. (1969), *Physiognomics in the Ancient World: Transactions of the American Philosophical Society* N.S. 59 Pt. 5.

Evans, W. M. (1980), 'From the l of Canaan to the land of Guinea: the strange odyssey of the sons of Ham', *The American Historical Review*, vol. 85, no. 1, pp. 15–44.

Fairfax, S. C. (1903–4), 'Diary of a little colonial girl', *Virginia Magazine of History and Biography*, vol. II, pp. 212–14.

Falk, Z. W. (1964), *Hebrew Law in Biblical Times*, Jerusalem.

Fallers, L. A. (ed.) (1964), *The King's Men*, London.

Faulkner, A. O. *et al.* (1982), *When I Was Comin' Up: An Oral History of Aged Blacks*, Hamden, CT.

Felkin, R. W. (1885–6), 'Notes on the Waganda Tribe of Central Africa', *Proceedings of the Royal Society of Edinburgh*, vol. 13, pp. 699–770.

Fernandez, J. W. (1982), *Bwiti: An Ethnology of the Religious Imagination in Africa*, Princeton.

Finley, M. I. (1959), 'Was Greek civilisation based on slave labour?', *Historia*, vol. 8, pp. 145–64 (twice reprinted in M.I. Finley (ed.), *Slavery in Classical Antiquity*, Cambridge 1960 and 1968, and, with reduced annotation, in Finley, *Economy and Society in Ancient Greece*, (ed.) B. D. Shaw and R. P. Saller, London 1981, Harmondsworth 1983).

——(ed.) (1960), *Slavery in Classical Antiquity: Views and Controversies*, Cambridge.

——(1965), 'La servitude pour dettes', *Revue historique de droit français et étranger*, 4th series, vol. 43, pp. 159–83.

——(1968), 'Slavery', *International Encyclopaedia of the Social Sciences*, vol. 14, pp. 307–13, New York.

——(1972), 'The extent of slavery', in R. Wink (ed.), *Slavery: A Comparative Perspective*, pp. 3–15, New York.

——(1975), *The Use and Abuse of History*, London.

——(1979), 'Slavery and the historians', *Histoire Sociale – Social History*, vol. 12, pp. 247–61 (repr. in trans. in Finley, *Mythe, Mémoire, histoire. Les usages du Passé*, (ed.) F. Hartog, Paris 1981, and in *Ancient Slavery and Modern Ideology*, London 1980, Harmondsworth 1983).

——(1980,1983), *Ancient Slavery and Modern Ideology*, London.

——(1981, 1983), *Economy and Society in Ancient Greece* (eds.) B. D. Shaw and R. P. Saller, London.

——(1985), *The Ancient Economy*, London.

Fisher, A. G. B. and Fisher H. J. (1970), *Slavery and Muslim Society in Africa*, London.

Fithian, P. V. (1943), *The Journal and Letters of Philip Vickers Fithian, 1773–1774: A Plantation Tutor of the Old Dominion*, (ed.) H. D. Farish, Williamsburg.

Fitzpatrick, J. C. (ed.) (1931), *The Writings of George Washington*, 39 vols, Washington, DC.

Fogel, R. W. and Engerman S. L. (1974), *Time on the Cross: The Economics of American Negro Slavery*. Boston.

Foner, L. and Genovese E. (1969), *Slavery in the New World: A Reader in*

Comparative History, NJ.

Fontaine, J. (1973), *Memoir of a Huguenot Family*, Baltimore.

Forde, D. (1963), *African Worlds: Studies in the Cosmological Ideas and Social Values of African Peoples*, London.

Foucault, M. (1972), *The Archaeology of Knowledge*, trans. A. Sheridan, London.

——(1981), 'The order of discourse', in R. Young (ed.), *Untying the Text: A Post-Structuralist Reader*, pp. 48–78, London.

Fouchard, J. (1972), *Les Marrons de la Liberté*, Paris.

Frazier, E. F. (1964), *The Negro Church in America*, New York.

Frederiksen, M. W. (1966), 'Caesar, Cicero and the problems of debt', *Journal of Roman Studies*, vol. 56, pp. 128–41.

Galenson, D. (1981), *White Servitude in Colonial America: An Economic Analysis*, Cambridge.

Gardner, R. G. (1980), 'Eighteenth-century Virginia Baptist manuscript Church books', *Virginia Baptist Register*, no. 19, pp. 910–15.

Garlan, Y. (1982), *Les Esclaves en Grèce Ancienne*, Paris.

Garnsey, P. (1970), *Social Status and Legal Privilege in the Roman Empire*, Oxford.

Gaspar, D. B. (1979), 'Runaways in seventeenth-century Antigua, West Indies', *Boletin de Estudios Latinomaericanos y del Caribe*, vol. 26, pp. 3–13.

Geggus, D. (1982), *Slavery, War and Revolution: The British Occupation of Saint Domingue, 1793–1798*, Oxford.

——(1985), 'Haiti and the abolitionists: opinion, propaganda and international politics in Britain and France, 1804–1838', in D. Richardson (ed.), *Abolition and its Aftermath: the Historical Context, 1790–1916*, pp. 113–40, London.

Genovese, E. D. (1965), *The Political Economy of Slavery: Studies in the Economy and Society of the Slave South*, New York.

——(1969a), *The World the Slaveholders Made: Two Essays in Interpretation*, New York.

——(1969b), 'The treatment of slaves in different countries: problems in the application of the comparative method', in L. Foner and E. D. Genovese (eds), *Slavery in the New World: A Reader in Comparative History*, pp. 202–10, NJ.

——(1971), *In Red and Black: Marxian Exploration of Southern and Afro-American History*, Knoxville.

——(1975), *Roll, Jordan, Roll: The World the Slaves Made*, London.

——(1979), *From Rebellion to Revolution. Afro-American Slave Revolts in the Making of the Modern World*, Baton Rouge and London.

——and Fox-Genovese E. (1983), *Fruits of Merchant Capital: Slavery and Bourgeois Property in the Rise and Expansion of Capitalism*, New York.

Gibson, C. (1964), *The Aztecs under Spanish Rule*, Standford.

Giddings, P. (1984). *When and Where I Enter: The Impact of Black Women on Race and Sex in America*, New York.

Godelier, M. (1981), 'The origins of male domination', *New Left Review*, no. 127, pp. 3–17.

Goody, J. (1980), 'Slavery in time and space', in J.L. Watson (ed.), *Asian and African Systems of Slavery*, pp. 16–42, Oxford.

Greene L. (1944), 'The New England negro as seen in advertisements for runaway slaves', *Journal of Negro History*, vol. 29, pp. 125–46.

Grégoire, H. (1826), *De la noblesse de la peau ou du préjugé des blancs contre la couleur des africains et celle de leurs descendants noirs et sang-mêlés*, Paris.

Grele, R. J. (ed.) (1975), *Envelopes of Sound: Six Practitioners Discuss the Method, Theory and Practice of Oral History and Oral Testimony*, Chicago.

Griggs, E. L. and Prator C.H. (1952), *Henry Christophe and Thomas Clarkson: A Correspondence*, Berkeley and Los Angeles; r.p. 1968, New York.

Groot, S. W. de (1963), *From Isolation towards Integration: The Suriname Maroons and their Descendants, 1845–1863*, The Hague.

Gruening, E. (1928), *Mexico and Its Heritage*, London.

Gschnitzer, F. (1964), *Studien zur griechischen Terminologie der Sklaverei* I, Mainz.

Gutman, H. G. (1976), *The Black Family in Slavery and Freedom, 1750–1925*, Oxford.

Gwaltney, J. (1980), *Drylongso: A Self-Portrait of Black Americans*, New York.

Hallam, H. R. K. (1977), *The Life and Times of Rabih Fadl Allah*, Ilfracombe.

Hart, J. (1982), *Herodotus and Greek History*, London.

Harvey, W. W. (1827), *Sketches of Hayti from the Expulsion of the French to the Death of Christophe*, London.

Henige, D. (1982), *Oral Historiography*, London.

Herskovitz, M. J. (1966), 'What has Africa given America', in *The New World Negro*, pp. 168–74, Bloomington.

Higman, B. W. (1976), *Slave Population and Economy in Jamaica, 1807–1834*, Cambridge.

——(1984), *Slave Populations of the British Caribbean, 1807–1834*, Baltimore.

Hill, C. (1963), *Society and Puritanism in Pre-Revolutionary England*, New York.

——(1982), 'Science and magic in seventeenth-century England', in R. Samuel and G. Jones (eds), *Culture, Ideology and Politics*, pp. 176–93, London.

Hill, R. E. (1980), 'This little light of mine', *Radcliffe Quarterly* (December).

——(1984), 'Lifting as we climb: black women's organizations, 1890–1935', *Radcliffe Quarterly*, (March).

Hill, R. L. (1959), *Egypt in the Sudan, 1820–1881*, London.

Hilton, R. et al. (eds) (1978), *The Transition from Feudalism to Capitalism*, London.

Hindess, B. and Hirst P.Q. (1975), *Pre-Capitalist Modes of Production*, London.

Hoetink, H. (1972), 'Caribbean race relations', in R. Winks (ed.), *Slavery: A Comparative Perspective*, pp. 139–143, New York.

Holly, J. T. and Harris, J. D. (1970), *Black Separatism and the Caribbean, 1860*, Ann Arbor.

Holmes, C. F. (1971), 'Zanzibari influence at the southern end of Lake

Victoria: the lake route', *African Historical Studies*, vol. 4, pp. 477–503.

Holt, P. M. (1970), *The Mahdist State in the Sudan, 1881–1898*, Oxford.

Hopkins, K. (1978), *Conquerors and Slaves*, Sociological Studies in Roman History, vol. I, Cambridge.

Humphreys, S. C. (1983), *The Family, Women and Death: Comparative Studies*, London.

Hurmence, B. (1984), *My Folks Don't Want Me To Talk About Slavery: Twenty One Oral Histories of Former North Carolina Slaves*, Winston-Salem, NC.

Iliffe, J. (1979), *A Modern History of Tanganyika*, Cambridge.

Inglis, B. (1973), *Roger Casement*, London.

Isaac, R. (1982), *The Transformation of Virginia, 1740–1790*, Chapel Hill, NC.

Jackson, B. S. (1970), 'Some comparative legal history: robbery and brigandage', *Georgia Journal of International and Comparative Law*, vol. 1, pp. 45–103.

——(1972), *Theft in Early Jewish Law*, Oxford.

——and Watkins, T.eF. (1984), 'Distraint in the laws of Eschnunna and Hammurabi', in *Studi in onore di Cesare Sanfilippo*, vol. 5, pp. 409–19, Milan.

Jackson, G. P. (1943), *White and Negro Spirituals: Their Life Span and Kinship*, Locust Valley, NY.

Jakobsen, R. (1956), *Fundamentals of Language*, The Hague.

James, C. L. R. (1963), *The Black Jacobins: Toussaint l'Ouverture and the San Domingo Revolution*, New York.

James, W. (1975), 'Sister-exchange marriage', *Scientific American*, vol. 233, pp. 84–94.

——(1977), 'The Funj mystique: approaches to a problem of Sudan history', in R. K. Jain (ed.), *Text and Context: The Social Anthropology of Tradition*, pp. 95–133, Philadelphia.

——(1979), *Kwanim Pa: The Making of the Uduk People. An Ethnographic Study of Survival in the Sudan-Ethiopian Borders*, Oxford.

——(1986), 'Lifelines: exchange marriage among the Gumuz', in D. Donham and W. James (eds), *The Southern Marches of Imperial Ethiopia: Essays in History and Social Anthropology*, pp. 119–47, Cambridge.

Joachim, B. (1971), 'Le néocolonialisme à l'essai', *La Pensée*, vol. 156, pp. 35–51.

Johnson, C. H. (ed.) (1969), *God Struck Me Dead: Religious Conversion Experiences and Autobiographies of Ex-Slaves*, Philadelphia.

Johnson, D. H. (1982), 'The isolation of the southern Sudan: a re-examination of the evidence', *Heritage. A Journal of Southern Sudanese Cultures*, vol. 1, no. 2–3, pp. 94–100.

Jones, A. H. M. (1964), *The Later Roman Empire, 284–602*, 3 vols, Oxford.

——(1972), *The Criminal Courts of the Roman Republic and Principate*, Oxford.

Jones, J. (1985), *Labor of Love, Labor of Sorrow*, New York.

Jones, M. A. (1983), *The Limits of Liberalism in American History, 1607–1980*, Oxford.

Jordan, W. D. (1968), *White over Black: American Attitudes toward the Negro, 1550–1812*, Chapel Hill, NC.

Joseph, G. M. (1982), *Revolution from Without: Yucatán, Mexico and the United States, 1880–1924*, Cambridge.

Kagwa, A. (1934), *The Customs of the Baganda*, trans. E. Kalibala, New York.

——(1952), *Mpiza za Baganda*, London.

Kapteijns, L. (1985), *Mahdist Faith and Sudanic Tradition: the History of the Masalit Sultanate, 1870–1930*, London.

Katz, F. (1980), *La servidumbre agraria en México en la epoca porfiriana*, Mexico.

Kilson, M. and Dusser De Barenne (1971), 'West African society and the Atlantic slave trade, 1441–1865', in N. Huggins, M. Kilson, D. Fox (eds), *Key Issues in the Afro-American Experience*, vol. 1, pp. 39–53, New York.

Klein, H. (1971), 'Patterns of settlement of the Afro-American population in the New World, in N. Huggins, M. Kilson, D. Fox (eds), *Key Issues in the Afro-American Experience*, vol. I, pp. 99–115, New York.

——(1978), *The Middle Passage: Comparative Studies in the Atlantic Slave Trade*, Princeton.

Kloosterboer, W. (1960), *Involuntary Labour since the Abolition of Slavery: A Survey of Compulsory Labour throughout the World*, Leiden.

——(1972), 'Involuntary labor since abolition', in R. Wink (ed.), *Slavery: A Comparative Perspective*, pp. 193–214, New York.

Knight, A. (1986), *The Mexican Revolution*, 2 vols, Cambridge.

Knight, F. W. (1970), *Slave Society in Cuba during the Nineteenth Century*, Madison.

Kolchin, P. (1977–78), 'The process of confrontation: patterns of resistance to bondage in nineteenth-century Russia and the United States', *Journal of Social History*, vol. II, pp. 457–490.

Korngold, R. (1945), *Citizen Toussaint*, London.

Kruse, H. H. (1981), *Mark Twain and 'Life on the Mississippi'*, Amherst.

Kulikoff, A. (1986), *Tobacco and Slaves: The Development of Southern Cultures in the Chesapeake Colonies, 1680–1780*, Chapel Hill, NC.

Lacerte, R. K. (1975), 'The First Land Reform in Latin America', *Interamerican Economic Affairs*, vol. 28, no. 4, pp. 77–85.

Laclau, E. (1977), *Politics and Ideology in Marxist Theory*, London.

Lascu, N. (1969), 'Intorno ai nomi degli schiavi nel teatro antico', *Dioniso*, vol. 43, pp. 97–106.

Lauffer, S. (1955/56), *Die Bergwerkssklaven von Laureion*, Mainz.

Leacock, E. (1972), Introduction to F. Engels, *The Origin of the Family, the State and Private Property*, New York.

Lefort, C. (1978), *Les formes de l'Histoire*, Paris.

Leitch, V. B. (1983), *Deconstructive Criticism: An Advanced Introduction*, London.

Levine, L. W. (1977), *Black Culture and Black Consciousness: Afro-American Folk Thought from Slavery to Freedom*, New York.

Lévy-Bruhl, H. (1934), *Quelques problèmes du trés ancient droit romain*, Paris (pp.

15–33 reprinted in M. I. Finley, (ed.) *Slavery in Classical Antiquity: Views and Controversies*, pp. 53–72, Cambridge).

——(1960), 'Théorie de l'esclavage' [1931], in M. I. Finley (ed.), *Slavery in Classical Antiquity: Views and Controversies*, pp. 151–69, Cambridge.

Lewis, J. (1983), *The Pursuit of Happiness: Family and Values in Jefferson's Virginia*, New York.

Lewis, N. and Reinhold M. (1966), *Roman Civilisation*, sourcebook, 2 vols, New York.

Lewy, J. (1958), 'The biblical institution of *deror* in the light of Akkadian documents', *Eretz Israel*, vol. 5, pp. 21–31.

Lombardi, J. V. (1969), 'Manumission, maumisos, and aprendizaje in republican Venezuela', *Hispanic American Historical Review*, no. 49, pp. 656–78.

Lonsdale, J. (1981), 'The state and social processes in Africa', American African Studies Association paper.

Lotze, D. (1959), *Metaxu eleu therōn kai Doulōn. Studien zur Rechtsstellung unfreier Landbevölkerung bis zum 4. Jht. v. Chr.*, Berlin.

——(1985), 'Zu neuen Vermutungen über abhängige Landleute im alten Sikyon', in H. Kreissig and F. Kühnert (eds), *Antike Abhängigkeitsformen in den griechischen Gebieten ohne Polisstruktur und den römischen Provinzen*, Berlin.

Lovejoy, P. E. (ed.) (1981), *The Ideology of Slavery in Africa*, Beverly Hills and London.

——(1983), *Transformations in Slavery: A History of Slavery in Africa*, Cambridge.

Lugard, F. (1893), *The Rise of our East African Empire*.

MacCary, W. T. (1969), 'Menader's slaves: their names, roles and masks', *Transactions and Proceedings of the American Philological Association*, vol. 100, pp. 277–94.

McCreery, D. J. (1976), 'Coffee and class: the structure of development in liberal Guatemala', *Hispanic American Historical Review*, vol. 56, pp. 438–60.

——(1983), 'Debt servitude in rural Guatemala, 1876–1936', *Hispanic American Historical Review*, vol. 63, pp. 735–59.

McDaniel, G. W. (1982), *Hearth and Home: Preserving a People's Culture*, Philadelphia.

Machell, P. (1896), 'Memoirs of a Soudanese soldier (Ali Effebdi Gifoon)', *Cornhill Magazine*, n.s. vol. 1, nos. 439–442, pp. 30–40 and 484–92.

Macherey, P. (1978), *A Theory of Literary Production*, trans. G. Wall, London.

Main, G. L. (1982), *Tobacco Colony: Life in Early Maryland, 1650–1720*, Princeton.

Mair, L. (1934), *An African People in the Twentieth Century*, London.

Manigat, L. F. (1962), *La Politique agraire du gouvernement d'Alexandre Pétion*, Port-au-Prince.

——(1977), 'The relationship between marronage and slave revolts in St Domingue-Haiti', in V. Rubin and A. Tuden (eds), *Comparative Perspectives on Slavery in New World Plantation Societies*, pp. 420–38, New York.

Marissal, J. (1978), 'Le commerce Zanzibarite dans l'Afrique des Grands Lacs au XIXe siècle', *Rev. franc. d'Hist. d'outre-Mer*, vol. 65, pp. 212–335.

Martin, E. B. and Ryan T. C. I. (1977), 'A qualitative assessment of the Arab slave trade of East Africa, 1770–1896', *Kenya Historical Review*, vol. 5, pp. 71–91.

Marx, K. (1964), *Pre-Capitalist Economic Formations*, (ed.) E. J. Hobsbawm, London.

Masson, O, (1973), 'Les noms des esclaves dans la Grèce antique', *Actes du colloque 1971 sur l'esclavage*, pp. 9–23, Besançon.

Mathews, D. G. (1977), *Religion in the Old South*, Chicago.

Mauss, M. (1954), *The Gift: Forms and Functions of Exchange in Archaic Societies*, trans. I Cunnison, London.

Meillassoux, C. (1975) (ed.), *L'Esclavage en Afrique Pre-coloniale*, Paris.

——(1986), *Anthropologie de l'Esclavage*, Paris.

Meldon, J. A. (1908), 'Notes on Sudanese in Uganda', *Journal of the African Society*, vol. 7, no. 26, pp. 123–46.

Mendelsohn, I. (1949), *Slavery in the Ancient Near East*, New York.

Meyers, A. R. (1977), 'Class, ethnicity, and slavery: the origins of the Moroccan 'Abid', *International Journal of African Historical Studies*, vol. 10, no. 3, pp. 427–42.

——(1983), 'Slave soldiers and state politics in early 'Alawi Morocco, 1668–1727', *International Journal of African Historical Studies*, vol. 16, no. 1, pp. 39–48.

Miers, S. and Kopytoff I. (1977) (eds), *Slavery in Africa: Historical and Anthropological Perspectives*, Madison.

Millar, F. G. B. (1984), 'Condemnation to hard labour in the Roman Empire, Augustus to Constantine', *Papers of the British School at Rome*, vol. 52, pp. 124–47.

Mintz, S. and Price R. (1976), *An Anthropological Approach to the Afro-American Past: A Caribbean Perspective*, Philadelphia.

Mommsen, Th. (1887–88), *Römisches Strafrect*, Leipzig.

Montague, L. L. (1940), *Haiti and the United States, 1714–1938*, Chapel Hill, NC.

Morgan, E. (1975), *American Slavery – American Freedom: The Ordeal of Colonial Virginia*, New York.

Morton, R. (1976), *Slaves, Fugitives and Freedmen on the Kenya Coast, 1873–1907*, unpublished PhD thesis, Syracuse University, New York.

Mulira, E. M. K. (1954), *Economic Development and Tribal Change*.

Mullin, G. W. (1972), *Flight and Rebellion: Slave Resistence in Eighteenth-Century Virginia*, New York.

Nash, G. B. (1974), *Red, White and Black: The Peoples of Early America*, Englewood Cliffs, NJ.

Navarro, M. G. (1968–69), 'La guerra de castas de Yucatán', *Historia Mexicana*, vol. 18, pp. 11–34.

——(1977–78), 'El trabajo forzoso en México, 1821–1917', *Historia Mexicana*, vol. 27, pp. 588–615.

Nicholls, D. (1974), *Economic Dependence and Political Autonomy: The Haitian Experience*, Montreal.

——(1979), *From Dessalines to Duvalier: Race, Colour and National Independence in Haiti*, Cambridge.

——(1985), *Haiti in Caribbean Context: Ethnicity, Economy and Revolt*, London.

Norusis, M. J. (1982), *SPSS, An Introductory Guide*, New York.

Nyakutura, J. (1970), *Aspects of Bunyoro Customs and Tradition*, trans. Zebiya Kwamya Rigby, Nairobi.

——(1973), *Anatomy of an African Kingdom: a History of Bunyoro-Kitara*, trans. Teopista Muganwa, (ed.) G. N. Uzoigwe, New York.

O'Fahey, R. S. (1973), 'Slavery and the slave trade in Dār Fīr', *Journal of African History*, vol. 14, no. 1, pp. 29–43.

——and Spaulding, J. L. (1974), *Kingdoms of the Sudan*, London.

——(1980), *State and Society in Dār Fīr*, London.

——(1982), 'Fur and Fartit: the history of a frontier' in J. Mack and P. Robertshaw (eds), *Culture History in the Southern Sudan*, pp. 75–87, Nairobi.

Oliva, P. (1971), *Sparta and her Social Problems*, Amsterdam and Prague.

——(1981), 'Heloten und Spartaner', *Index*, vol. 10, pp. 43–54.

Patterson, O. (1967), *The Sociology of Slavery: An Analysis of the Origins, Development and Structure of Negro Slave Society in Jamaica*, London.

——(1977a), 'On slavery and slave formation', *New Left Review*, no. 117, pp. 31–68.

——(1977b), 'Slavery', *Annual Review of Sociology*, vol. 3, pp. 407–49.

——(1982), *Slavery and Social Death: A Comparative Study*, Cambridge, MA.

Paul, S. M. (1970), *Studies in the Book of the Covenant in the Light of Cuneiform and Biblical Law*, Leiden.

Perkins, L. (1984), 'Shapes of a better future: Afro-American women of vision and courage', in *Women of Courage: A Catalog of an Exhibition of Photo-graphs based on the Black Women Oral History Project*, Cambridge, MA.

Perlman, M. L. (1970), 'The traditional systems of stratification among the Ganda and the Nyoro of Uganda', in A. Tuden and I. Plotnicov (eds), *Social Stratification in Africa*, pp. 125–61, London.

Perry, W. S. (1969), *Historical Collections Relating to the American Colonial Church*, [1870], 4 vols, New York.

Petrone, G. (1983), *Teatro antico e iganno: finzioni Plautini*, Palermo.

Pettit, A. G. (1974), *Mark Twain and the South*, Lexington.

Phillips, A. (1984), 'The laws of slavery: Exodus 21:2–11, *Journal for the Study of the Old Testament*, vol. 30, pp. 51–66.

Piattelli, D. (1984), 'Effetti giuridici dell'affrancazione degli schiavi alla luce dei documenti aramaici di Elefantina', in *Atti del XVII Congresso Internazionale di Papirologia*, pp. 1233–44, Naples.

Pinchbeck, R. (1926), *The Virginia Negro Artisan and Tradesman*, Richmond.

Pipes, D. (1980), 'Black soldiers in early Muslim armies', *International Journal of African Historical Studies*, vol. 13, no. 1, pp. 87–94.

——(1981), *Slave Soldiers and Islam: The Genesis of a Military System*, New Haven and London.

Poulantzas, N. (1975), *Political Power and Social Classes*, trans. T. O'Hagan, London.

Price, R. (ed.) (1973), *Maroon Societies*, New York.

Pritchard, J. B. (1969) (ed.), *Ancient Near Eastern Sources Relating to the Old Testament*, Princeton.

Pritchett, W. K. (1956), 'Attic stelai', *Hesperia*, vol. 25, pp. 276–81 (and vol. 30, 1961, pp. 26–7).

——(1971), *The Greek State at War*, vol. 1, Berkeley.

Ransom, R. L. and Sutch, R. (1977), *One Kind of Freedom: The Economic Consequences of Emancipation*, Cambridge.

Rawick, G. P. (1972) (ed.), *The American Slave: A Composite Autobiography*, Westport, CT.

Rice, D. (1977), 'Enlightenment, evangelism and economics: an interpretation of the drive towards emancipation in British West India', in V. Rubin and A. Tuden (eds), *Comparative Perspectives on Slavery in the New World*, Annals of the New York Academy of Science, vol. 292, pp. 123–31.

Richards, A. I. (1954), (ed.), *Economic Development and Tribal Change*, Cambridge.

Ricoeur, P. (1981a), *Hermeneutics and the Human Sciences: Essays on Language, Action and Interpretation*, (ed.) and trans. J. B. Thompson, Cambridge.

——(1981b), 'The Hermeneutic function of Distanciation', in Ricoeur (1981a) 131–44.

Robertson, C. C. and Klein, M. A. (1983) (eds), *Women and Slavery in Africa*, Madison.

Roscoe (1911), *The Baganda*, London.

Rosiers, Compte de (1819), *Hayti reconnaissante, en réponse à un écrit imprimé à Londres, et Intitulé: l'Europe chatiée, et l'Afrique vengée*, Sans Souci.

Rubin, V. and Tuden, A. (1977) (eds), *Comparative Perspectives on Slavery in the New World*, Annals of the New York Academy of Science, vol. 292.

Salt, H. (1967), *A Voyage to Abyssinia and Travels into the Interior of that Country*, [1814], London.

Schlaifer, R. (1936), 'Greek theories of slavery from Homer to Aristotle', *Harvard Studies in Classical Philology*, vol. 47, pp. 165–204.

Schuver, J. M. (1883), *Reisen im Oberen Nilgebiet*, Supplement no. 72 to *Petermanns Geographische Mitteilungen*, Gotha.

Schwartz, S. B. (1970), 'Resistance and accommodation in eighteenth-century Brazil: the slaves' view of slavery', *Hispanic American Historical Review*, no. 57, pp. 313–33.

——(1974), 'The manumission of slaves in colonial Brazil: Bahia 1684–1745', *Hispanic American Historical Review*, no. 54, 603–35.

Scott, J. C. (1976), *The Moral Economy of the Peasant: Rebellion and Subsistence in Southeast Asia*, New Haven, CT.

Shockley, A. A. (1978), 'Oral history: a research tool for black history', *Negro History Bulletin*, vol. 41, (Jan/Feb).

Simpson, E. N. (1937), *The Ejido, Mexico's Way Out*, Chapel Hill.

Smith, N. D. (1983), 'Aristotle's theory of natural slavery', *Phoenix*, vol. 37, pp. 109–23.

Snodgrass, A. M. (1980), *Archaic Greece; The Age of Experiment*, London.

——(1984), 'The ancient Greek world', in J. Bintliff (ed.), *European Social Evolution. Archaeological Perspectives*, pp. 227–33, Bradford.

Sobel, M. (1979), *Trabelin' On: The Slave Journey to an Afro-Baptist Faith*, Westport, Connecticut.

——(forthcoming), *Like the Garden of the Lord, Like the Land of Egypt: Black and White World Views in Eighteenth-Century Virginia*, Princeton.

Soghayroun, I. (1981), *The Sudanese Muslim Factor in Uganda*, Khartoum.

Southall, A. (1975), 'General Amin and the coup: great man or historical inevitability?', *Journal of Modern African Studies*, vol. 13, no. 1, pp. 85–105.

Spaulding, J. (1982), 'Slavery, land tenure and social class in the northern Turkish Sudan, *International Journal of African Historical Studies*, vol. 15, no. 1, pp. 1–20.

——(1985), *The Heroic Age in Sinnar*, East Lansing, Michigan.

Spenser D. (1984), 'Soconusco: the formation of a coffee economy in Chiapas', in T. Benjamin and W. McNellie, *Other Mexicos: Essays on Regional Mexican History, 1876–1911*, pp. 123–143, Albuquerque.

Stanzel, F. K. (1984), *A Theory of Narrative*, trans. C. Goedsche, Cambridge.

Ste. Croix, G. E. M. de (1972), *The Origins of the Peloponnesian War*, London.

——(1975), 'Early Christian attitudes to property and slavery', *Studies in Church History*, pp. 1–38.

——(1981; corr. imp. 1983), *The Class Struggle in the Ancient Greek World, From the Archaic Age to the Arab Conquest*, London.

——(1984), 'Class in Marx's conception of history, ancient and modern', *New Left Review*, no. 146, pp. 94–111.

Stephenson, W. H. (1938), *Isaac Franklin: Slave Trader and Planter in the Old South*, Baton Rouge.

Stewart, W. (1951), *Chinese Bondage in Peru: A History of the Chinese Coolie in Peru, 1849–1874*, Durham, NC.

Stowe, H. B. (1852), *Uncle Tom's Cabin, or, Life Among the Lowly*, Boston.

——(1853), *The Key to Uncle Tom's Cabin: Presenting the Original Facts and Documents Upon which the Story Is Founded*, Boston.

Sutch, R. (1975), 'The breeding of slaves for sale and the westward expansion of slavery '1850–1860', in S. L. Engerman and E. D. Genovese (eds), *Race and Slavery in the Western Hemisphere: Quantitative Studies*, Princeton.

Tadman M. (1977), *Speculators and Slaves in the Old South: A Study of the American Domestic Slave Trade, 1820-1860*, unpublished PhD thesis, University of Hull.

——(1979), 'Slave trading in the ante-bellum South: an estimate of the extent of the inter-regional slave trade', *Journal of American Studies*, vol. 13, pp. 195–220.

——(forthcoming), *Speculators and Slaves: Slave Trading, Accommodation and Resistance in the American South, 1790–1865*.

Thomas, K. (1971), *Religion and the Decline of Magic: Studies in Popular Belief in Sixteenth and Seventeenth Century England*, London.

Thompson, A. O. (1976), 'Some problems of slave desertion in Guyana, c. 1750–1814', Occasional Paper No. 4, ISER.

Thompson, E. P. (1967), 'Time, work-discipline and industrial capitalism', *Past and Present*, vol. 38, pp. 56–97.

Thompson J. B. (1984), *Studies in the Theory of Ideology*, Cambridge.

Thompson, P. (1978), *The Voice of the Past: Oral History*, New York.

Tosh, J. (1970), 'The northern interlacustrine region', in R. Gray and D. Birmingham (eds), *Pre-Colonial African Trade*, London.

Treu, K. (1983), 'Zu den Sklavennamen bei Menander', *Eirene*, vol. 20, pp. 39–42.

Turner, J. K. (1911), *Barbarous Mexico*, Chicago.

Turton, A. (1980), 'Thai institutions of slavery', in J. Watson (ed.), *Asian and African Systems of Slavery*, pp. 251–292, Oxford.

Tutino, J. (1979), 'Life and labour on north Mexican haciendas: the Querétaro-San Luis Potosí Region, 1775–1810', in E.C. Frost *et al.* (eds), *El trabajo y los trabajadores en la historia de México*, pp. 337–78, Mexico.

Twaddle, M. (1972), 'The Muslim revolution in Buganda', *African Affairs*, no. 71, pp.54–72.

——(in press), 'The ending of slavery in Buganda', in S. Miers and R. Roberts (eds), *The Ending of Slavery in Africa*, Madison.

Uzoigwe, G. N. (1972), 'Precolonial markets in Bunyoro-Kitara', *Comparative Studies in Society and History*, vol. 14, pp. 422–55.

Vidal-Naquet, P. (1981, corr. impr. 1983), *Le chasseur noir. Formes de pensée et formes de société dans le monde grec*, Paris.

Vlach, J. M. (1978), *The Afro-American Tradition in Decorative Arts*, Cleveland.

Volosinov, N. N. (1973), *Marxism and Language*, New York.

Walbank, F. W. (1951), 'The problem of Greek nationality', *Phoenix*, vol. 5, pp. 41–60.

Walker, S. S. (1972), *Ceremonial Spirit Possession in Africa and Afro-America*, Leiden.

Warburg, G. R. (1981), 'Ideological and practical considerations regarding slavery in the Mahdist state and the Anglo-Egyptian Sudan, 1881–1918', in P.E. Lovejoy (ed.), *The Ideology of Slavery in Africa*, Beverly Hills and London.

Warmington, E. H. (1935), *Remains of Old Latin*, Cambridge, MA.

Washington, G. (1976–79), *The Diaries of George Washington*, (ed.) D. Jackson *et al.*, 6 vols, Charlottesville.

Waters, K. H. (1985), *Herodotus the Historian*, London.

Watson, A. (1985), (ed.), *The Digest of Justinian*, 4 vols, Philadelphia.

Watson, E. (1861), *Men and Times, or the Revolution; or Memoires of Elkanah Watson, Including Journals of Travels in Europe and America, 1777–1842*, New York.

Watson, J. L. (1980a), 'Slavery as an institution, open and closed system', in J. L. Watson (ed.), *Asian and African Systems of Slavery*, pp. 1–15, Oxford.

——(ed.) (1980b), *Asian and African Systems of Slavery*, Oxford.

Weber, M. (1964), *The Theory of Social and Economic Organisation*, trans. and ed. by A. M. Henderson and Talcott Parsons, London.

Webster, T. B. L. (1969), *Monuments Illustrating New Comedy*, Bulletin of the Institute of Classical Studies. Supplement 24.

Weinfeld, M. (1972), *Deuteronomy and the Deuteronomic School*, Oxford.

Weld, T. D. (1839) (ed.), *American Slavery as It Is: Testimony of a Thousand Witnesses*, New York; reprinted 1969, New York.

Wells, A. (1984), 'Yucatán: violence and social control on henequen plantations', in T. Benjamin and W. McNellie (eds), *Other Mexicos: Essays on Regional Mexican History*, pp. 213–241, Albuquerque.

Welwei, K. W. (1974–77), *Unfreie im antiken Kriegsdienst*, 2 vols, Wiesbaden.

Westermann, W. L. (1955), *The Slave Systems of Greek and Roman Antiquity*, Philadelphia.

Whitehead, D. (1981), 'The serfs of Sicyon', *Liverpool Class. Monthly*, vol. 6, pp. 37–41.

Wiedemann, T. (1981), *Greek and Roman Slavery*, London.

Wilberforce, R. I. and Wilberforce, S. (1838), *The Life of William Wilberforce*, London.

Williams, J. (1978), 'John Williams' Journal, (ed,) J. S. Moore, *Virginia Baptist Register*, vol. 17, pp. 795–813.

Williams, R. (1977), *Marxism and Literature*, Oxford.

——(1981), *Culture*, London.

Williamson, J. (1980), *New People: Miscegenation and Mulattoes in the United States*, New York.

Willis, J. R. (1985) (ed.) *Slaves and Slavery in Muslim Africa*, 2 vols, London.

Wilson, E. H. (1983), *Hope and Dignity: Older Black Women of the South*, Philadelphia.

Wood, P. H. (1974), *Black Majority: Negroes in Colonial South Carolina from 1760 through the Stono Rebellion*, New York.

——(1978), "I did the best I could for my day": the study of early black history during the second reconstruction, 1960–1976', *William and Mary Quarterly*, Third Series, vol. 35, pp. 185–225.

Work, J. (1940), *American Negro Songs and Spirituals*, New York.

Wrightson, K. and Levine, D. (1979), *Poverty and Piety in an English Village: Terling, 1525–1700*, New York.

Wrigley, C. C. (1964), 'The changing economic structure of Buganda', in L. A. Fallers (ed.), *The King's Men*, pp. 16–63 London.

Yetman, N. R. (1984), 'Ex-slave interviews and the historiography of slavery', *American Quarterly*

Young, R. (1981) (ed.), *Untying the Text: A Post-Structuralist Reader*, London.

Zulueta, F. de (1946–53), *The Institutes of Gaius*, Oxford.

Index